C.V. Wedgwood (1910–1997) was a noted British historian and expert on the English Civil Wars, as well as a successful lecturer and broadcaster. She was created a DBE in 1968, and in 1969 became the third woman to be appointed a member of the British Order of Merit. Her biography, *William the Silent*, was awarded the 1944 James Tait Black Memorial Prize and her iconic *The Thirty Years War* remains in print over 70 years after first publication.

'The best narrative historian writing in the English language.'
Lawrence Stone, *New York Review of Books*

'Her gifts are splendid and altogether exceptional. She is a great craftswoman and a great writer.' Sir John Plumb

'Most distinguished, [she] is the dream of the history fan. A scholar of unimpeachable diligence and accuracy, she also possesses the double literary gift of lucid exposition and brilliant portrayal.'
The Chicago Sunday Tribune

Tauris Parke Paperbacks is an imprint of I.B.Tauris. It is dedicated to publishing books in accessible paperback editions for the serious general reader within a wide range of categories, including biography, history, travel, art and the ancient world. The list includes select, critically acclaimed works of top quality writing by distinguished authors that continue to challenge, to inform and to inspire, These are books that possess those subtle but intrinsic elements that mark them out as something exceptional.

The Colophon of Tauris Parke Paperbacks is a representation of the ancient Egyptian ibis, sacred to the god Thoth, who was himself often depicted in the form of this most elegant of birds. Thoth was credited in antiquity as the scribe of the ancient Egyptian gods and as the inventor of writing and was associated with many aspects of wisdom and learning.

A KING CONDEMNED

The Trial and Execution of Charles I

C.V. Wedgwood

TPP

TAURIS PARKE
PAPERBACKS

New paperback edition published in 2011 by Tauris Parke Paperbacks
An imprint of I.B.Tauris and Co Ltd
6 Salem Road, London W2 4BU
175 Fifth Avenue, New York NY 10010
www.ibtauris.com

Distributed in the United States and Canada Exclusively by Palgrave Macmillan
175 Fifth Avenue, New York NY 10010

First published in 1964 by Collins

ISBN: 978 1 84885 688 2

A full CIP record for this book is available from the British Library
A full CIP record is available from the Library of Congress

Library of Congress Catalog Card Number: available

Printed and bound in Great Britain by CPI Cox & Wyman, Reading, RG1 8EX

TABLE OF CONTENTS

FOREWORD

In the 1940s Veronica Wedgwood began the research for the writing of a proposed trilogy of books covering the period from the late 1630s, when Charles I could consider himself 'the happiest King in Christendom', to the Restoration of his son in 1660. The first volume, *The King's Peace*, which concluded with the passage of the Grand Remonstrance in November 1641, appeared in 1955; the second, *The King's War*, which continued the story through to January 1647 and detailed the King's defeat and surrender, was published in 1958. The third volume, still contemplated at that latter date, never appeared. Instead Wedgwood devoted her energies to the completion of the detailed account of the last ten weeks of the King's life, first published in 1964 – in England as *The Trial of Charles I*; in the USA as *A Coffin for King Charles: the Trial and Execution of Charles I* and here, for this new edition, *A King Condemned*.

Wedgwood's relationship with academic historians was not an easy one, and the immediate reception of this work by the professionals in their flagship journals was cool, even condescending. Both Conrad Russell and Carolyn Edie neglected to mention the extraordinary mastery – a critical mastery that would have done credit to the most 'dryasdust' academic expert on the period – of the rich seam of documentary evidence, particularly of the pamphlets that poured from the presses in this climacteric period. In England, Russell acknowledged that the work was 'well written' and added 'something to our knowledge', but regretted that the work displayed little interest in the political theory of the regicides. In America, Edie, while warmly praising the book's lively presentation, also noted that issues of republican theory had been neglected, and expressed suspicion of the reliance on a 'narrative method' – the 'major problem' of the book.[1] Both reviewers conform to a frequently expressed view that Wedgwood's oeuvre as a whole emphasised 'recording history rather than illuminating it'.

This was a charge that Wedgwood had already challenged in her introduction to *The King's War*. Concentration on 'what happened and how it happened', she wrote, was a necessary prelude to properly posed analytical questions, and 'often by implication answers' such questions 'of why it happened'.

Thirty years after writing his dismissive review, Russell, having undertaken a narrative history of the period 1637–1642, emphasised the considerable merit that he now recognised in Wedgwood's method – 'the enormous strength which comes from refusing to ask the question why without first asking the question how'.[2] These virtues clearly emerged in the next major analysis of the trial and execution of the King, a volume of eleven essays published in 2001, which originated in a conference to mark the 350th anniversary of these events in 1999.[3]

Several of the essays followed up on issues raised by Wedgwood – the journalism of the period and the reporting of the trial; the response of the European governments to the regicide. Others took up the challenges posed by the early reviewers to analyse the political and constitutional theories that underpinned the trial. But three of the essays undertook the detailed analysis of what happened and how it happened, and two of them came to very different conclusions from Wedgwood's work.[4]

Veronica Wedgwood, following a rich stream of contemporary opinion, argued that, from the moment of the army's devastating intervention in late November–early December 1648, seizing Charles from the Isle of Wight and purging Parliament of those who were still attempting to negotiate with the King, the denouement of trial and execution ineluctably followed. Some of the army leaders, particularly Cromwell, were cautious and sought to paste a veneer of legality around their revolutionary actions – purging rather than dissolving parliament; constructing a court consisting largely of civilians; allowing the King every opportunity to plead to the charges once the court was in session. Charles, in Wedgwood's account, recognised that his doom was foreordained, and refused to give his implacable enemies the pleasure of rehearsing his evils in a formal trial. He accepted martyrdom in a superb performance in which he presented himself as the defender of his people's rights against illegal military despotism.

In arguing this, Wedgwood rejected an alternative argument that had been suggested by S.R. Gardiner, the great Victorian historian of the period. For Gardiner, the delay between the army's coup and the execution was indicative of more than Cromwell's cautious attempt to create a broad-based consensus in favour of the trial, and he argued that there was evidence to suggest that the army were still trying to cut a deal with Charles until late December 1648. Adamson and Kelsey, writing in 1999, built on this, and rejected Wedgwood's account. Negotiation between the 'frighted junto' that ruled England and the King continued into January. For Kelsey the trial itself was part of this ongoing process of negotiation: if the King would plead to the charge against him, so recognising the legitimacy of the High Court of Justice, he would acknowledge his subordination to the authority that had established the court, the 'Rump' of the House of Commons; with that premise conceded it would be possible to re-establish King Charles, as a ceremonial figure-head, a 'Doge of Venice'.[5]

Methodologically, Adamson and Kelsey follow Wedgwood's lead. Their mastery of the dense array of evidence is as assured as hers, and, with her, they emphasise what happened, in an intense analysis of chronological detail, and how it happened. Their answer to the question of why it happened is very different from hers. From their perspective, the religious zeal and political radicalism of the army, a zeal of which the soldiers boasted in the aftermath of the execution – 'we were extraordinarily carried forth to desire Justice upon the King, that man of blood' – was largely rhetorical persiflage. In fact, the policies of the army were tentative and negotiable. Cromwell was seeking a genuine settlement; his manoeuvres were not indicative of the 'artifice' in which, according to the French ambassador he excelled, designed simply to maintain a pose of moderation and consensus and to retain the co-operation of troubled conservative civilians. Charles becomes a reckless gambler, who presented with a series of opportunities extending through the trial itself, saw them only as indicative of the weakness of and divisions among soldiers and MPs, overplayed a strong hand, and was surprised when the High Court moved to convict him.

I have argued against these interpretations, challenging in detail the evidence upon which they are erected.[6] Ultimately I prefer the account provided by Wedgwood. And this is not because she wrote well, the point conceded by all her critics. The elegance, the wit of her writing was not simply a question of style; it was not mere window dressing. It stemmed from her sensitivity to and imaginative recreation of the characters and motivations of the actors. In this work she provides a series of brilliant sketches of minor players, like the King's attendants Herbert and Mildmay, the Leveller leader, Lilburne, the religious zealots, Harrison and Peters. But it is in her characterisations of Cromwell and Charles, particularly the latter, that her mastery of text, context and of human nature appears most assured. She was no uncritical admirer of Charles. She recognises his duplicity and the devious tenacity that so offended Cromwell. But her portrayal of Charles in the last weeks of his life is utterly compelling. The King was consoled by religious faith and by his sense that a loving God was punishing him for his contemptible behaviour in permitting the sacrifice of Strafford to his enemies in 1641. Accordingly, he accepted and brilliantly played out the role of martyr, and in doing so established his, and the monarchy's, role as the avatar of the law and liberty that his opponents claimed to uphold.

Clive Holmes
Lady Margaret Hall

---

1 Russell in *English Historical Review*, vol. 81 (1966), pp. 594–5; Edie in *American Historical Review*, vol. 73 (1967–8), pp. 1148–9.

2 Russell's comments were made in a radio broadcast in August 1995; his *Fall of the British Monarchies, 1637–1642*, was published in 1991.

3 Jason Peacey (ed.), *The Regicides and the Execution of Charles I*.

4 The three essays are John Morrill and Philip Baker, 'Oliver Cromwell, the Regicide and the Sons of Zeruiah' (pp. 13–45); John Adamson, 'The Frighted Junto: Perceptions of Ireland, and the Last Attempts at Settlement with Charles I' (pp. 36–70); Sean Kelsey, 'Staging the Trial of Charles I' (pp. 71–93). The latter two challenge Wedgwood's account.

5 Kelsey developed this argument further in a series of articles published between 2003 and 2007: the most important are 'The death of Charles I', *Historical Journal*, vol. 45 (2003), pp. 727–54; 'The trial of Charles I', *English Historical Review*, vol. 118 (2003), pp. 583–616.

6 'The trial and execution of Charles I', *Historical Journal*, vol. 53 (2010), pp. 289–316.

INTRODUCTION

In the course of my researches for the third volume of my history of the Civil Wars I became deeply interested in the King's trial—an event which is at the same time very well documented and yet full of problems. So much is known, and yet so much is hidden. Why did Fairfax *do* so little, and Cromwell—at least in public—*say* so little? How effectively, and to what purpose, did government censorship operate? In seeking the answers to these and other problems, I found I had accumulated the material for a study of the King's trial which could best be treated in a book to itself, rather than as a part of a general history of the Civil Wars.

The Trial of Charles I is not therefore intended as part of the larger series of which *The King's Peace* and *The King's War* are the first two volumes. It is a book in its own right, and though short, I hope may prove both interesting and useful.

In the dedication I give the best thanks I can to the friend under whose hospitable roof I finished *The King's Peace* and, more recently, wrote the first draft of this present book. My thanks are also due to the Principal and Fellows of Lady Margaret Hall, Oxford, where I completed the final draft.

I have also to thank Mr. Oliver Millar for his invaluable help with the illustrations, Mr. David Piper for much useful advice and Mr. R. E. Hutchison of the Scottish National Portrait Gallery for information about Weesop's painting of the execution. Among colleagues and friends who have assisted me in discussion or provided me with clues in the form of references, are Dr. Leslie Hotson, Miss Mary Coate, Miss Anne Whiteman and Mr. Christopher Hill. I have also enjoyed some stimulating argument with Mr. Hugh Ross Williamson, whose vigorous account of *The Day They Killed the King* is built up from rich contemporary material.

During the course of this book I have worked in the British Museum, the Public Record Office, the House of Lords Record Office, the Bodleian Library, the Ashmolean Museum, the Library of University College London (with its notable collection on London topography) and of course the London Library; I offer my sincerest thanks for much patience, help and courtesy at all these places.

CHAPTER ONE

PROLOGUE

THE TRIAL and execution of King Charles I amazed all Europe in 1649. Since then, monarchs have perished by popular decree in more violent and far-reaching revolutions, and the conception of monarchy for which King Charles both lived and died has vanished from the earth. Where the institution survives to-day it does so in a form that he would not recognise.

The startling events which took place in England in the winter of 1648-9 foreshadowed things to come. Kings had been killed before, had fallen victims to conspiracy, had been deposed, had been murdered. The grandmother of Charles I, Mary, Queen of Scots, had been tried and executed; but not while she was a reigning Queen, not in her own country or by her own subjects. She had long been deposed from the throne of Scotland, she was a prisoner in England and was judged and condemned by her captors.

King Charles was brought to trial by his own people, under his title as King—an act which defied tradition and seemed to many a fearful blasphemy against a divinely appointed Sovereign. A Royalist wrote on the eve of the trial:

Never was such damnable doctrine vented before in the world, for the persons of sovereign Princes have ever been held sacred . . . even among the most barbarous Nations; and though in many Kingdoms they have been regulated by force of arms and sometimes . . . deposed and afterwards privately murdered, yet in no History can we find a parallel for this, that ever the rage of Rebels extended so far to bring their Sovereign lord to public trial and execution, it being contrary to the law of Nature, the custom of Nations, and the sacred Scriptures. . . . What Court shall their King be tried in? Who shall be his Peers? Who shall give sentence? What eyes dare be so impious to behold the execution? What Arm be stretched out to give the stroke against the Lord's Anointed, and shall not wither like that of Jeroboam, when he lifted it up against an anointed prophet?[1]

Answers were given, within a few weeks, to all these questions. Men were found to sit in judgment, to pronounce sentence, and to strike off the head of the King. Charles was never deposed. In the charge against him he is described as "King of England", in the warrant for his execution he is still "King of England". The last words of the executioner, uttered without irony, as the King laid his head on the block were "an' it please Your Majesty."[2] Those who tried him, struck not only at the man but at the office. In the words of John Cook, who as Solicitor General prosecuted the King, they "pronounced sentence not only against one tyrant, but against tyranny itself."[3] The King had sinned as King, and as King he paid for it. Certain bold and consistent principles inspired what the Regicides did.

Yet in other ways the King's trial was a hurried and ill-considered expedient. For the King had to die. As Oliver Cromwell said, in a confused and cryptic speech defending the act to the House of Commons, "providence and necessity had cast them upon it."[4] The death of the King had been no part of the original purpose when Civil War broke out between King and Parliament in 1642. *Then* his opponents had declared themselves to want nothing more than his honour and safety provided that his methods of ruling the country were changed. Six years later, by the logic of events (the "providence and necessity" of which Cromwell spoke) nothing less than his death would solve the problem. How had this happened?

When in the summer of 1642 Charles on the one side and the leaders of Parliament on the other, began to raise forces for war, the King's opponents had believed that, once they were victorious in the field, he would grant all their demands. They wanted him to consult them in his choice of ministers and to put the control of the armed forces into their hands. They also wanted him to reform the Church by abolishing bishops and making Parliament arbiter of ecclesiastical affairs. These concessions would have transformed Parliament from an advisory body—which was what it had always been in practice, into the governing power of the nation which it had long striven to be. The King would remain as the respected figurehead, but effective power—civil, military, and ecclesiastical—would be exercised by the gentry, the lawyers, and the merchants of the House of Commons, strengthened by the wealth and influence of the Lords.

The King's opponents assumed that, once his armies were defeated, he would accept their conditions as the price of peace and personal freedom. They were wrong. Defeated, powerless, and a prisoner, Charles continued to resist their demands. He believed that God had given him the paramount authority in the realm—and as his Tudor predecessors had exercised such authority it may be added that history was on the whole on his side. Since he was convinced that the political power of the monarchy was divinely ordained, he believed that he would be committing a grave sin if he abandoned any part of it. He was prepared to risk his freedom and his life (and the lives of many of his subjects) rather than allow the sacred authority of the sovereign to be impaired. What he had received from God, he must hand intact to his son.

He was a brave man, but he was also secretive and devious. He played for time, with evasions, with pretences of concessions. In the circumstances in which he found himself—powerless, cut off from his friends, a prisoner—this was natural enough. But his continual delays in reaching an agreement, his attempts to make division between his opponents, to raise new allies at home and abroad, and to kindle a second war, exasperated his enemies. Meanwhile the country, lacking any accepted government, slipped towards anarchy. In the spring of 1648 the King's under-cover plots came violently to the surface in a new outbreak of war. An army invaded from Scotland and risings occurred in South Wales, Kent, East Anglia, and the North. After a long summer of fighting the Royalists were everywhere defeated.

The outbreak of the second war convinced the King's more ruthless antagonists that no peace could be made while he lived. Before setting out to subdue the Royalists, many of the principal soldiers of the Parliamentary Army met for three days of prayer and consultation. At the end of these they solemnly undertook "to call Charles Stuart, that Man of Blood, to an account for that blood he had shed and mischief he had done, to his utmost, against the Lord's cause and people in these poor nations."[5]

The King was aware of his danger. Since the beginning of his captivity he had faced with unfaltering calm the possibility that he would be killed—secretly done to death, perhaps, behind the walls of his prison. But some of his opponents, the best of them, were men of courage and high principle. Secret murder they abhorred. They too believed that God was on their side, and that a wicked King was an acceptable sacrifice. They dared, therefore, to try him openly and execute him in public. They defied the theory of Divine Right because they saw little in the Scriptures to support, and much to contradict it. For them, as for the King, religion and politics were closely linked. They invoked the Bible to support their action, but they also declared that the authority of the People was above that of the Sovereign, and attempted to show that a King, like any other man, could be tried by the

Common Law of England. In the opinion of many contemporaries they challenged the vengeance of God by an act of unexampled blasphemy. But in the opinion of some (admittedly a minority) they dealt justly in the sight of the Lord.

On 20th November, 1648, the Puritan Army—Cromwell's Army—laid before the House of Commons their demands that the King be brought to trial. On the following 30th January his head was struck off on a scaffold erected in the open street outside his own Banqueting House of Whitehall.

It is the purpose of this book to describe the events of those ten weeks. During that time an Army of 40,000 men, dominated by a resolute group of officers (chief among them Oliver Cromwell and his son-in-law Henry Ireton) took over the effective government of the country, purged and manipulated Parliament, created the necessary revolutionary procedures to try the King, while suppressing other revolutionary motions not to their purpose, brought the King to judgment in Westminster Hall in defiance of almost all legal opinion, secured fifty-nine signatures to his death warrant, and an executioner to carry out the sentence, and finally proclaimed England a Republic.

The sequence of events is ingenious and exciting, the protagonists on both sides remarkable—the serene and lonely King; the formidable Cromwell, with the fanatic soldiers under his command; John Bradshaw and John Cook the two lawyers who undertook the one to be his judge and the other prosecutor. For the Royalists, the King's death was the blackest act in the annals of mankind since the Crucifixion, a monstrous crime perpetrated by a gang of miscreants who blackened the fair name of England with everlasting infamy. But those who killed the King had a high conviction that they were right, that they had struck a blow against tyranny which would "live and remain upon record to the perpetual honour of the English state, who took no dark or doubtful way, no indirect by-course, but went in the open and plain path of Justice, Reason, Law and Religion."[6]

CHAPTER TWO

THE GRAND DELINQUENT

November - December 1648

KING CHARLES I kept his forty-eighth birthday at Newport in the Isle of Wight on Sunday, 19th November, 1648. James Ussher, Archbishop of Armagh and primate of Ireland was selected to preach before the Court. He disconcerted his listeners by rhapsodising on the sanctity and grandeur of sovereignty. "The King is not only glorious, but glory; not only powerful, but power," he said. The forty-ninth year of a man's age, into which His Majesty was now entering, was accounted a year of jubilee by the Jews: "It must be the desire and prayer of every loyal heart that the King may have a jubilee indeed."

The King, who personified glory and power, was a small, weary, grey-haired man who sat for a great part of the sermon with his hand over his face. Some of the spectators thought he was embarrassed by Ussher's exaggerated phrases, so far remote from his actual condition this 19th November, 1648.[1] Defeated in a war with his Parliament, he had been a prisoner for two and a half years. His captivity was honourable; he was treated with ceremony and attended by a small Court, but the harsh reality was veiled rather than concealed. He knew better than his courtiers the dangers that threatened him, and when he covered his face during Ussher's sermon it may have been to hide a conflict of feeling that for once he could not control. Unknown to those present, he had taken during the last forty-eight hours, alone and open-eyed, a decision that brought his life into imminent peril.

An ironic fate inspired his Court preachers at the most

critical moments of his reign. When he ascended the throne, John Donne, the Dean of St. Paul's, had chosen, for his first sermon to the young King, the theme of martyrdom. At his Coronation the old Bishop of Carlisle had preached on the text "Be thou faithful unto death, and I will give thee a Crown of life."[2] Donne too had been unconsciously prophetic: "The last thing Christ bequeathed to thee was His Blood . . . refuse not to go to him the same way too, if His Glory require that Sacrifice." That sacrifice was now required, and King Charles sat with his hand over his face while Ussher extolled his glory and wished him a jubilee.

He was by this time inured to misfortune. In the last years he had grown to look old and strained; his cheeks sagged, he had deep pouches under his eyes, his hair and beard were very grey. He had been gradually deprived of everything that he most valued and of the people on whom he most depended. In his days of prosperity he had moved freely between half a dozen great palaces, hung with tapestries, embellished with cabinets of rarities, decorated with the grandest paintings of Titian, Mantegna, Correggio, and Van Dyck. Now his lodging was the private house of a loyal gentleman, Sir William Hopkins, in the little town of Newport, and his magnificent Court had dwindled to a few small rooms and a handful of attendants. The luxuries with which he had once been surrounded had gone; the hunting parties which had been his principal pleasure were not permitted, for fear of his escape; the hawks, the hounds, the horses were reduced to the needs of his modest household and restricted life. He still had his dogs, his spaniel, Rogue, and his favourite greyhound, Gypsy. Greyhounds, he said, love their masters as much as spaniels do, "yet do not flatter them so much."[3]

At times he played bowls. He enjoyed discussions on serious subjects with his attendants. He also read much—the Bible, books of devotion, George Herbert's poems, Spenser's *Faerie Queen*, translations of Tasso and Ariosto, and he turned the pages of the commentary on Ezekiel by the Jesuit Villalpandus, perhaps not so much for their devotional content as for the splendid architectural plates showing the learned Jesuit's conception of the Temple at Jerusalem, a majestic classical fantasy much admired at the time. As an escape from the dreary prospect before him, the King also considered plans for rebuilding Whitehall brought to him by Inigo Jones's assistant, John Webb.[4]

The King had not seen his wife, whom he dearly loved, for more than four years; for the last twelve months he had not seen any of his children. In these unhappy conditions, his moods, always variable, wavered between resignation and illusory hope. He had always had a taste for intrigue, and his plots were unceasing and often of a self-contradictory complexity. He became used to writing a feigned hand, to sending and receiving coded letters which were hidden in a laundry basket, or slipped into the finger of a glove. He had to be watchful and on his guard, distrustful of strangers who offered to serve him, for fear that they were spies. He could gauge a man's loyalty, he said, by the way he kissed his hand.[5]

Meanwhile humble people, and especially women, moved by his distress found ways of showing him reverence. A young housewife, curtsying low, put into his hand the most beautiful rose in her garden. The country people brought their children to be cured by the royal touch. A girl, blind in one eye, on whom he laid his hand, cried out that her eye was restored. Experiments with a candle showed that indeed, to some extent, it was. The King maintained his habitual restraint, but was visibly moved by the incident.[6]

During that summer of 1648, a series of Royalist risings which he had in part engineered, had been each in turn put down. The commander in chief of the Parliamentary Army, Lord Fairfax, dealt with the revolt in Kent and Essex; Lieutenant General Oliver Cromwell crushed the Royalists in Wales and their Scottish allies in the North. The King, waiting in the Isle of Wight for news of his friends, accepted with stoicism their successive defeats, and felt no compunction for having once again plunged his country into war and caused the deaths of many of his subjects. In his own view, he had no choice: it was his duty to regain, by whatever means, the power he had lost.

Differences of interest and opinion deeply divided his enemies. The religious terms of "Presbyterian" and "Independent" were currently applied to the two major groups in Parliament. The Presbyterians were the conservative opponents of the King, who wanted to restore him as King, after securing to Parliament the control of the armed forces, and reforming the Church by the abolition of Bishops and the purification of ritual. During the war many of them had hoped for a compromise peace. The Independents, as their name implied, believed in wider toleration, and a general freedom for congregations to choose their own ministers and worship in their own way outside the ancient parochial system. With this religious view, political opinions of a more adventurous kind were sometimes, though not always, associated. Led in the House of Commons by Sir Harry Vane, and by Oliver Cromwell when he was not with the troops, the Independents had consistently demanded the vigorous prosecution of the war and, since its conclusion, their Parliamentary strength had been increased by the election of a number of Army officers to fill the places left vacant by expelled Royalist members. They were a minority in Parliament, but a large one, and dangerous, because they represented the interests and beliefs of the Army.

A third group—more deliberately organised and having already some of the characteristics of a modern political party—existed outside Parliament. The Levellers, as they were called, had come into prominence in the ranks of the Army and in the City of London during the last three years. Their acknowledged leader was John Lilburne, a prolific and eloquent pamphleteer, and their programme included the reform of the franchise and of justice, general freedom of religion, and the abolition of tithes.

During the Royalist risings of the summer, the Independents in Parliament had been weak because Cromwell and a score of other soldier-members had been absent on campaign. The Presbyterians had thus regained control of the House. Fearing the fanaticism and violence of the Army they had resolved to reach an agreement with the King while they had the power to do so, and to confront the Army at the conclusion of the fighting with a peace treaty already signed. Whether this plan could have succeeded is doubtful, but there was at least a chance that it might do so, and that the King and the Presbyterian-Parliament, offering to the nation the hope of peace and order once again, would prevail against the discontent of Independents and Levellers and the demands of the victorious Army.

The Treaty would have to be made speedily if made at all, and by November 1648 King and Parliament had reached no terms. The Parliamentary Commissioners stood stiffly to their demands—the King must give up his immemorial right to command the armed forces of the Kingdom; he must send a selected few of his most ardent supporters into exile; he must submit to the reform of the Church according to Parliament's decree. He, for his part, would yield none of these things, and looked upon the Treaty solely as a means of regaining his personal liberty and thereby the freedom of action he needed to work for the overthrow of his victorious enemies. In letters which he sent privately to his eldest son— a boy of eighteen who had taken refuge in the Netherlands— he spoke his opinions frankly, never doubting that the failure to reach agreement, on this occasion as on all previous ones, was the fault of his opponents and not his own.[7]

In public he had given his word that he would not escape during the Treaty, but in secret his plans and projects for escaping were continual, although useless.[8] In public he was indignant when he was accused of encouraging the Irish to come to his help, asserting that the accusation was a deliberate attempt "to persuade our people that, whilst we were treating

18

of peace with them, we were preparing for war by others."
But he wrote secretly to the Marquis of Ormonde, his principal
supporter in Ireland, urging him to continue his efforts to
help him, and assuring him that he would repudiate any terms
agreed to at Newport as soon as he was at liberty to do so.[9]

Yet he believed that he wanted peace and was doing all
that was possible, as a Christian and a King, to secure it. Once
at least during the negotiations one of his secretaries, the
devoted Philip Warwick, saw him sunk in desperate grief,
his eyes brimming with tears.[10]

The duplicity for which he has often been blamed was,
in the last years of his life, the only weapon left to him for
the defence of the things in which he believed. His sovereign
authority was, for him, an article of faith. God had entrusted
him with power that was sacred. God, who knew the secrets
of all hearts and from whom nothing was hidden, had decreed
that the safety of the people rested in the will of the sovereign.
The claims made by his subjects to have a voice in the government independent of his own seemed to him to be blasphemous.
Those who made them were, in his opinion, either wicked
men or the dupes of wicked men. He had never been able
to believe in any more respectable reason for their conduct.

Holding such convictions, he must of necessity think
himself blameless in all actions of whatever kind which aimed
at restoring his power and saving his people from the consequences of their folly. In the Civil War between himself
and Parliament, he saw Parliament alone as guilty of all the
blood which had been shed. He had, it is true, after long
argument at Newport agreed to a clause in the Treaty exoner-
ating his opponents and by implication admitting his own
and his adherents' guilt in the war. But this, as he wrote to
his son, was an admission wrung from him by the hard necessity of his condition as a prisoner.[11] It did not in any way
represent his conviction in the matter, nor did he imagine
that any dispassionate, honest man could possibly agree with it.
As for the renewal of war in the past months, and the Army's

accusation of him as a Man of Blood, he regarded this as the vicious propaganda of scoundrels.

He was aware that his greatest danger was not from Parliament but from the Army, which, though in theory under the authority of Parliament, was in practice not to be controlled by any but its own leaders. So long as the Army was still engaged in suppressing the Royalists he was safe to negotiate with Parliament, and he did not doubt that, if they reached agreement, the Army would have to accept their decision, so strong was the popular desire for peace. But if the fighting came to an end before any settlement had been reached, then the Army would not hesitate to break up the negotiations and take the law into their own hands. In the week immediately preceding Archbishop Ussher's birthday sermon, he knew that this had happened.

II

By the middle of October, feeling in the Army ran strong against the Treaty. The regiment commanded by Henry Ireton, Cromwell's son-in-law, offered a petition to the commander in chief, Lord Fairfax, in which they expressed their indignation that any treaty should be made with a King who had "betrayed the trust reposed in him and raised war against the nation to enslave it, violating his oaths and trampling under foot our laws." It was their earnest desire "that impartial and speedy justice may be done upon all criminal persons and . . . that the same fault may have the same punishment in the person of King or Lord as in the person of the poorest commoner." They would not even tolerate any defence of the King, and requested that all who spoke on his behalf should be treated as traitors, "till he shall be acquitted of the guilt of shedding innocent blood."[12]

The example of Ireton's regiment was followed by others. Pamphlets and news-sheets reported that the King at Newport had avowed his responsibility for the war, and had thus in effect admitted his guilt for the blood of his slaughtered subjects—a number variously over-estimated at anything up to three hundred thousand.[13]

At this juncture a party of Royalists from one of their few remaining strongholds, the castle of Pontefract, attempted to kidnap and hold to ransom Colonel Rainborough, an outspoken Republican and the hero of the Levellers. By an unlucky accident they killed him. This gratuitous murder of an unarmed man provoked a storm of indignation among the soldiers against the King and his bloody Cavaliers. Threatening talk and threatening petitions multiplied.

The soldiers who guarded the King were under the command of moderate-minded men who did not share this vengeful spirit. Colonel Robert Hammond, Governor of Carisbrooke, who had been in charge of the King for nine months, had grown to have—if not affection and respect for him—at least a conscience about his fate. If the Army intended harm to the King, was he, as Governor, to be a party to it? Did he not owe something to the man who had once been a sovereign ruler, and whom he had come to know as a courteous gentleman? He appealed for advice to his cousin—the most powerful man in the Army, and some thought the most powerful man in England: Oliver Cromwell.

Cromwell was not, in rank, the most powerful man in the Army or in England. He was Lieutenant General under Fairfax, and when Hammond wrote to him he was not even at the Army Headquarters, but far away in the North, where he had taken over the unfinished task of Rainborough and was besieging Pontefract. Yet by this time there was general agreement among those who reported the affairs of England in private letters, public newspapers or the secret Press of the Royalists that Old Noll, Duke Oliver, King Cromwell—for they called him by all these names—was the power to be reckoned with.

Oliver Cromwell is, of all the dominating figures in

English history, perhaps the hardest to interpret. His letters and speeches reveal the power of his personality and the practical side of his genius—his mastery of military organisation and of strategy. But outside the military field the reasoning which governed his actions is far from clear. He compelled his intellect to work through the medium of prayer, and he disguised the complex cerebral mechanism of memory, association and deduction in the cloudy language of vision and prophecy. Thus the workings of his powerful and concentrated mind presented themselves to him as the outcome of spiritual guidance. In all except practical matters his speech was impulsive and confused. He beat down opposing arguments by the force of his own convictions, only very rarely by an exposition of the logic behind them.

We have very little evidence from his own mouth for the part he played in the death of the King and none which fully explains his intentions and his aims. In seeking to understand what he did and why he did it we are compelled to study contemporary hearsay and conjecture (of which there was much) and to accept, though with reservation, the accounts of his conduct given by those of the Regicides who, many years later, when on trial for their lives, pleaded that he had compelled them to kill the King.

From his own hand or his own lips a few phrases only survive, though strong ones. In this autumn of 1648 he described the King as "this Man against whom the Lord hath witnessed." Nine years later, when he himself refused to take the title of King, he said of the destruction of the monarchy: "I will not dispute the justice of it when it was done, nor need I now tell you what my opinion is in the case if it were *de novo* to be done."[14]

The beliefs and motives of the King never showed more clearly than in these last days. The motives of Cromwell are by contrast enigmatic and uncertain.

He had been born a year earlier than King Charles, the son of a small landowner whose family had first amassed, and then lost, considerable wealth since the Reformation. The Cromwells were of Welsh origin, the descendants of Morgan Williams, an innkeeper and brewer of Putney who had married the sister of Thomas Cromwell, Henry VIII's minister and the secular architect of the Reformation. They had taken his name out of gratitude and respect for a man towards whom few except themselves had felt either of these things.

Oliver Cromwell had experienced in his thirties the agony and relief of a spiritual conversion, and since that time had guided his conduct by prayer and the Scriptures. As a Member of Parliament in the early years of King Charles he had been an opponent of the Court. He was a conscientious and serious rather than an influential member in the opening months of the Parliament which, in 1640, began the ferocious attack on the King and his ministers culminating in Civil War. But he was associated with many of the leaders of the Puritan opposition by ties of kindred and marriage, and when Parliament needed forces to fight a war he had immediately raised a troop of horse.

In war, unexpectedly, he discovered a natural genius. His methods of training transformed his rough rural recruits into disciplined soldiers. He insisted on promotion by merit regardless of birth. Under his influence those whom he called "plain russet-coated captains" often rose to high rank. The Royalists sneered at Colonel Harrison, once a lawyer's clerk, at Colonel Pride, allegedly a drayman, at Cornet Joyce, the gallant little tailor who had personally arrested the King.

But the quality of the troops was undeniable. "Europe has no better soldiers," said an experienced Scottish professional on the eve of the battle of Marston Moor. After that great victory, on 2nd July, 1644, Cromwell's reputation was secure. Under his influence, Parliament consolidated their forces into the New Model Army, a national force in which his ideas of training, discipline, and promotion prevailed, and in which the religious views of the Independents predominated.

They made Thomas Fairfax commander in chief. He was heir to a great estate in Yorkshire and the most distinguished professional soldier in the country. He appointed Cromwell his Lieutenant General of Horse, and together they carried the New Model Army to victory. By the spring of 1646 King Charles had fled, to throw himself on the mercy of the Scots, and the war was at an end.

No sooner was the fighting over than tension developed between Army and Parliament, and between both of them and their allies of Scotland. The King as a prisoner was a valuable possession in this three sided cold war of threats and bargains. First the Scots bartered him to the English Parliament in return for payment for their troops. Parliament, in possession of the King, and dominated by the Presbyterians, attempted to disband the Army, which it feared as an instrument of the Independents and which it was unwilling and unable to pay. At the height of the quarrel between Army and Parliament, the King was seized by a party of soldiers under Cornet Joyce and brought in triumph to the Army Headquarters. It was widely believed that Cromwell had inspired this action.

Fairfax and Cromwell moved the King to his own palace at Hampton Court with every sign of friendship, occupied London, expelled a number of Presbyterians from Parliament, secured an Independent majority and began to negotiate a peace with the King on their own terms. But the King distrusted them, and escaped before the Treaty was completed, only to be recaptured in the Isle of Wight. His precipitate action proved fatal to the Treaty and—in the end—to him.

Cromwell's reputation with his men was jeopardised by this unsuccessful overture to the King. There were mutterings of betrayal and a flare-up of mutiny. But during the fighting of 1648 he had regained and enhanced his reputation by the speed and skill with which he quelled the Royalist insurgents and the Scottish invaders. At Preston, his army outwitted and overwhelmed forces three times their own size. It was the most amazing of all their victories, and they had not men enough to guard the prisoners.

Fairfax played a far less spectacular part in the south-east, at the long siege of Colchester. Cromwell was the acknowledged hero of the Second Civil War, the strongest single influence in the Army, and therefore, in the approaching crisis, the man whose will must prevail.

It was to this formidable cousin of his that Robert Hammond, custodian of the King in the Isle of Wight, now turned for advice.

Cromwell's answer was an uncompromising condemnation of the Newport Treaty. "Look to thy heart," he wrote to Hammond, "thou art where temptations multiply . . . Peace is only good when we receive it at our Father's hand; it's dangerous to snatch it, most dangerous to go against the will of God to attain it." The defeat of the Royalists—he argued—was a sure sign that God had cast out the King.[15]

A few days later he called a meeting of his officers in the North. They declared their solidarity with the rest of the Army in condemning the treaty and demanding that justice be done "upon all persons whatsoever." It was Cromwell's first formal indication of where he stood.[16]

Naturally Cromwell condemned the treaty. He had taken part in the meeting of the Army on the eve of the Second War which had branded Charles as a Man of Blood and vowed to bring him to justice for the murder of his subjects. He had therefore accepted the necessity of trying the King as early as the previous May. But he was deeply concerned that human as well as divine justice should be done, as far as possible within the framework of Parliamentary government and the English Common Law.

This pre-occupation with the legal aspect of the matter was characteristic of Cromwell, and seems to be the explanation of his apparent hesitations during the next weeks. He was never in doubt about the necessity of bringing the King to a reckoning. But it would seem that the strategy he envisaged to secure this end was different from that advised and enforced by some of his colleagues. Hence, in the slower and more complex sphere of politics, he was compelled (as he had often been in the field) to modify his plan to meet unexpected and sometimes unwelcome contingencies.

It would be no new thing for the Army to take control of Parliament. Eighteen months earlier, when Parliament had refused to meet the soldiers' demand for pay, they had marched on London and frightened away their principal opponents in the House of Commons. But the march had been preceded by a direct appeal to the Army on the part of their supporters in Parliament led by the Speaker. Thus their action could be interpreted rather as a liberation of Parliament undertaken at the request of its members than as an unconstitutional interference with government.

It seems possible that Cromwell hoped for some such sequence of events once again. The Presbyterians had a by no means overwhelming majority—even in the House as it stood. With the war at an end, the Army officers who were also members of Parliament (about twenty of them) would resume their seats. Their votes, added to those of their civilian friends, would bring the supporters and the antagonists of the Army in the House of Commons very nearly to an equality. It should not prove impossible, if they watched for their opportunity, to get the Treaty of Newport voted down in Parliament, and the protection of the Army invoked.

Certainly in his letter to Hammond Cromwell was concerned to show that the minority in Parliament had both a right and a duty to assume power. But the time was not quite ripe, and Cromwell, by remaining in the North may have hoped to discourage premature action by his colleagues in the South.

If so, he was unsuccessful. It seemed to Ireton, and to others—the stalwart Republican Edmund Ludlow, the fanatic Harrison—that delay was dangerous. If the Army did not assert its power over Parliament and forcibly break off the Treaty, they might be too late. As Harrison argued: "We fully understand that the Treaty betwixt the King and Parliament is almost concluded upon; at the conclusion of which, we shall be commanded by King and Parliament to disband, the which if we do, we are unavoidably destroyed ... and if we do not disband, they will by Act of Parliament proclaim us traitors, and declare us to be the only hinderers of settling peace in the nation."[17]

In Cromwell's absence, Ireton was the steersman. Fairfax, the Lord General, played an ineffective part. His judgment in war was accurate and swift, but he was at sea in politics. By tradition, he respected Parliament and would have supported the Treaty but he was incensed, like any good commander, by Parliament's ill-usage of his Army. Pay was always in arrears, and his men were compelled to live at free quarter on the people. By this oppressive arrangement the civilian inhabitants were compelled to feed and lodge the troops, while they continued to pay a weekly assessment to Parliament for the cost of the war. The monstrous injustice of it exasperated the soldiers almost as much as their unwilling hosts. They were, after all, Englishmen who had fought for the liberties of the people—or so they had been told. Now, to find themselves imposed as a burden on their countrymen was not what they had expected.[18]

Fairfax hated injustice, was proud of his troops and aware of their deserts. He was torn between his natural loyalty to Parliament and his duty to his men. He was also in a state of considerable perplexity about the real intentions of Ireton and his other masterful subordinates.

Ireton had spent the greater part of October in partial retirement at Windsor, drawing up a Remonstrance from the Army to Parliament. The presentation of this document, which denounced the Treaty and asked for justice on the King, would precipitate the crisis. By early November, its contents were before Fairfax and his Council of Officers, with Ireton strongly urging immediate action. Fairfax hung back, and

was not alone in his doubts. In the end they decided to postpone this ultimatum to Parliament, and try, once more, a
direct approach to the King.

Ireton may have agreed the more readily because he
knew that it could not succeed. The proposals sent by Fairfax
and his Council went much further than anything yet suggested by the Parliamentary Commissioners at Newport.
The Army averred that it would restore the King "to a
condition of safety, honour and freedom" if he would agree
to regular biennial Parliaments who were to control the Army,
all matters relating to defence, and the appointment of the
principal ministers. Charles was, in effect, to cease to be
King in any sense that he understood, and to become merely
the principal official in a country governed by Parliament.[19]

Ireton took the precaution of accompanying this message
to the King with a private and pressing letter to Colonel
Hammond warning him to keep a close watch on his prisoner.[20]
It was impossible that Charles should not recognise these
terms as a final ultimatum, a forewarning that the Army had
sealed his fate; it was probable therefore that he would try
to escape.

This message the King received, understood and rejected
in the third week of November at Newport. He made
tentative plans for escape, but Hammond was too watchful.[21]
He knew by the time Archbishop Ussher preached his birthday
sermon, that his last ordeal was approaching and made ready
to meet it as became a King and a Christian.

III

Fairfax could no longer hold back the soldiers' demand for
justice on the King. He may not any longer have wished to
do so, for it is possible that he was still under a misapprehension
as to the Army's intentions. It is also possible that he thought
the projected trial of the King was merely another turn of the

screw to compel Charles, after two years' delay, to yield what he had always refused: a cruel but essential trick to gain by fear and force the settlement that neither Parliament nor Army had been able to gain by argument.

Had not Henry Ireton—by design, or by accident?—concluded the petition for justice signed by his regiment with one strange, suggestive phrase: " . . . till he shall be acquitted of the guilt of shedding innocent blood." Did not this indicate that the King's condemnation was not a foregone conclusion? That there might be some other outcome—submission, acquittal, reconciliation?

It does not appear that Ireton himself had any such thoughts. But others did. Almost until the final hour, there were some who confidently asserted that the trial could not end in the King's death. Fairfax was, at least for a time, one of them.

Such a belief would explain the ease—almost the eagerness—with which he now proceeded in the course traced for him by Ireton. On the King's rejection of their offer the Council met again, accepted Ireton's proposed Remonstrance, and sent it to Parliament. Fairfax signed a covering letter to the Speaker urging him to place it before the House without delay.

This lengthy document condemned the King's policy, exposed the folly of attempting to treat with him, summed up the Army's plans for justice, peace and reform, and openly demanded "that the capital and grand author of our troubles, the person of the King, by whose commissions, commands or procurement, and in whose behalf, and for whose interest only, all our wars and troubles have been, with all the miseries attending them, may be speedily brought to justice, for the treason, blood and mischief he's therein guilty of."[22]

The Remonstrance was brought to Westminster on 20th November by a deputation of officers led by the formidable Colonel Isaac Ewer, who had distinguished himself in the recent war by taking Chepstow Castle and killing the governor. The Presbyterian party in the House of Commons should have known, when they read the words which condemned their Treaty and called for justice on the King, that the hour of doom had struck, for them as well as the King. But with a desperate obstinacy they played for time and refused to discuss the Remonstrance for a week. Colonel Ewer and his fellow officers received this news impassively, but some of the soldiers who attended them lay in wait for members when the House rose, and shadowed them to their lodgings, with muttered threats.[23]

Almost immediately the major points of the Remonstrance were published in newspapers and pamphlets. So also were further petitions from regiments up and down the country, clamouring for justice on the King.[24] Parliament had no power to stop this, for the chief censor of the Press was himself a strong supporter of the Army.

In the Isle of Wight the King had a moment of wry, ironic satisfaction. "The thundering declaration of the Army," as he described it in a letter to his son, was a judgment on the Presbyterians; they had failed to make terms with him, and now they too were bound for destruction. As for himself, he faced with serenity the fast approaching end:

> We know not but this may be the last time we may speak to you or the world publicly. We are sensible in to what hands we are fallen; and yet (we bless God) we have those inward refreshments the malice of our enemies cannot perturb; we have learned to busy ourself in retiring into ourself, and therefore can the better digest what befalls, not doubting but God's Providence will restrain our enemies' power and turn their fierceness to his praise.[25]

If the King was calm, Colonel Hammond was not. He had appealed in vain to Parliament to transfer him to some easier post. "Though hitherto it hath pleased God miraculously to guide me through this difficult employment, yet I find in myself an utter disability to proceed in it as things

30

now stand and are likely to continue. . . ." So the poor man had written just before the Remonstrance was sent to the House of Commons.[26] In his despairing perplexity at the threat to the King's life he appealed again to Cromwell.

He can have had little comfort from the answer. Cromwell advised him to follow the guidance of God, though he did not state explicitly where—in his view—that guidance led.

"We in this Northern Army were in a waiting posture, desiring to see what the Lord would lead us to"—so Cromwell wrote. The Remonstrance had now gone before Parliament. He himself might have wished it to be delayed a little longer, "yet seeing it is come out, we trust to rejoice in the will of the Lord, waiting his further pleasure." Now and again, in this long, rambling letter Cromwell drew near to an explicit statement. God, he argued, had shown His judgment on the King by overthrowing his supporters in the field. The victories which the Army had won over them in the last summer, the many providences they had experienced "hang so together, have been so constant, so clear and unclouded." Could any honest man still believe that good would come of a treaty with the King? "Good?—by this Man against whom the Lord hath witnessed?" Cromwell was within an inch of telling Hammond that the King must die, but again he swerved: "The Lord be thy counsellor, dear Robin," he wrote.[27]

Through the windings of this long letter the goal is discernible. God had pronounced sentence on the King, the Army must find means to execute it. But what means and in what manner? To judge by his letter to Hammond, the Remonstrance had come sooner than Cromwell expected. It would have suited better with his desire to keep the whole business within a convincing framework of Parliamentary procedure, if the Remonstrance had been deferred until the Army had stronger support in the House of Commons—his own for instance.

It is possible that he had stayed so long in the North in the belief that no official demand for the King's death would be made until he was there to guide its reception in the House. If this was so, then he had miscalculated. But whatever his reasons had been it was clear that he must now rejoin his colleagues in the South without delay. Fairfax too had an urgent need of him now that the initial move had been taken towards the King's trial. Writing from his headquarters at Windsor, the Lord General required Cromwell's attendance "with all convenient speed" so as to give "a merciful further-ance . . . to the very great business now in agitation."[28]

In the Isle of Wight the King was still obstinately exchang-ing opinions with the Commissioners of Parliament as though the Treaty were not irrevocably doomed. In the intervals he studied the Remonstrance of the Army and jotted down some notes on it. He pondered on the concessions he had made at Newport, more especially on the formal statement he had been compelled to endorse that the war was not of Parliament's making. Could this be regarded as a confession of guilt and used in evidence against him? He was certain that he could not be brought to trial by any legal means. "By the letter of the Law, all persons charged to offend against the Law ought to be tried by their peers or equals: what the Law is, if the Person questioned is without a Peer? And if the Law seems to condemn him, by what Power shall judgment be given and who shall give it."[29]

On 28th November, the Parliamentary Commissioners took their leave of the King, to carry his answers to West-minster. Charles did not expect to see them again; it was clear to him (as it was indeed to them) that the Army would prevent their return. The parting scene was public, at Newport Town Hall, and all the leading gentry of the Isle were there to witness it.

The Commissioners went through the motions of respectful leave taking as if all things were still normal, but the King, not knowing whether he would ever again be allowed to speak before an audience of his people, uttered a more solemn farewell:

> My Lords, you are come to take your leave of me, and I believe we shall scarce ever see each other again; but God's Will be done. I thank God, I have made my peace with him, and shall, without fear, undergo what he shall be pleased to suffer men to do unto me. My Lords, you cannot but know that, in my fall and ruin, you see your own, and that also near to you. I pray God send you better friends than I have found. I am fully informed of the whole carriage of the plot against me and mine, and nothing so much afflicts me as the sense and feeling I have of the sufferings of my subjects and the miseries that hang over my three kingdoms drawn upon them by those who, upon pretence of public good, violently pursue their own interests and ends.

Among those present was the Royalist Sir John Oglander, a kindly, eccentric, true-hearted old gentleman at whose house the King had dined about a year before, on the only occasion during his captivity in the Isle of Wight when he had been permitted to ride abroad in comparative freedom. Not a listener remained unmoved to hear the King speak so, wrote Sir John in his diary; he may have exaggerated, but most of those present were moved, and some shed tears.[30]

This was the last act of the failed Treaty of Newport. On the following day, preaching before the King, his small Court, and the officers of the garrison, one of his faithful adherents Dr. Henry Ferne chose a text from the prophet Habbakuk: "Though it tarry, wait for it, because it will surely come, it will not tarry." Public peace must surely come in the end, he said, but it might come sooner to a just man dying. Perhaps to the King it would come sooner, and not only peace, but more than peace: "a Crown of Glory that cannot fade away, a Kingdom that cannot be moved."

Charles listened attentively and later sent for the text of the sermon to study in private.[31]

Forty-eight hours after the Commissioners left, the Army took drastic action. First the bewildered Colonel Hammond was summoned away on a peremptory command signed by Fairfax. Then, on the evening of 30th November, in pitch darkness and driving rain, two hundred infantry and forty horsemen crossed from the mainland to the Isle of Wight and occupied Newport. They were commanded by that same Colonel Ewer who had, ten days earlier, laid before Parliament the Army's demand that the King be brought to trial.

The King had word of it first from Henry Firebrace, a faithful servant who had already once attempted to contrive his escape, and who was in the habit of smuggling out some of his letters. Charles was indeed writing to the Queen when the anxious Firebrace came in to warn him that the town was full of soldiers and he feared for his life. Charles refused to believe that murder was intended but he sent for Colonel Cooke, the youthful officer who commanded his guards at Newport, and asked him if there was a design to carry him off. Cooke knew of no such thing and, having become deeply attached to the King, was distressed at this new threat. From eight o'clock until nearly midnight he hurried to and fro in the pelting rain from Newport to Carisbrooke and back finding out what he could. Hammond's deputy, Major Rolph, gave him some assurance that the King would not be moved that night. More than this he could not learn, but the activity among the soldiers convinced him that the King was in danger.

He returned, to find Charles closeted with two devoted courtiers, the Duke of Richmond and the Earl of Lindsey who had been permitted to attend on him during the time of the Treaty. By this time, the house was guarded at every door and window, with sentinels outside the King's bedroom, and the whole place thick with the smoke of slow-matches. With the help of Cooke, who was now wholly in the King's

34

interest, escape might still have been possible. The Duke of Richmond, putting on a soldier's dark-coloured cloak, experimentally demonstrated that it was possible to walk unchallenged in Cooke's company right through the guards. But he and Lindsey pleaded with the King in vain. Charles argued that he had given his parole to Hammond and would not break it, even when Cooke pointed out that Hammond was no longer in command and certainly had nothing to do with the present danger. The King's sense of honour worked intermittently but strongly, and it may have held him back; he may also have felt that his chance of success was too slender to be worth the risk of an undignified recapture.

He sent Lindsey and Cooke away. He kept Richmond with him, his cousin, courtier and friend; it would be the last time he would have an attendant whom he loved and trusted to wait on him through the night, and he must have known it. Outside the rain beat down, masking the movements of the troops. Parliament would never have ordered this military occupation of Newport; he was in the hands of the Army, of those who called him The Grand Delinquent and The Man of Blood, and intended shortly to kill him. By now, it was one o'clock. He went quietly to bed.[32]

Next morning, before the first glimmer of wintry daylight, Colonel Ewer and Major Rolph were at his door with orders to remove him immediately. In half an hour he was ready. There was no time even to eat the breakfast hurriedly ordered by his attendants before the coach was at the door and the soldiers insisted that he should start. Firebrace knelt to kiss his hand as he came downstairs, but as the King paused for this last courtesy, he was jostled forward with an impatient "Go on, Sir." Rolph attempted to ride in the coach with him but Charles would not allow it. "It is not come to that yet," he said. "Get you out." But Richmond was forbidden to come. Escorted by the soldiers he drove to the quayside and embarked on the short crossing to Hurst Castle. This small and gloomy fortress stands at the extreme point of a spit of shingle running out into the Solent to the south of Lymington. The King had been distressed when he parted from Richmond, but he showed no further emotion on the journey.[33]

All hope of escape was at an end. Though the King managed occasionally still to smuggle out a coded letter, his opportunities were too limited to be of much avail to him.[34] The servants of his own choosing whom he had been allowed to have with him at Newport—Richmond, Lindsey, Hertford, and Southampton—had now been separated from him. He had only the attendants whom his captors could trust, correct in outward bearing but without sympathy for his cause or his person. Taking his daily exercise on the windswept beach of pebbles, or on the leads of the castle, he could see the sails of the Parliamentary squadron which patrolled the coast— ships of the English Navy which in the far-off days of peace had been his pride and joy;[35] and which now in ceaseless vigilance blockaded his solitary prison against rescue from Ireland or France or the Netherlands.

Fairfax had sent orders that he was to be treated with all civility.[36] The formalities were observed. In the cramped space of the little fortress the King was waited on by sixteen attendants, two gentlemen of the bedchamber, a carver, cup bearer and sewer, two pages, three cooks, and half a dozen other servants. He dined alone and in state, in the best room available, seated beneath a canopy, served on bended knee.[37]

IV

Having taken possession of the King, the Army now took possession of London, Parliament, and the government of the country. They waited ten days, in vain, for the House of Commons to answer their Remonstrance. Ostrich-like, the Presbyterian majority refused to discuss it. At Windsor, Fairfax and his officers met for a long day of prayer and consultation, punctuated by the arrival of more petitions for justice from regiments stationed in South Wales and the North. The Northern petition was sent by Cromwell, with a letter urging upon Fairfax, in his usual cloudy language, the necessity of carrying out the evident will of God.

> I verily think and am persuaded they are things which God puts into our hearts. I shall not need to offer anything to your Excellency: I know God teaches you . . . I hold it my duty, having received these petitions and letters, and being desired by the framers thereof, to present them to you. The good Lord work his will upon your heart enabling you to it; and the presence of the Almighty God go along with you.[38]

When he wrote those words Cromwell had not yet received the urgent command of Fairfax to join him in the South and be present at "the very great business now in agitation." Cromwell's exhortations to the Lord General to do God's work, and the Lord General's appeal to Cromwell to come to his aid must have passed each other by on the road. Before Cromwell came southward, Ireton had already propelled the Lord General into action. For, as Ireton saw it, no time was to be lost.

On 30th November, the Remonstrance was reissued as an appeal to the City of London. The Army had waited in vain for Parliament to respond; they proposed now to march on London, dissolve Parliament by force and form a provisional government pending a new election. They required £40,000 from the City towards the pay of their men. Fairfax signed the letter, but the guiding mind and the strong hand were Ireton's.[39]

Appalled by the threat of military occupation, the Mayor sat up all night in council and sent a distracted message to the House of Commons. Here the die-hard Presbyterians still held out and one of them, the pedantic lawyer William Prynne, urged his colleagues to declare the Army rebels. The majority had sense enough to refrain from offering needless provocation to an armed force which they had no power to resist.[40]

The march on London had begun. As the Army advanced, Parliament made a last-minute effort to halt them with an offer of £40,000.[41] But this was the sum that they intended to exact from the City, and knew that they would get. Twice the amount would not have stopped them now. The head of the column was already at Kensington, three miles from the Parliament House. On 2nd December, the troops occupied Westminster.

Next day was Sunday and nothing further happened, though conservative pastors in City pulpits denounced the Army, and its own preachers extolled its righteousness. On Monday Parliament reassembled without interruption, and for the next forty-eight hours the Commons continued to function, with grave uneasiness, but unmolested.

Only now did they hear from the Isle of Wight that the King had been moved to Hurst Castle "without their knowledge and consent" as they protested. They debated the Army's removal of the King far into the night and with great heat but all that came of their argument was a mild message of protest to Fairfax.[42] On the following day, 5th December, they received the Commissioners for the Treaty who had taken almost a week to journey to London from Newport. The delay had been partly caused by their fear of interception by Army patrols whom they knew to be on the watch for them; in order to evade them they had travelled in small groups and by devious ways, thus greatly lengthening the journey.[43]

With the King no longer in their power and the Army at the door, the House continued to debate the question of the Treaty. In this futile argument one Commissioner, the Republican, Sir Harry Vane, averred that he saw no hopes at all of bringing the King to acceptable terms. He was opposed by his fellow Commissioners, but strongly supported by two eloquent and highly intelligent members of the House, both colonels in the Army, John Hutchinson and Edmund Ludlow. The longest speech of all came from William Prynne, exhaustively condemning the actions and views of the Army, and demonstrating at inordinate length the necessity of going on with the Treaty. Not a modest man, he was convinced that his arguments had swayed the House, and the majority, whatever they felt about his immense oration, were in favour of pursuing the Treaty in despite of the Army. After they had voted to this effect, they seemed to offer a belated recognition to the menacing presence of the soldiers quartered round them: they appointed a deputation to wait on Fairfax for the purpose of preserving "a good correspondence" between Parliament and the Army.[44]

The General received them after an unusually long delay and laconically suggested that if they wanted friendship with the Army they should give their attention to the neglected Remonstrance. While the official representatives of the House were seeing Fairfax, Ireton and Harrison were discussing with the Speaker, William Lenthall, with Edmund Ludlow and other members of Parliament, what to do next. In the manifesto sent to London only forty-eight hours before, Ireton had declared an intention of dissolving Parliament and arranging a new election. But he now found that the Army's best supporters in the House advised—indeed insisted—that there be no forcible dissolution. Their reason for this was a desire to maintain an appearance of respect for Parliament and to lessen the chances of the collapse into anarchy which might occur if a new election took place.

The men who together worked out the next move, not without vehement discussion, had much the same interests at heart. Ludlow and Speaker Lenthall, as well as Ireton, were men of property who wanted to preserve economic stability and the social order. At least, had they been questioned on these points, they would have said so. But these were not, in fact, things which they much considered: they took them for granted. In their minds they were deeply exercised about the duplicity of the King, his infringement of the subjects' rights as they conceived of them, and above all, the Will of God. What they did during these next weeks, tended to the preservation of property and the social order at the expense of the King's life. But that was not the *reason* for their actions. They talked, with deep and heartfelt sincerity, of the religious, moral, and constitutional issues, and in this genuine conviction they carried with them all the purely religious extremists— men like Colonels Harrison and Pride—and left behind only the relatively small group who wanted, not only the death of the King, but more far-reaching changes as well.

So now, on this December evening, what exercised their minds was how, with the least appearance of irregularity, they could gain control of the central government. Ireton's plan for the forcible dissolution of Parliament seemed to Ludlow and others an unnecessary breach of the law. The present Parliament had been legally called by royal warrant in 1640. Before the outbreak of the war, when the constitutional authority of King, Lords and Commons was still functioning without an open breach, a bill had been presented to the King prolonging the life of this Parliament until such time as it should willingly dissolve itself. The King had given his consent. Legally, therefore, this Parliament was indissoluble by any outside authority.

The members who supported the Army, combined with those who were malleable or indifferent, formed a minority of a reasonable size, and included some of the strongest personalities in the House. The Speaker, William Lenthall, was on the whole on their side. It would be possible—so Ludlow and his friends argued—to exclude the irreconcilable Presbyterians and still keep a House of Commons in being large enough to perform its normal functions. The exclusion of unsatisfactory members was, moreover, a familiar proceeding as Royalist members had been expelled from this Parliament in its earlier years, first singly or by twos and threes, and later by the dozen. One way and another nearly two hundred members had been turned out in the last eight years. They had of course been expelled from within, by the vote of their colleagues. What was now proposed was an exclusion—a purge—imposed from without by the Army—a measure more drastic than any that had hitherto been used, but much less drastic and much more defensible than a dissolution.[45]

The decision taken, they spent the night of 5th December preparing lists of those who were to be excluded. Meanwhile, in the streets of Westminster, at orders from Ireton, the Army took control. The City Trained Bands—citizen volunteers who formed no part of the Army—had long had the duty of patrolling the approaches to Parliament. When a party of them marched up as usual at dusk on 5th December, they found their places occupied by men from the regiments quartered nearby. Jests and laughter broke out, and an exchange of good-natured greetings as the newcomers told the London men to go home to their shops and their wives; in future they could safely leave their military duties to the Army. Had they had any doubts about giving up their charge, these were laid to rest by their own commander, Philip Skippon, who had been general of the infantry in the Army and threw all his influence on to their side during the next critical days.[46]

Before daylight next morning Ireton had strengthened the guards round the Parliament House and stationed men to watch every entrance. This done, he reported to Fairfax. If the General made any comment on the dispositions of his subordinate it is nowhere recorded. Probably he preserved his usual silence.

So it happened that members of Parliament coming to take their places in the House on 6th December, found the approaches no longer guarded by the familiar Trained Bands, but by two regiments of the dreaded Army.

At the top of the stairs into the Parliament House stood Colonel Pride. Common repute said that he had begun life as a foundling left on the parish of St. Bride's (hence his name) and had worked in his youth as a brewer's drayman. Nothing in fact is known of his origins, but by 1648 he had become an officer and a gentleman with a good presence and civil manners. At the door of the Parliament House, hat in hand, he politely inquired the name of each member as he arrived. What happened next was not always polite. The name was checked off on a list and if the member was one of those marked down as an opponent of the Army, he was forbidden to enter the House. In order to prevent any mistakes, Lord Grey of Groby—"that grinning dwarf" as he was unkindly described—stood beside Colonel Pride to identify the members. He had been himself a member of the House of Commons since it first assembled in 1640 and was a consistent supporter of the Army.

Some of the excluded members were sent home, but forty-one, including the long-winded William Prynne, were detained all day and all the ensuing night in a large basement room usually known as "Hell". It proved to be a region of ice, rather than a region of fire. The weather was a penetrating, sleety drizzle, and the prisoners, compelled to squat or sleep on bare benches or the draughty floor, complained piteously of their treatment. Next day they were moved to better quarters in two Westminster taverns, and little by little over the next weeks, most of them were released.

Some members, warned of what was happening, stayed away from the House. Two—John Birch and Edward Stephens—by a slip in the organisation managed to take their seats. But, when they incautiously looked out at the door to see what was going on, Pride's men dragged them over the threshold, deaf to their piercing shrieks of "Privilege! Privilege!" Those who were left in the Commons sent a protest to Fairfax asking for the release of their colleagues, but this was a formal gesture, for the House was now composed only of the friends of the Army. A sneering Royalist called them "a little pretty nimble box of instruments" fit to carry out the Army's designs. The official statement of the Army was different in tone. Fairfax and his general Council of Officers issued a declaration that they had liberated the faithful and trustworthy members of Parliament from an oppressive faction and enabled them to carry out their duties to the nation without the "interruptions, diversions and depravations" of self-interested and corrupt colleagues.[47]

On the following day, 7th December, Cromwell at last rode in from the North. He declared that he had known nothing of the Purge but he approved the result.[48] The first part of the statement was almost certainly true, the second part may not have been. The surviving evidence of his actions and his opinions at this time is tantalisingly incomplete, but the fragments seem to suggest that he had had a more subtle plan for maintaining the appearance of Parliament's authority than this forcible purging of the House. Had the crisis been postponed until after his return he might, with the help of Vane, have marshalled the Army's friends within the House more effectively than had hitherto been done, and so, by some well-timed motion from the floor of the House have secured the expulsion of the forty or so rigid Presbyterians who stood in their way. By doing this the Army's control of Parliament would have been established from within instead of being violently imposed from without. But it was too late now for any redeeming manœuvre and Cromwell accepted with a good grace a situation which he could not alter.

It was noticed that he made his first entrance into the purged House—from which he had been absent since May on campaign—arm in arm with Henry Marten, a convinced Republican whose eloquence, wit and ingenuity often influenced the Commons. He had not always been on good terms with Cromwell, but their present unanimity of purpose was emphasised when Marten began the business of the day by moving a vote of thanks to General Cromwell for his services in the field.[49]

The troops had meanwhile, to the considerable dismay of the Londoners, occupied the City and seized the deposits of cash at Goldsmiths' Hall and Weavers' Hall to meet arrears of pay. On the whole, the men were well-behaved, although they made a bonfire of the panelling and choirstalls of St. Paul's, for the weather was very cold. To spare the citizens as far as possible, they were quartered in empty buildings or warehouses, sleeping on the bare floors. Fairfax, anxious lest the bad conditions might breed discontent and disorder, ordered the citizens to provide bedding so that every two soldiers could share a mattress, a bolster and a pair of sheets and blankets.[50] He busied himself with matters of organisation and discipline, issued orders for the civil behaviour of the troops, and rarely attended the Council of Officers where the policy of the Army took shape: the Council of Officers which was now, through its control of Parliament, the effective government of England.

In the House of Commons on 13th December, the Treaty negotiations at Newport were voted "highly dishonourable and destructive to the peace of the Kingdom." Two days later the Council of Officers voted that the King be moved to Windsor, "in order to the bringing of him speedily to justice," —in accordance with their Remonstrance of 20th November. They appointed a small Committee to consider how his trial should be managed, and sent Colonel Harrison to fetch him away from Hurst Castle. At this meeting Ireton was present, Fairfax was not, and Oliver Cromwell presided.[51]

CHAPTER THREE

GRANDEES, PRESBYTERIANS, AND LEVELLERS

1648

"THE ENGLISH Nation are a sober people, however at present infatuated," King Charles had written from Newport to his son.[1] They were not so infatuated as to be unable to mock at their plight. One of the most popular ballads in London at the time was a string of doggerel verses deriding the idea of majority rule, the conflicting claims of the sects and the rumours about the fate of the King:

> Now thanks to the Powers below
> We have even done our do,
> The Mitre is down and so is the Crown,
> And with them the Coronet too. . . .
> There is no such thing, as a Bishop or King,
> Or Peer but in name or show.
> Come clowns and come boys, come hobbledehoys,
> Come females of each degree,
> Stretch out your throats, bringing in your votes,
> And make good the anarchy. . . .
> We are fourscore religions strong,
> Then take your choice, the major voice
> Shall carry it, right or wrong;
> Then let's have King Charles, says George,
> Nay, we'll have his son, says Hugh,
> Nay, then let's have none says jabbering Joan,
> Nay, we'll all be Kings, says Prue.[2]

But ballads and gaiety were declining, not merely because of the Puritan triumph. A foreign visitor who returned to England after the civil wars found that the people, whom he remembered as friendly and good-humoured, had become "melancholy, spiteful, as if bewitched."[3] They had cause for gloom. There had been no settled government for over six years; taxation to pay for the war had been introduced by Parliament in 1643 on a nation-wide basis and had continued ever since. The hated Excise, a purchase tax, enhanced the price of most essential goods, while every household in the country had to contribute to the so-called "weekly assessment" to pay the running expenses of the war. The King's adherents from the highest, almost to the lowest, had had to "compound", or in other words to pay fines which were somewhat arbitrarily calculated in relation to their resources and the extent to which they had actively participated in the fighting. The lamentations of gentlemen and their wives who found themselves in debt and difficulty on this account were the loudest, but the greatest sufferers were the lesser men—yeoman farmers or small tradesmen who might find themselves reduced to abject need as a result of their loyalty or their indiscretion. Some of the victors had all too evidently made money out of the war, but the poorer sort were no better off. The men of the unpaid Army bitterly resented having to live at free quarter and thus oppressing the very people whose liberties they were supposed to defend. Limbless soldiers and widows and children of the slain begged in the streets or thronged about the doors of Parliament. If some of these unfortunates were not what they claimed to be, it was none the less true that beggary had much increased. So had highway robbery, and all the other familiar symptoms of a long period of disorder.

Trade and industry had been much depressed in the war. The wool trade had been interrupted because for several years the King had held key positions which cut off London from the graziers and clothiers of the Cotswolds and the

Berkshire downs. The cloth industry of the West Riding had been dislocated by fighting in the earlier part of the war. The northern mines had been damaged by flood, and the coal export of Newcastle—a Royalist stronghold—had been choked for two years by a Parliamentary blockade. The Navy, fulfilling its first duty of preventing foreign help from reaching the King, had proved inadequate to protect English shipping—and that of London in particular—from Irish and Flemish pirates operating sometimes under the protection of the royal flag.

A series of three disastrous harvests had caused widespread distress and the price of wheat, barley and oats was the highest of the century. The summer of 1648 had been continuously and disastrously wet from the beginning of May until mid-September,[4] adding anxiety about floods, crops and livestock to the disturbance and destruction of renewed fighting.

The mood of London by the winter of 1648 was one of glum and resentful endurance, and in so far as it is possible to generalise about a people this was the prevailing mood throughout the country. The Royalists, after their second defeat, were leaderless and hopeless. This negative attitude goes far to explain the events of the next eight weeks. For anyone who reads pamphlets, newspapers, or letters written by the King's adherents at this time cannot but be struck by the discrepancy between the strength of the emotions expressed and the feebleness with which they were translated, or rather not translated, into action. During this critical winter the leaders of the Army alone, and occasionally the Levellers, had the resolution necessary to carry out their dangerous designs. It is true that they also had the physical force to do so. But too much can be made of this. Their military power would no doubt always have ensured their ultimate success. It does not explain why no attempt was made, however foolhardy, however futile, to cross their designs. It has been said often, and with truth, that the majority of the English people did not want their King's execution. It needs also to be remembered that whether they wanted it or not, the majority of the English people were prepared to accept it. They were shocked by it; in private talk, and even in public, they repudiated it. But from the removal of the King from Newport until his death on the scaffold, not one of the King's subjects risked his life to save him.

They were not indifferent. On the contrary they were greedy for news and were on the whole well supplied, both with information and propaganda. King Charles during the years of his power had forbidden the importation into England of the corantoes or news-books which had begun to circulate abroad, especially in the Low Countries. The production of such things at home was naturally prohibited. But with the collapse of his government, and the popular thirst for news stimulated by the Civil War, the weekly papers soon became a familiar part of daily life. They were free-lance affairs, for the most part run by editors and printers in alliance, sold at a penny a time, and competing furiously with each other. Many were short-lived, as editors and printers lost interest, were crowded out by more efficient competitors, or got into trouble with the government—for Parliament soon began to notice the dangers of unrestricted circulation of news.

At the end of 1648 there were six regular and fairly well established papers, licensed by the government censors. The less popular had a circulation of about a thousand, the most successful twice or even three times that number.[5] They were all weeklies, but as each had a different publication day, Londoners could buy a paper any day of the working week. Although London was the centre from which they all came (in the war the King had issued his official newspaper from Oxford) the country was not ill-served with news. The carriers' carts which, at regular intervals, left London with packages, goods, and letters for every part of the country, now also carried bundles of news-books, which would be bought, shared out, handed on and read aloud to audiences at inns and ale-houses, and in the parlours of farmhouses and manor houses, sometimes also in pulpits, over all the country. By 1648 the news reached even the farthest parts of England with a regularity unknown to previous generations. The seizure of the King by the Army, his trial and death would be followed, in some detail, week by week by almost all his literate subjects and by quite a number of the illiterate as the bundles of news-sheets arrived from London.

The most generally popular newspaper of the period seems to have been *A Perfect Diurnall*, which came out every Monday and was edited and largely written by Samuel Pecke, "a bald-headed buzzard . . . a tall thin-faced fellow, with a hawk's nose, a meagre countenance and long runagate legs, constant in nothing but wenching, lying and drinking."[6] The description comes from a rival journalist and may be unjust. Whatever his personal faults Pecke was a newsman of ability whose paper was always full, informative and fairly free of deliberate inaccuracy.

The other papers in steady demand were John Dillingham's *Moderate Intelligencer* and Richard Colling's *Kingdoms' Weekly Intelligencer*, both of which, in the coming crisis, showed a cautious bias in the King's favour. Colourless and less efficient was Daniel Border's *Perfect Weekly Account*. Fiercely critical of the King was a newspaper edited by an extreme sectary, Henry Walker's *Perfect Occurrences*. Walker had been a pamphleteer of eccentric sectarian opinions since the beginning of the troubles and had distinguished himself, on the eve of the war, by leaping on to the King's coach and thrusting an abusive leaflet through the window. He had a Cambridge degree and some pretensions to learning and was amusing his readers at this time by giving them each week the name of some eminent public figure transliterated into Hebrew with a suitable exposition of its meaning in that language.[7]

The senior censor, appointed during the Army's first period of political dominance, in 1647, was Gilbert Mabbott. The son of a Nottingham shoemaker, he had been secretary to Fairfax, and his sympathies were—like those of many intelligent small tradesmen—with John Lilburne and the Levellers. Soon after he became censor Mabbott had tried to suppress Dillingham's *Moderate Intelligencer* on the grounds of an incautious Royalist joke at Parliament's expense. His plan seems to have been to eliminate Dillingham and then to gain control of this lively and well-established journal for himself. The manœuvre failed and Dillingham managed to establish his right to possession of his own paper. Mabbott remained in occupation of half its title however, and from the summer of 1648 produced a weekly called *The Moderate*.[8]

The Moderate is by far the most interesting newspaper for this critical period. In his position as censor Mabbott could express his views without fear of being suppressed, and was thus able to present his news with comments which conveyed a distinct policy. *The Moderate* expressed the hopes and misgivings of the Levellers and gave detailed attention to their petitions and manifestos. It was no respecter of persons and Mabbott went further than any other editor in publishing scurrilous rumours about the King. *The Moderate* persistently hinted during these weeks that there had been a "black wench" in the Isle of Wight with whom the King had solaced his loneliness. But, these offensive slanders apart, Mabbott used his position at the centre of affairs to acquire much interesting news which he presented intelligently. He had also, through the closely integrated Leveller party, a means of distribution denied to his competitors. Leveller agents saw to it that his paper was more widely circulated than any other in the ranks of the Army. If its circulation was rather more specialised than that of Pecke's *A Perfect Diurnall* it seems to have been, at this time, nearly as large.

Apart from the licensed Press, three Royalist papers appeared with difficulty and at irregular intervals—*Mercurius Melancolicus*, *Mercurius Elencticus* and the irrepressible *Mercurius Pragmaticus*, familiarly called "Prag". Their editors were by this time well-known by sight to the spies and informers of London as well as to the whole pack of government "blood-hounds", appointed by Parliament to track down illicit pamphleteers at eighteen pence a day. None the less they contrived to dodge arrest, and to lurk in back alleys and friendly taverns sometimes for weeks together, and to print their sheets on small movable presses that could be easily concealed. They even prevailed on hawkers to sell them although the penalty for any man or woman caught so doing was to be whipped as a common rogue. George Wharton, who combined astrology with editing *Mercurius Elencticus* had been in prison for part of the autumn. The title (and profits, such as they were) of *Mercurius Melancolicus* seem to have been pirated and filched to and fro between at least three editors of whom Martin Parker the veteran and popular ballad-writer was one. The most efficient of the Royalist sheets was *Pragmaticus*, edited with a fair amount of regularity by Marchamont Nedham who had been in the course of his life a schoolmaster and a doctor, but had found his vocation in the war as a sharply satirical commentator on current affairs.

In general these "resistance" news-sheets hardly justified the risks involved in their production and sale. There was little in them but abuse of Army and Parliament, scandal about their leaders and occasional misinformation about Royalist victories at sea, or projected help from foreign monarchs. *Pragmaticus* was the exception; Nedham did not fall behind in abuse, for which he had a pretty talent, developed during the war when he had edited one of the leading Parliamentary news-sheets and made merry at the expense of the Cavaliers. He had also, unlike his fellow Royalist editors, some useful sources of information at the heart of affairs, possibly left over from his Parliamentarian past. His accounts of debates in Parliament, though derisive, are full and well-informed.[9]

The King's fate was the principal topic of discussion among his subjects. Few of them, in spite of the constant threat of the Army, seem to have practised even an elementary caution about expressing their views in public. Political and religious opinions were bandied about with a bold indifference to consequences: not that the consequences were likely to be very serious. The clandestine news-sheets occasionally produced rather unconvincing tales of troopers who had trampled on London citizens for expressing Royalist views, but in a period of such uncertainty, the government (whoever and whatever it was) was not likely to prosecute any but the most persistent and dangerous critics. The denunciations of ale-house and fireside politicians were not worth their attention, though sometimes provocative conduct might lead to a brawl. Lord Middlesex dining with a party of Cavaliers at the White Horse tavern in the City had expressed his feelings for some troopers in the street below, by emptying a chamber pot on their heads. Not surprisingly, this led to a fight, in which the Cavaliers, far outnumbered, had the worst of it and some of them were held prisoners for the night. But nothing further happened.[10]

On another occasion the Earl of Northampton, who had fought devotedly for the King, happened to meet an old enemy in arms, Sir William Brereton, in a narrow lane near London. Some years before Brereton had refused after a battle to yield up the body of Northampton's father for burial. For this unpleasant and unchivalrous conduct the family had never forgiven him. Northampton at once drew his sword and challenged him. Brereton refused to fight, but before he could make his undignified escape Northampton had given him some vicious cuts about the head and shoulders. For this outrage he was threatened by Parliament with exclusion from pardon; but the threat was not carried out.[11]

It was not from the broken Royalists that the Army expected their most serious troubles to come. As they took over the government of the country and set all in motion for the trial of the King, the opposition that they chiefly feared was from the Presbyterians, whom they had ousted from Parliament but had not silenced, and from the Levellers whose demands for radical changes of government they had not yet accepted.

The effective strength of the Presbyterians had been broken by the purging of Parliament. The Army, while it let the lesser members go, very prudently kept the more influential in prison. Three of these were soldiers of some distinction—Sir William Waller, Edward Massey, and Robert Browne. Waller had been one of Parliament's leading generals in the first years of the war. Massey, a young man famous for his defence of Gloucester against the King in 1643, had attempted to organise a new Presbyterian force, to challenge the power of the Army. In this he had been assisted by Browne, an eminent citizen and sheriff of London who, during the war, had commanded the midland forces for some months. With these three safely shut away, there could be no more danger of the Presbyterians raising a rival Army.

Noisier, but on the whole less dangerous, were two furious polemicists of the Presbyterian party—William Prynne and Clement Walker, both of whom had been excluded at the Purge. Walker had already published a violent attack on Cromwell and his supporters called *A History of Independency*, and his pen was busy with more venomous stuff as soon as the Army seized power. William Prynne, a rigid Puritan, had published criticism of the King's religious policy and the Queen's participation in masques, and had been a victim of no less than two sentences in the Star Chamber during the absolute rule of the King. He had lost his ears, been branded on the cheek, had stood in the pillory and had been prohibited from practising law. Reinstated when Parliament met in 1640, he had enjoyed for some years a just prominence for his sufferings and had had his vengeance by prosecuting Archbishop Laud. But he was a meticulous legalist who would not countenance the infringements of Parliamentary privilege that had once been practised on a small scale by the King and were now being practised on a large scale by the Army. He and Walker, sometimes singly, sometimes together launched a series of protests against "the present unParliamentary junto", "Cromwell's journeymen", the despicable "Rump" —this was Walker's name for it—that now sat at Westminster.[12]

Meanwhile the Presbyterian ministers in the London churches preached in wrath and grief on the Army's capture of power. Edmund Calamy at St. Mary Aldermanbury drew large and wealthy audiences—" seldom less than sixty coaches" were to be seen waiting on the day of his weekly "lecture". William Jenkyn, that "sententious, elegant preacher" and Cornelius Burges, a more theatrical performer and something of a demagogue, attracted the middle and lower ranks of citizens.[13] Obadiah Sedgwick at St. Paul's, Covent Garden, told his fashionable parishioners of the misdeeds of the Army; they were already well aware of them, because the arcade of their beautiful Piazza had been turned into an improvised stable where the soldiers tied "their horses to the doors of noblemen's, knights' and gentlemen's houses."[14] Thomas Watson, with greater courage, preached a sermon before the remnant of the House of Commons at St. Margaret's, Westminster, in which he told them they were no Parliament at all. Their indignation, though real, was mild: they abstained from their usual practice of recording a vote of thanks, but took no other action.[15]

The Presbyterian ministers were a majority in London but there was an eloquent minority of Independent preachers to cry up the Army as the instrument of God's judgment. Many curious Londoners crowded into the Courtyard at Whitehall to hear the famous Army chaplain Hugh Peter preach in the open-air to the troops. He was well known for his lively, popular style and graphic gestures. They were not disappointed. The soldiers listened attentively while he declared that the kingdom was their mother, in grave danger; but Parliament, the wicked elder son, had locked her in and kept the key, so that the Army, the younger son, had no other way to rescue her but by breaking down the door.

He concluded by assuring them that the General, or any of the officers, would willingly answer any questions that troubled them.[16]

Well known to the Londoners and much more impressive than Hugh Peter was John Goodwin, minister of an Independent congregation in Coleman Street, who in the triumphantly named pamphlet *Right and Might Well Met* welcomed the coming of the Army to apply an exceptional remedy to exceptional circumstances and protect the people against the treachery and hypocrisy of the Presbyterians.[17]

Some few sectaries, however, of a mystical turn of mind were shocked that the Army of Saints should have yielded to gross sensual ambition, and seized political power. Such a one was William Sedgwick, who had a few months before presented his religious meditations, *Leaves from the Tree of Life*, to the King, only to have them returned with the comment that "the author stands in need of some sleep". This slighting conduct notwithstanding, Sedgwick was shocked at the threat to Charles's life. In an open letter to Fairfax he assured him that the Army might conceivably and in some unexplained fashion be doing the Lord's work, since God knew how to use enemies as well as friends. Nebuchadnezzar, or even the Devil himself, unwittingly did the Lord's work. But the Army was in no other sense an instrument of Heaven. On the contrary they were full of pride and vainglory and their thoughts were bloody.[18]

For reasons that were not mystical at all but practical the Levellers also looked upon this new turn of events with suspicion, seeing in it the will and guidance of Cromwell and his son-in-law Ireton and fearing that so far from securing liberty, justice and peace, the result would be a military tyranny under Cromwell.

The upheavals of the war had released new forces and stimulated new demands among the people. The Leveller movement was strongest in London and was, or had been, stronger still in the Army. The rank and file of the Army

were young men—sons of yeomen, sons of tradesmen, sons
of craftsmen. They represented that part of the people of
England who had rarely, until now, raised their voices in
politics. Most of the cavalry could read but the infantry were
nearly all illiterate. But since the Parliamentary forces had
been reformed into the New Model Army in the spring of
1645, these soldiers—many of them still at the most formative
and suggestible age—had been exposed to moral, spiritual,
and intellectual influences which had given them not only
discipline as a body, but confidence and enlightenment as
men. The sermons which they had heard convinced them
that they were fighting for a righteous cause. The victories
which they had won proved that their watchword, *God with
us*, expressed an undoubted truth. Free exposition of the
Bible and free discussion taught the more intelligent to exercise
and to trust their own powers of reasoning. They grew to
value themselves more highly as Christians and as citizens.

In the interval between the two wars pamphlets of all
kinds had circulated in the Army; religious ideas and political
doctrines had been freely discussed and the name and principles
of John Lilburne had grown familiar to all. The soldiers
began to ask for much more than the privileges of Parliament
and the reform of the Church for which the war had been
fought. They wanted an enlarged franchise, more frequent
Parliaments, a simpler and better administration of justice
and the abolition of trading privileges which hampered the
poorer tradesmen. The principal points of the programme
were set out in the *Agreement of the People* in October 1647—
a document sponsored by the Army Levellers, and intended
as a basis for peace.

The mistimed attempt to escape on the part of the King,
a Leveller mutiny in the Army, equally mistimed and quickly
suppressed by Cromwell, and finally the outbreak of the
Second War had caused the Agreement to be shelved. By the
winter of 1648-9 the Levellers were weaker in the Army
than they had been a year before, and they had lost their

most important partisan among the officers, the sharp-tongued Colonel Rainborough who had been killed by the Cavaliers at Doncaster.

The Leveller following in the ranks had been inspired and organised during the two years' interlude of peace. After six months of renewed fighting the hard core remained, but many of those who had accepted Leveller ideas in the inactive months when talk or argument was the chief interest of the day, lost interest when they were in action once more. The officers whom they had criticised as "Grandees" in the interlude of peace, were now once again their leaders in battle, who took the decisions, who risked their lives with them, who brought them victory. The Leveller movement waned in the Army as the old confidence and the traditional obligations between leader and led, gentry and tenantry, masters and servants reasserted themselves under the primitive stresses of war. When the war was over, a burning resentment against the King, who had been responsible for this second outbreak with all its useless bloodshed, was felt alike by officers and men. Hence the petitions for justice on the Grand Delinquent, the King.

But this bold resolution, to destroy the King, overshadowed the more important but less startling demands of the previous year. The Leveller leader John Lilburne, who had not been concerned in the summer's fighting, realised this and saw at once how his old enemies the "Grandees" might turn this to their advantage by concentrating all action and all attention on the destruction of the King, and subsequently refusing to meet any other demands for reform.

Lilburne had first attracted public notice as a young man, little more than a boy, when he had received a savage sentence from the King's government for distributing a book against the bishops. Flogged through the streets and pilloried at Westminster, he had addressed the crowd with considerable eloquence, and defiantly distributed copies of the offensive pamphlet even during his punishment. He was a slender,

febrile, attractive youth with a quick brain and an unquench-
able spirit.

When the Long Parliament met, Cromwell took up his
case and secured his release. Later when the Civil War broke
out, Lilburne distinguished himself as a soldier and rose to
the rank of lieutenant colonel. In 1645 he resigned on a point
of conscience, being unwilling to take the oath imposed on the
officers of the New Model Army. From this time on his
distrust of Cromwell grew. Lilburne now, in pamphlet and
petition, argued in favour of social reforms—the reorganisation
of justice, the extension of the franchise, more frequent
Parliaments, and the abolition of the trading privileges which
hampered the small men. As his methods of attack were often
both libellous and personal, he constantly and noisily ran
foul of the law. Never silent, seldom out of prison, he became
steadily more popular and more influential with the small
tradesmen of London whose cause he championed, and with
the troops. He himself disliked the name "Leveller" because
neither he nor his followers believed in "levelling"; they
believed in a society which would give opportunity and
justice to lesser men and a ladder for rising in the world.
Cromwell, once his benefactor, was now denounced as a
"Grandee", "a silken Independent", a traitor to the Cause for
which the war had been fought. Lilburne distrusted equally
the officers who were men of rank and property—like Cromwell himself, Ireton, Ludlow, Whalley—and the men who,
like Harrison, Okey, Pride and others, had risen through
merit. Those who were not "Grandees" by birth had become
so by interest and were Cromwell's "creatures".

When the war broke out afresh in the summer of 1648
Parliament released Lilburne from prison, not out of any love
for him or his ideas, but so that he should make trouble for
Cromwell and thus undermine the unity of the Army.

They misread Lilburne's character. He was passionately
centred upon himself. Everything he wrote came out of his
own experience and was illustrated by references to his own

achievements and sufferings, and to the unjust machinations of his enemies. But he did not want much for himself; he did not want revenge. He wanted freedom for men like himself, reform of the law, and the restriction of privilege. He knew that if he divided the Army and undermined Cromwell he would merely strengthen the power of Parliament, which, in his own words, stood for "nothing worth praising or liking . . . in reference to the People's Liberties or Freedoms."

Immediately upon his release he wrote to Cromwell: "I am no staggerer from my first principles that I engaged my life upon, nor from you, if you are what you ought to be, and what you are now strongly reported to be." While the war lasted he kept Parliament in mind of the Levellers' demands by stimulating a petition for the abolition of tithes, and of commercial privileges; for the release of prisoners for debt; for the reform of the criminal law, especially in relation to capital punishment; for better treatment of the poor. As soon as the Cavaliers were defeated he wrote peremptorily to Cromwell to insist that the freedom of the people under a just government was "the sole intended end of the wars".

The answer came indirectly. Instigated apparently by Cromwell, a group of his supporters led by young Colonel Tichborne saw Lilburne at the Nag's Head tavern in London. Here they declared that in their view the first thing to be done was to cut off the King's head, and to purge or to dissolve Parliament. Lilburne was incensed. The King was an evil man and Parliament a mockery, but if the Army destroyed them both, "they would devolve all government in the kingdom into their wills and swords", a situation under which the state of the people might be a greater slavery "than ever it was in the King's time". There must be safeguards: nothing should be done to the King until a free Parliament had been elected on a reformed franchise, so that the people's will could be truly known. At this the "Gentlemen Independents", as Lilburne styled them, grew "most desperately cholerick" but they agreed in the end, after a second discussion, to set up a committee, part Army and part civilian, to consider the best way of implementing the Leveller programme.[19]

In consequence of this some concessions to Leveller opinions were made by Ireton in drafting the Remonstrance which, on 20th November, the Army had presented to Parliament. But Lilburne was still not satisfied. Journeying to Windsor to confront the "Grandees" with further arguments, he found Ireton at the Garter Inn preparing to march on London. He was indignant. This was a project, he said, of "the most desperate mischievousness". To seize on Parliament, to bring the King to trial—these were useless and vicious gestures unless the Army would first give "some good security to the nation for the future settlement of their liberties and freedoms." Ireton was impatient and angry, but Colonel Harrison ("fine and gilded Harrison" as Lilburne sneered) was conciliatory, and this was fortunate, because Lilburne was on the point of stirring up his followers in London to demonstrate against the Army. In the end he was pacified with a plan for a new *Agreement of the People* to be worked out by representatives of Parliament, the Army, and the Levellers.[20]

In this way the acquiescence of the Levellers had been secured for the first move towards the trial of the King. But Lilburne had been outmanœuvred. His judgment had been right when he had argued that "some good security to the nation" needed to be laid down *before* and not *after* the march on London. Once the "Grandees" had taken power into their own hands by establishing themselves in the capital and controlling Parliament, they would see to it that no *Agreement of the People*, worked out in co-operation with the Levellers, should take the government out of their own capable hands.

These then were the dangers that faced Cromwell and the Army in planning the trial of the King. The defeated and depressed Royalists, the eloquent and irreconcilable Presbyterians, both of them opposed the King's trial on every ground of duty and morality. Lastly, the more subtly dangerous Levellers, who approved the King's trial, even the King's execution, but only as part of a more far-reaching revolution which the "Grandees", the present architects of the nation's fate, had no intention of permitting.

CHAPTER FOUR

RIGHT AND MIGHT WELL MET

December 15, 1648 - January 6, 1649

AT HURST CASTLE the King talked freely to his captors having no longer anything to lose by indiscretion. He was calm, even cheerful. The bitter resignation which seems to have been his mood in the last days at Newport had given place to a surprising optimism. He reminded them that no law existed by which a King could be tried. If the Army seriously threatened his life, they would certainly be opposed by the City magnates; foreign princes might also intervene and there would in all probability be an invasion from the Royalists in Ireland.[1] These things sounded plausible and Charles may have believed them. It was hard, it was nearly impossible, for a man who had been convinced all his life that he acted under a divine mandate to accept the idea that he could be tried and condemned by the people over whom God had placed him. He was still certain that the majority of his subjects wanted to see him restored to his throne, and that the Army said much more than they meant in their Remonstrance. He too seems, for a time, to have believed that the threat of a trial was intended to frighten him into abandoning the God-given rights of the Crown.

In London a Declaration purporting to be from his hand had appeared among the illicit broadsheets for sale in the streets. No printer's name was given for fear of prosecution. The King may have entrusted such a message to one of the devoted courtiers who was with him on his last night at Newport— Richmond or Lindsey. Or he may have smuggled it from

Hurst whence, on one occasion at least, he appears to have got a message away to a loyal servant outside. It is also possible that the words were written by a journalist working for the Cavaliers. The Declaration, whether it came from the King or not, expressed his point of view with dignity—his conviction that he was blameless and his resignation to the will of God.

> There is nothing [that] can more obstruct the long hoped for peace of this Nation, than the illegal proceedings of them that presume from servants to become masters and labour to bring in democracy. . . . I once more declare unto all my loving subjects (and God knows whether or not this may be my last) that I have earnestly laboured for peace, and that my thoughts were serene and absolute, without any sinister ends, and there was nothing left undone by me, that my conscience would permit me to do. . . .[2]

Colonel Harrison, fulfilling his orders to transfer Charles to Windsor, as a preliminary to his trial, reached Hurst Castle after dark on 7th December. He made the necessary arrangements with the governor for the King's removal thence, and left the following day to see to the security plans for the rest of the journey. Charles did not see him and was not consulted but he expressed pleasure on learning that he was to go to Windsor.[3]

Three days later he set out, riding all the way under strong guard. He dined on the first day near Redbridge at the house of Lady Knollys. At Winchester, where he spent the night, the Mayor and Aldermen received him with all ceremony as though this were a holiday progress in the days of his power. The mace was handed to him and formally returned, and he was escorted into the city where many of the local gentry in their best attire had gathered to kiss his hand. After he had left, the Mayor was reprimanded by the governor for what he had done and tendered his apologies to Parliament, but there seems to have been no attempt by those in charge of the King to interfere with the proceedings at the time.[4]

From Winchester the King's journey lay across the open downland where there had been much fighting at the turning point of the war. He rode by the long village of Alresford which had been burnt from end to end during the battle in March 1644—the first serious defeat that his armies had suffered. Beyond Alresford the wide landscape gives place to more crowded and hilly country. They stopped to dine at Alton, where the grass of five summers had by now blurred the traces of an outpost in the churchyard, scene of a heroic stand by a party of outnumbered Cavaliers.

All along the highway groups of men and women gathered to see the King go by; some of them raised a cheer, and some shouted "God preserve Your Majesty." Between Alton and Farnham, he noticed a well-equipped troop of horse drawn up at the roadside. The officer in command was a fine-looking man, handsomely apparelled in a velvet hat and new buffcoat with a "crimson silk scarf about his waist, richly fringed." Signing to his attendant Herbert, the King asked who this might be, and learnt that it was Colonel Harrison, the fanatic whom he believed had wished to murder him, and who had first called him by the accusing name "that Man of Blood".[5]

That evening, when the King was lodged at Farnham, he spoke with Harrison. Charles was gracious and flattering. He had some skill in physiognomy he said, and he could see that Harrison was a valiant man. He had heard that he had been involved in a plot to murder him, but he did not credit this now that he had met him. Handsome Harrison ("fine and gilded" in John Lilburne's phrase) answered courteously. As for plots and murders, "he hated all such base, obscure under-takings." The King could set his mind at rest; what was yet to befall him "would be open to the eyes of the world."[6]

At Farnham, as at Winchester, gentry and country-folk crowded in to see the King and some brought sick children to receive the healing royal touch.[7] Harrison seems to have made no attempt to stop them. The number and efficiency of his troops was security enough.

Next day they rode towards Bagshot. It was miry weather, better for horses than coaches. A coach from the West Country with a dozen passengers aboard had overturned on Bagshot Heath only a week before, fatally injuring one of the travellers, a merchant of Exeter. The Royalists were putting about a story that, just before the accident, he had been telling his companions that hanging was too good for the King. For this blasphemy God had, within the instant, struck him dead.[8]

At Bagshot the King dined at the Lodge with Lord and Lady Newburgh, spirited young people and notoriously Royalists. He had suggested this himself and Harrison had presumably agreed because there was nowhere else so convenient. He trusted to his own and his soldiers vigilance to circumvent any plan of escape that might be attempted either by Newburgh or, more probably, by his wife. She had been, ten years before, Lady Catherine Howard, a wilful girl and one of the admired beauties of the court, who had eloped with the King's cousin, Lord D'Aubigny. After his death at Edgehill, she had been conspicuous in the famous plot to seize London in 1643, and had carried messages through the enemy lines concealed in her bosom.

The Newburghs received the King with the warmest welcome their house and the season could afford. To Colonel Harrison and his men they were careful and correct, though they noticed with resentment that he posted guards at every door. During dinner it was reported from the stables that the King's horse had gone lame. Lord Newburgh immediately volunteered to supply him with a fresh mount. He was a keen racing man and his horses were famous. But Harrison was not taken by surprise. He had expected the Newburghs to have a scheme for rescuing the King and was confident that if Charles tried to get away on Lord Newburgh's fastest horse, he would not succeed.

By the time dinner was over, the winter afternoon was drawing towards dusk and a steady rain was falling. Harrison marshalled his men very closely round the King and drew his attention to the quality and good condition of their horses. Knowing that he had no chance against them, Charles did not try to escape.[9]

Through darkness, cold and driving rain the King reached Windsor to be greeted by the shouts of drenched Royalists waiting in the streets—"God bless Your Majesty and send you long to reign." After he had gone by they went off to dry themselves by drinking his health at the Garter and other inns so noisily that a party of musketeers came down from the castle to disperse them.[10]

Meanwhile the King had been received into the castle by the nervous and courteous governor, Colonel Whichcot. As he entered the outer enclosure, he saw the Duke of Hamilton kneeling in the mud. Once his Master of the Horse, and for many years his most trusted and least trustworthy adviser on Scottish affairs, Hamilton had ended his disastrous career by leading the Scottish invasion of the previous summer to ignominious defeat. He, too, was now a prisoner at Windsor. Yet he had done something to redeem his errors. He had been expected, after his capture, to buy his life by incriminating the King as the author of the invasion. The London news-sheets had confidently reported that he had offered to do so, even that he had done so. He had in fact refused to speak.[11]

Now, as the King came by, he tearfully kissed his hand, with nothing to say but "My dear Master. . . ."

"I have been so indeed to you," said the King. What more he would have said Hamilton was never to learn. The guards closed in and the King went on, leaving Hamilton to follow him "with his eyes as far as he could see him, knowing he was to do so no more."[12]

Within the castle the King found that his own bedchamber had been prepared for him, with a good fire on the hearth.

Somewhere in that dark, ancient rabbit warren of a castle others beside himself, men who had served him, were imprisoned as he was. He asked who else was there, but made no comment when he was told. Instead he walked to the fire and stood for a long time silent, leaning on the back of his chair.[13] His thoughts may have been with Hamilton, for so many years his courtier, companion and friend. That high-coloured, confident, voluble man, so free always with advice which was always wrong, so big in talk about all that he would do for his master, so pitiable in action: he had seen him now for the last time, broken, grey-haired, kneeling in the rain.

But his thoughts may have gone, as they often did in these days, to one who had long been dead: a dominating and difficult man whom none of them (certainly not Hamilton) had liked in his days of power—the eloquent, masterful Strafford, the minister whom he had himself sent to the block eight years ago to appease Parliament and the people. During the last months he had several times said that he felt no guilt for any of the bloodshed in the Civil War because he had been fighting for a righteous cause, but the blood of Strafford lay heavy on his conscience because he had consented to his death in the knowledge that he was innocent. For this sin—more heinous in a King than in an ordinary man—God had not ceased to punish him.[14]

While the King was on his journey to Windsor, the Council of the Army and the vestigial House of Commons made preparations for his trial, amid a hubbub of rumour and speculation. It was still widely believed that there would be no trial, or certainly no execution. Perhaps they "would work him by terror to renounce the regal dignity." Perhaps the whole proceeding was a plot of Cromwell's who would in the end denounce his associates and restore the King "on his own shoulders".[15] Or perhaps the Grandees meant to reinstate the King with reduced powers, like a "doge of Venice"—and then to turn upon and exterminate their real enemies the Levellers.[16] Another more lugubrious suggestion, was that the King was to be dressed in his royal robes and publicly divested of them in Westminster Hall.[17]

This latter fantasy may have had some connection with the widely reported arrival at Windsor of the King's tailor bearing a trunk load of new clothes. The order for these had been put in hand during the Treaty of Newport. The handsome suits trimmed with gold and silver lace, the sumptuous fur-lined gown and the black velvet cloak lined with satin had been planned against his return to Westminster as King. They were in time for his trial. More cheerfully, they were in time for Christmas Day, when the King, still dining under his canopy in formal state, made himself fine for the occasion.[18]

It was almost the last time that the ceremonies were observed. Considerations of expense and of security prompted an alteration. Immediately on the King's arrival at Windsor, Harrison was recalled to play his part on the Army Council where he was a principal supporter of Cromwell. Since it was felt that the safety of the King required more attention than the governor of Windsor Castle would be able to spare from his other duties, Colonel Matthew Tomlinson was sent down to replace Harrison. Tomlinson was young, little more than thirty, a Puritan squire from Yorkshire. As the King's watchdog for the last five weeks of his life he was cool, efficient and on the whole well-mannered. The King found him tolerable, if scarcely sympathetic. He had instructions to reduce the number of the King's personal attendants to six, to keep the door of his room continually guarded, to arrange for at least one officer to be with him, night and day, except when he was at his devotions, and to permit him to take exercise only on the terrace.[19]

Even at Hurst, even on the last journey to Windsor, the ancient tradition that the people had a right to see their King had been maintained. His formal meals had always been the occasion for visitors to enter the room and watch from a distance while his servants went through the rituals—setting his chair, holding his gloves, uncovering the dishes and formally tasting what he ate and drank as a precaution against poison, carving his meat, pouring his wine and presenting plate or cup, napkin or rose-water on bended knee. In the cramped gloom of Hurst Castle, a few visitors had found their way in. At Farnham and Winchester the room had been packed.

But Tomlinson had orders that no one was to enter any of the King's apartments except those appointed to guard or to wait on him and their personal servants. No awed, curious, friendly or hostile visitors would ever again gape at him as he sat alone under his canopy, delicately eating with his fingers or sipping from his cup of claret and water.

The maintenance of the King's state in these conditions was an unnecessary expense and on 27th December, orders were sent from the Army Council to omit all ceremonies in future. Charles received the news without emotion but indicated that he would eat in his own room, choosing (so his principal attendant, Thomas Herbert, records) merely what dishes he wanted from the daily bill of fare.[20] He was still by modern standards subjected neither to material privation nor discomfort. But he was cut off from all sympathetic companionship, except that of his dogs. His attendants had been appointed by Parliament ever since the beginning of his captivity; only at Newport, during the Treaty, had he enjoyed for a brief interlude the attendance of some of his old courtiers. But at Hurst, as before at Carisbrooke, those who waited on him were the nominees of his opponents who performed their tasks correctly but without warmth. The King's patience and dignity in his oppressed condition sometimes softened their feelings, but it was chiefly among the lower servants that a rash desire to help him was sometimes born, or a well-placed bribe from a Cavalier secured the delivery of a message from friends.

Some of those who waited on him felt nothing but dislike. Anthony Mildmay who served him as carver throughout this period, described the King spitefully in a letter to his brother as "the most perfidious man that ever lived." He found waiting on him "insupportable", yet he continued in his place, presumably in hope of a reward from his real masters in Parliament and Army. The brother to whom he wrote had been for many years Master of the King's Jewel House, but he had supported Parliament in the war and had notoriously disposed of some of the King's possessions for his own profit. Very probably the King did really contrive to make Anthony Mildmay's attendance on him as insupportable as he could, for he regarded the brothers as a pair of ungrateful rogues. But though the number of the King's servants was reduced, first at Hurst Castle and more drastically at Windsor, Mildmay was not withdrawn: the Army knew they could trust him.[21]

The King was slightly more fortunate in Thomas Herbert, who many years later was to compile an exculpatory account of his service in which he emphasises his devotion. He was not devoted, though he seems to have been efficient and civil. A sly, hard man with a keen sense of his own advantage, he was indignant, soon after Christmas, to find that his own servant, handsomely bribed by a Cavalier agent, had brought in two letters from the Queen and hidden them in the King's close stool. They were found before they reached the King. The servant was questioned and named the agent—a Major Bosvile who had found means of getting letters to the King on earlier occasions, and for whom the Army's bloodhounds were soon combing the back-streets of Southwark. As for Herbert, the Army knew that there "was not the least occasion" to suspect him personally.[22]

A much more sympathetic character was the intellectual James Harrington. A man of great learning, who derived his political views from his classical studies, he was also something of an eccentric. He had considerable charm, a lucid brain and a ready tongue, and the King appears to have enjoyed an occasional battle of wits with him. He for his part was said, during the Newport Treaty, to have expressed admiration for the King's defence of the Episcopal system. On arrival at Windsor the King's attendants were required to swear to report anything they might hear of Royalist plans for the King's escape. Harrington, though willing to promise to do nothing personally to assist the King, would not undertake to tell tales of anyone else and so was compelled to leave.[23]

II

At Whitehall the plans for the King's trial went forward. In the once crowded precincts of Parliament, business was sluggish and attendance so slack that the House of Commons often had difficulty in raising the necessary quorum of forty. The House of Lords was still more diminished, and mocking journalists said that when the whole half-dozen peers had arrived, they sat telling tales by the fireside.[24] The centre of activity was not in Parliament but in the Army Headquarters at Whitehall. The King's one-time palace had become a confused mixture of barracks, offices and conference rooms. Here Fairfax—His Excellency the Lord General—paced the corridors in anxious bewilderment and maintained a prudent silence on all crucial matters. Here Cromwell came and went from the House of Commons, with those fellow-soldiers who were also members of Parliament—Harrison, Fleetwood, Hutchinson, Ireton, Ingoldsby, Ludlow, and Corbet. Here, when duty kept him late he occupied a richly furnished bedroom long left untenanted. Here Ireton and Harrison shared one of the smaller rooms where, after late and weary sessions, they sometimes slept in the same bed. Here the Army Council met to discuss each further step towards the trial of the King, and here on several occasions, its members met John Lilburne and the representatives of the Leveller party to consider what kind of government England should have when the King was dead.

Lilburne had lost no time in organising the joint meetings

of Levellers, soldiers, and Parliament men which had been suggested to him by Ireton and Harrison at Windsor to quiet him down before they marched on London. He had gone further—he had not only drawn up, but had printed the programme of reform which they jointly now placed before the Army Council.[25] If Lilburne imagined that it would be accepted with no further delay he was soon disillusioned. The officers of the Army Council were concerned for religious liberty, but they were not interested in, or were hostile to the Leveller demands for a more evenly distributed representation of the people in Parliament, for greater social and civil justice, and for the abolition of tithes, which made ministers of religion a burden to the poor. Lilburne was quick to see that the Grandees of the Army intended to smother his propositions under an avalanche of argument and then to modify or destroy his programme. It was noticeable that all representation of the men had been dropped by the Army Council for the last thirteen months. It was now simply a Council of Officers.

Four Leveller representatives were chosen to attend the discussions. But there was no limit on the number of the Grandees who came. Cromwell was rarely present but the men whom Lilburne called his "creature colonels" came and spoke frequently. Fairfax, who was in the chair during a long debate on 14th December, made no attempt to give the Levellers a hearing. He allowed Ireton to speak again and again, while Lilburne and his friends had difficulty in putting forward their case. Once John Evelyn, a determined sight-seer, slipped in to listen to the discussion, and found Ireton himself in the chair. He was shocked by the wickedness of the democratic propositions under discussion, but no less shocked by the "disorder and irreverence" of the debate—the uncivil language used by these "young, raw ill-spoken men."[26]

Some angry interchanges certainly took place. They talked, Lilburne said, far into the night, and he and his friends received much "base and unworthy language" from their opponents. In the end he furiously challenged them all and severally to single combat. Naturally they did not respond. Long before any agreement had been reached Lilburne withdrew, declaring that he scorned to come among such "a pack of dissembling, juggling knaves." A few days later he presented to Fairfax, *A Plea for Common Right and Freedom*. In this he complained of the unfairness of the debates, declared that the future happiness of the entire country was now in the hands of the Army, and warned the Lord General

> by all good means to prevent your and our being overgrown with destructive interests, or with persons promoting the same. . . . By breaking all authority you have taken upon yourselves the care, protection and restoration (of our just liberties.) . . . It highly concerns you in the position you have put yourselves, not to be straight or narrow hearted to your friends in point of liberty or the removal of known grievances, but to be as large in both as the utmost reasons of these knowing times can plead for or desire. . . .
>
> And therefore as in all your Remonstrances, papers, and declarations you have made the liberties of the people your banner and standard for which you have contested: so (now you having assumed all power into your own hands) let it appear to the world you meant so indeed; . . . since you are thus far engaged, do it with all your might that God may be glorified in your success, we and all good men encouraged to stand by you and the people enjoy their long wished for peace, whom we desire may be made absolutely free and happy by this Army . . . that so this Army, your Excellency, and the worthy officers thereof may be the joy and rejoicing of this nation to all future generations.[27]

Fairfax had no sympathy for John Lilburne's ideas. Whatever he might feel about the King's trial, he was at one with Cromwell and the other Grandees in thinking that the liberties of the people, their freedom and happiness depended on the preservation of the social hierarchy and the political rights of the privileged class to which he belonged. He believed in a modified religious toleration, but he did not believe that anything but anarchy could come of abolishing tithes, reforming the franchise, changing the frame of government and altering the administration of the law. He remained unresponsive.

It did not matter. Lilburne expected no answer and waited for none. Before the end of December he quitted London for the North. His retreat at this critical moment in the affairs of the Levellers calls for some explanation and the explanation which he himself offered may be true though it seems out of character. He was a poor man with a large family and he had, long since, been voted three thousand pounds by Parliament in respect of his sufferings in the time of the King's power. The money had never been paid. In December 1648 he had put before the House a proposition to enable him to raise it from the estates of Royalist delinquents in Durham. He was determined to get this arrangement ratified in Parliament before the King's death, suspecting that when the King was gone and the Grandees had "fully got up into the throne" he might whistle for his reward. Thus his attention was divided between the demands of his followers and this private matter of his own, and when on 18th December his grant was ratified, he left London for the North to collect his money, and returned only after the King's death.[28]

Even allowing for the dire poverty in which Lilburne, his long-suffering wife and growing family usually found themselves, this conduct seems odd in one who rarely counted the cost of his political actions. Other reasons for the withdrawal suggest themselves. He may not have wished to stay in London during the King's trial of which he did not approve. He probably also understood, with impotent anger, how completely the Grandees had outmanœuvred him by forcing the issue over the King. For if he chose to stay in London, to raise tumults among his supporters and make difficulties for Cromwell and the Army, who would benefit? In the end only the Royalists. By stirring up riots in London and disturbances in the ranks of the Army, he might hold up the King's trial and create something like anarchy in public affairs. But he would not thereby bring the Leveller programme any nearer to realisation and he would strengthen no one except the King's friends. All this he very probably realised. When he cursed the Army leaders for juggling knaves, it was because they had juggled him into a position whence he could strike no blow against them without harming his own cause even more than theirs.

III

With Lilburne gone, the Levellers were not likely to make serious trouble during the proceedings against the King. The state of the City of London, however, still gave cause for anxiety. The Presbyterian ministers continued vigorously to denounce the Army from their pulpits and to publish their denunciations in print. One sheriff of London, the militant Presbyterian Browne, had been arrested; but the majority feeling among the wealthier citizens remained sympathetic to the Presbyterian view and the excluded members. Furthermore the Lord Mayor had been elected, when hope ran high, both in Parliament and the City, that the Newport Treaty would succeed, and that the King would soon come home again to his capital. Presumably for this reason the City's choice had fallen on Abraham Reynardson, of the Merchant Taylors Company, a man of notorious Royalist sympathies. Reynardson had no doubt looked forward to receiving the King at Temple Bar in the presence of cheering multitudes as soon as peace was made. He would have been eminently suitable for the task. Instead he found himself confronted with a military occupation by an Army which threatened to murder his sovereign.

The presence of this Lord Mayor and a majority of Aldermen only a whit less hostile, made it essential that some means be found to control the City. This could best be done by packing the Common Council, the supposedly representative assembly of citizens, with friends of the Army. Once again Philip Skippon, the veteran commander of the Trained Bands, served the Army's cause. On the eve of the Purge he had used his influence to ensure the withdrawal of the Trained Bands from Westminster to make room for Colonel Pride's men. Now he rose in the House, where he represented the West country borough of Barnstaple, and "looking as demurely as if he meant to say Grace", moved that no citizen who had been in favour of the Treaty with the King should be eligible for the Common Council. This prohibition was enforced at the election which took place next day, and the Royalist Lord Mayor found himself saddled with a Common Council which overwhelmingly and even vindictively supported the Army.[29]

IV

What precisely did the Army want? Or Cromwell? Rumour had it that both Cromwell and Ireton were unwilling to proceed to extremities. Royalist sympathisers, aware of the latent hostility between Grandees and Levellers, hinted that the demand for the King's trial was a trick of Cromwell's to "make the Levellers vent all their wicked principles and intentions, that having declared themselves, they may become the more odious and abominable and so be the more easily suppressed." It was suggested, without any convincing reason, that Cromwell was himself the author of an anonymous letter to the Council of Officers, urging them not to kill the King, and thus put the Crown into the hands of Charles II—young, active, free and able to get help abroad. Another story was that the projected trial was a manœuvre

to enable the King to acquit himself and so to prepare the
way for his restoration by Cromwell and the Army. Con-
versely, it was asserted by others that he was to be tried and
condemned, and then worked on by the fear of death to buy
back his life and crown by giving up all his power—renoun-
cing not only his control over the Army and the Church,
but even his right to veto bills submitted to him by Parliament. The French agent in London reported in his despatches
that Cromwell had even attempted to convey such an offer
to him secretly by means of the Earl of Denbigh who had
gone to Windsor specially for that purpose.[30]

Rumour and speculation surrounded the deliberations of
the Army Council for bringing the King to justice, and little
can be said with certainty about their discussions on the fate
of the King. Against the cloud of conjecture which obscures
Cromwell's actions and motives we have the authentic
personal statement made by him in his letter to Hammond
in November. He had called the King "a man against whom
the Lord hath witnessed." He was unlikely therefore, a month
later, to have contemplated bringing him back to the throne
on whatever terms. He knew the King well by this time, and
did not underestimate either his personal courage or his
devious tenacity. His previous experience of negotiating with
him had convinced him once and for all that no peace made
with Charles would be permanent or safe.

Those who believed that he had plans for the King's
restoration as a puppet of the Army and of his own, misread
the situation. Cromwell's conduct during these last days of
December suggests not that he wished to save Charles, but
that he wished to bring him to justice with some plausible
appearance of legality and Parliamentary consent. Thus he
exerted himself on the one hand to accumulate evidence
against the King, and on the other to increase the number
of members attending the House.

It had been no part of his plan prematurely to break off the
Treaty at Newport. His reason is clear: the King in the first

clause of it had admitted his guilt in making war. This admission would have been vitally important at his trial. But since the Treaty was broken off, it was doubtful if any use could be made of it. Cromwell's next hope of evidence was from Hamilton, but here too in spite of hours spent in questioning him, he had received no help; Hamilton refused to admit the King's complicity in the Scots invasion.[31] With these two sources of evidence gone, Cromwell vainly tried to postpone the trial of the King until the leaders in the Royalist risings of the previous summer should have been tried. Once more, this was a reasonable plan if his chief intention was to secure evidence against Charles. Though none of the Cavaliers would willingly have incriminated the King, much might have been surprised out of them by skilful questioning. But here again Cromwell was overruled.

Meanwhile he was equally unsuccessful in his attempt to redeem the Parliamentary situation. Those who had organised Pride's Purge—that mixed group of Parliamentary republicans and Army officers—had intended to keep at least a respectable semblance of a Parliament in being and had acted with the tacit approval of the Speaker, William Lenthall. But they had gone the wrong way about it. Had the expulsion been engineered from within (as Cromwell probably intended) it would have appeared less nakedly illegal and would not have caused so drastic a reduction of the House. For what caused the present emptiness of the House was not so much the forcible exclusion of the members who had actively favoured the Newport Treaty, as the voluntary abstention of many others who were not implacably opposed to the Army's interests but who resented their assault on Parliamentary freedom. Among these were almost all the leading lawyers of the House—the immensely influential John Selden, and the two distinguished barristers who in the absence of a Lord Chancellor, had the custody of the Great Seal, Bulstrode Whitelocke and Thomas Widdrington. Significantly even Sir Harry Vane had absented himself since the Purge, although until that moment he had been in effect the leader of the Army's party in the House.

Cromwell now appealed to Whitelocke and Widdrington for help in a series of meetings recorded, with exasperating brevity, in Whitelocke's laconic memoirs. First, on 18th December, Cromwell, with Speaker Lenthall, met and consulted the two eminent lawyers. Next day they came to see Cromwell at Whitehall, where Whitelocke noticed with disapproval that he "lay in one of the King's rich beds." Thereafter Whitelocke records two more meetings, the second of them attended by several members of Parliament; he gives only a hint of their purpose which was, as he puts it "to frame somewhat in order to the restitution of the secluded members" and to moderate the temper of the Army. At the second and most fully attended of the meetings, they discussed "settling the Kingdom by Parliament, and not to leave all to the Sword." They considered whether they should dispense with a King altogether or set up the King's youngest son, the little Duke of Gloucester, whom they could educate and shape to their will.[32] If this was the outline of their debate, it is clear that Whitelocke and Widdrington, as well as Cromwell, were assuming as a starting-point the removal of King Charles by deposition or by death. Whitelocke's tantalising records hint at much more than they tell. It looks as though Cromwell, who had initiated the discussions and drawn in the two lawyers, hoped that they would think of means to make the trial of the King acceptable to some at least of the absent members. If Parliament could first be strengthened by the return of the voluntary absentees, and then persuaded to sanction the trial, the naked violence of the Army would be decently covered.

The plan came to nothing. The last and longest of the meetings broke up fruitlessly, and when the depleted House of Commons on 23rd December appointed a Committee to consider how the King should be tried, Whitelocke and Widdrington took coach and went down into the country "purposely to avoid this business." It was not by chance either that Henry Elsyng, the efficient and faithful Clerk of the Commons, suddenly pleaded ill-health and resigned his place. His real reason, which he admitted freely to his friends, was "because he would have no hand in the business against the King." He was replaced for the time being by John Phelps, a man much less experienced in the business of the House, who had been employed as clerk to the war-time committee for the relief of plundered ministers.[33]

With every passing day the potential support, or even the acquiescence of the most experienced Parliamentarians and lawyers was being withdrawn from the existing House of Commons and the projected trial of the King. The fanatic enthusiasts of the Army were indifferent to anything but the ruling of their own consciences. But Cromwell, who had sat in Parliament since 1628, and had taken up the sword to defend what he regarded as the laws of the land, was still anxious that the King's trial and death should be contrived as far as possible within a framework of legal and Parliamentary procedure. That the trial was politically essential and morally right he did not doubt, but the hope of making it appear right in any other way was fast receding. He expressed both his political doubt and his moral confidence in a debate in the Commons on 26th December. He argued that, if any man had suggested the trial of the King for worldly calculations only, "he should think him the greatest traitor in the world, but since providence and necessity had cast them upon it, he should pray God to bless their counsels, though he were not provided on the sudden to give them counsel."[34]

V

Cromwell's refusal to say more at this juncture indicates his willingness to leave the effective guidance of the House to the dominant republican members, especially Henry Marten and Thomas Scot. He was evidently anxious that the measures taken in Parliament to bring the King to justice should not be openly dominated by the Army. He was, none the less, more often in the House than with the Army Council at Whitehall, where he relied on Ireton to guide their deliberations in the right direction.

He was not there on 29th December, when a woman named Elizabeth Pool was admitted, claiming that she had a revelation from Heaven. She was an honest, seemly country-woman from Abingdon, who spoke with ardour, though in so allegorical a fashion that the Divine message was scarcely intelligible. The presence of God was with the Army, she proclaimed, and they must stand up for the liberty of the people as God had opened the way. She had had a vision of a sickly deformed woman "which should signify the weak and imperfect distressed state of the land." Beside this woman stood a man, whom she took to represent the Army, offering to cure her. The way of the cure was to be through humiliation, prayer and indifference to worldly ends. Inspired by her fervour, Colonel Harrison eagerly asked if more precise instructions had been vouchsafed to her. But Ireton, who perceived that she had nothing of practical importance to say, soon dismissed her with respectful thanks for her seasonable words.[35]

While Elizabeth Pool was speaking before the Council of the Army at Whitehall, Oliver Cromwell was in the House of Commons listening to the urgent debate on the manner of bringing the King to justice. Thomas Scot, one of the few London Aldermen of strongly Independent views, reported the recommendations of the Committee for the King's trial. They advised that a special Court should be appointed for the purpose, to consist of men representing the interests of the nation and empowered to act for the space of one month only. This plan seems to have been generally acceptable, though there was long wrangling over the use of words, and a phrase which described Charles

Stuart as "entrusted with the government of the Kingdom" was eliminated in favour of the briefer and less explanatory "Charles Stuart the now King of England."[36]

To speed up the arrangements the Committee was now enlarged to include several more of the soldiers, more especially Cromwell. Three days later, with Henry Marten acting as their brisk spokesman, they placed the completed draft of the ordinance for the King's trial before the House.

The causes for which he was to be brought to justice were set forth in the boldest language:

> Whereas it is notorious that Charles Stuart, the now King of England, not content with the many encroachments which his predecessors had made upon the people in their rights and freedoms, hath had a wicked design totally to subvert the ancient and fundamental laws and liberties of this nation, and in their place to introduce an arbitrary and tyrannical government, and that besides all other evil ways and means to bring his design to pass, he hath prosecuted it with fire and sword, levied and maintained a cruel war in the land, against the Parliament and Kingdom, whereby the country hath been miserably wasted, the public Treasure exhausted, trade decayed, thousands of people murdered and infinite other mischiefs committed. . . .
>
> Whereas also the Parliament, well hoping that the restraint and imprisonment of his person, after it had pleased God to deliver him into their hands, would have quieted the distempers of the Kingdom, did forbear to proceed judicially against him; but found by sad experience, that such their remissness served only to encourage him and his complices in the continuance of their evil practices and in raising of new commotions, rebellions and invasions. . . .

All in all, the King was accused of having "traitorously and maliciously" plotted to enslave the English nation, and for the terror of any future rulers who might attempt the same wickedness, he was to be put on trial for his life before a special Court consisting of about a hundred and fifty members presided over by the two Chief Justices.[37]

The Ordinance passed without a division, but the Commons as an afterthought bolstered up their legal position by declaring that it was treason on the part of a King to levy war on his subjects.[38] In the meantime they selected Lord Grey of Groby to carry up their ordinance to the House of Lords. Eldest son of the aged Earl of Stamford, Grey had opposed the King in the House and in the field for the past seven years.

The haste of the Commons proved abortive. The House of Lords was found not to be in session. They were much reduced in numbers. None of the Royalist peers had attended for many years, and most of the indifferent or neutral had withdrawn. The attendance in the House was now rarely above half a dozen, with the Earl of Manchester, in the absence of a Chancellor, acting as Speaker. On New Year's Day they had decided to take a holiday. The ordinance "touching the King" would have to wait.

The peers were not the only people celebrating the New Year as a holiday. In spite of Puritan preaching and propaganda directed for the past seven years against the noisy celebration of "the twelve days of Christmas", many Londoners still clung to their old convivial habits, and eschewed all work between Christmas Day and Epiphany. Surreptitious dramatic performances had even begun again, at first in private houses. But actors and audiences had grown so bold that by the New Year four of the old theatres were open. This defiance of an ordinance against play-acting in force for the last seven years, could not go unpunished. Two parties of soldiers were despatched to break up the performances. At the Fortune theatre they found nothing but a rope-dancer, and at the Red Bull no one at all for actors and audience had been forewarned and had quickly vanished.

But at Salisbury Court they found a play in full swing, interrupted the performance and carried the players prisoners to the Headquarters at Whitehall in their theatrical finery. It was not an ill-natured business; all down the Strand people cheered the actors, the soldiers allowed them to respond and even to perform a sort of spontaneous pantomime as they went along. One of them was in crown and robes, and his attendants alternately discrowned and re-crowned him with appropriate gestures, eliciting groans, jeers, laughter and applause from the crowd. Only at the fourth theatre, the Cockpit, did the actors show fight, a mistaken policy as they were roughly handled, were arrested and had their wardrobe and properties confiscated.[39]

Next day the House of Lords reassembled, all twelve of them as befitted so serious an occasion. Few, if any, of those present cared much for the King. He had brought himself to his present plight by errors of policy in which the judgment of these last remaining peers had been against him. All had been in opposition to the Royal policy in the months which preceded the war. But some of them now saw it as their duty to uphold the laws of the land against outrage from this rogue remnant of the Commons.

So it happened that Manchester, who at the outset of the Civil War had raised and led the forces of the Eastern counties against Charles, now opened the debate with an emphatic statement that the King alone had power to call or dissolve Parliament, and that it was therefore absurd to accuse him of treason against a body over which he exercised the ultimate legal authority.

The Earl of Northumberland, who had supported Parliament throughout the war, now doubted whether one in twenty of the people of England was satisfied that the King and not Parliament had begun the conflict; without settling that point, he argued, it was impossible to accuse the King of treason. The Earl of Pembroke, never conspicuous for courage, excused himself from uttering an opinion at all, but the Earl of Denbigh who, like Manchester, had raised troops against the King at the beginning of the war, waxed eloquent against his trial. He would rather be torn in pieces, he averred, than have any part in so infamous a business.

Unanimously, therefore, the House of Lords rejected the ordinance. They then adjourned for a week, and most of them departed with all speed into the country.[40] They can hardly have expected their action to be effective against men so set upon their course as the Commons now were. It was said that Grey of Groby, at the news that the Lords had rejected the bill, proclaimed that he would himself perform the executioner's office rather than let the King escape from justice.[41] Whether he spoke such words or not the House of Commons was prepared to take the sole responsibility for the King's death. They declared their right to proceed without further reference to the Lords, revised their proposed list of the King's judges by removing the names of the peers, and hurried the amended bill through its first and second reading at a single session.[42]

This assumption of full Parliamentary powers by the remnant of the House of Commons was wholly unjustifiable. But although the remaining members were the constant object of abuse and derision by Presbyterians and Royalists, they were by no means a despicable body of men. A few, of course, were time-servers bound to the cause of the Army by fear or self-interest. Little can be said for Henry Mildmay, the dishonest embezzler of the King's jewels, or Cornelius Holland, once also a servant of the Crown who had profitably taken over one of the Royal estates at a low rent, or the feeble John Downes who had agonising doubts, but did not wish to forego the confiscated Church land that he had bought during the war.[43]

But there were many, both civilians and soldiers, of integrity and vision and courage, who had weighed what they believed to be the merits of the case, who knew the dangers, and who acted out of the highest motives of religion and public duty. Such was the austere and upright Colonel Hutchinson, who prayed earnestly for guidance before he undertook to be one of the King's judges, and found that he received no warning, "but a confirmation in his conscience that it was his duty to act as he did."[44] Such also was the convinced Republican Edmund Ludlow, who wanted to see the people of England "preserved in their just rights from the oppression of violent men," meaning the Cavaliers, who was convinced that an accommodation with the King was both politically unsafe and contrary to the will of God because it was written in the Book of Numbers that "the land cannot be cleansed of the blood that is shed therein but by the blood of him that shed it."[45] Colonel Harrison, who had assured the King that nothing dark or underhand would be done to him, had spoken out of a deep and holy pride in the act that was to be committed; never, to the dreadful moment of his death, would he regret or be ashamed of his part in it. These were all men of the Army, but some members of the House, not soldiers, felt as strongly—Henry Marten, for instance, that high-spirited, witty, extravagant *enfant terrible* of the House, whose good nature more than once saved Royalist victims from death. Under the surface irresponsibility, and the regrettable habit of wenching which shocked his Puritan colleagues, Marten was a man of deep feeling, with an unshaken belief in Republican principles; he had long regarded the King as responsible for the war and believed that he should be sacrificed for the good of the people. And John Carew the Devonshire landowner, that devout visionary who worked for the Fifth Monarchy of the Book of Daniel and the rule of the Saints on earth; and Alderman Thomas Scot, who was to thank God—eleven years later—as he prepared for the hangman's noose and the disembowelling knife that He had vouchsafed to call him to so good a Cause.[46]

While the Presbyterian ministers of London denounced the actions of the Army and the Commons, as against God and against the law, some Independent ministers defended them with eloquence less eccentric and arguments more persuasive than those of Hugh Peter. John Goodwin, the popular minister of Coleman Street, preached vehemently in support of the Army and published a closely reasoned defence of their conduct. Taking up the title of an angry Presbyterian manifesto called *Might Overcoming Right* he called his pamphlet *Right and Might Well Met*.

In it he argued the necessity that the King must perish in the interests of the nation whom he had deluded and betrayed, and whom, under pretence of the Treaty, he would certainly betray again. In purging Parliament and taking the government out of the hands of those who insisted on trusting, and treating with, the King, the Army had obeyed a more compulsive and more sacred law than anything written in the statute book. They had obeyed an immutable law of nature, created by the God of nature, to ward off the imminent destruction of the people.[47]

This argument of the natural law of self defence echoed a dictum which John Calvin had derived from St. Paul, and which the Dutch had used in justification of their revolt from Spain in the previous century.[48] The idea of a natural law implanted by God in the hearts of all men, was thus no bold innovation of the Independents, but sound Calvinist doctrine sanctified by its use in the most famous and successful of all Protestant revolts. Goodwin was, in effect, citing one of their own precepts to justify the Army's conduct to their Presbyterian critics.

Among laymen the paper contest raged no less fiercely than among the clergy. William Prynne ushered in the New Year with his *Brief Memento to the Present Unparliamentary Junto*, in which he denounced the Army's conduct at his usual interminable length as contrary to law, precedent, and Protestant tradition. On the Army's side a soberly named pamphlet *Rectifying Principles* was signed by the initials S.H.— it was probably the work of Milton's friend the Baltic refugee Samuel Hartlib. Half a work of propaganda, which recapitulated and denounced the policy of the King—his taxation, his monopolies, his alliance with Popish Spain—it also set forth a political theory to justify his trial. "The State at large is King," wrote this author, "and the King so-called is but its steward or Highest Officer."[49]

Some theory of this kind was essential to dissolve the band of allegiance between King and subject. On 4th January, the House of Commons proclaimed their own doctrine on the subject. The people, they declared, were under God, the source of all just power, and Parliament represented the people.[50] The first, theoretical, half of this statement was impressive; the second, practical, half was open not only to contradiction but to ridicule since everyone knew that the House of Commons so far from being a free assembly of freely chosen representatives was the tool of the Army— "Noll Cromwell's journeymen" as a Royalist newspaper scornfully called them.[51]

But the claim to represent the people was not absolutely false, was even in some ways less palpably false than the claim of any normally constituted Parliament of that time would have been. The Army, which controlled this Parliament, was a very fair cross-section of the younger generation of Englishmen, drawn from all parts of the land, from labourers, tradesmen, yeomen and gentry; it was a much more representative body of the English people than any Parliament that had ever met, or any that was to meet for many generations. In so far as the controlled and diminished House of Commons had no will but that of the Army, its actions may not have been so remote from the will of the people as the Royalists, the Presbyterians and the excluded members liked to think.

The Declaration of the House of Commons that the people were the source of all just power was printed and widely distributed within the next few days. Meanwhile the Council of the Army showed more concern to guide their actions by the will of God. Once again, they consulted the prophetess from Abingdon about the fate of the King. "You may bind his hands and hold him hard under," she said. The Almighty seemed to have given no mandate for his death. One of the officers, Colonel Rich, asked her a question that troubled many of them. What should they do if the King refused to acknowledge the right of his subjects to try him, and so would not answer the charge? She was confused by the legal terminology and gave only an indistinct answer. Disappointed, they thanked her and let her go.[52]

Into the midst of these unprecendeted actions of Parliament, these upheavals of tradition, these visions and arguments, two unexpected figures suddenly intruded. Their names appear as Ebenezer and Joanna Cartwright, a widow and her son who had lived for many years in Amsterdam, "being conversant with some of Israel's race called Jews." Polite and hopeful, at this time of universal change, the pair of them offered to the Army—these upholders of Fifth Monarchy, these warrior-statesmen who took their arguments from Isaiah and Daniel and the Book of Numbers—a request for the toleration of Judaism in England and the return of their people, exiled since the middle ages.[53]

They addressed their appeal to Fairfax. But the unhappy General was in no state to consider any problems but his own. He was rarely present now at the Council of Officers although the policy of the Army, and so of the nation, was being shaped there. His absence indicated the extent of his bewilderment. Until the march on London he had, in appearance at least, guided the actions of the Army. Though he was to say later that his name had been set down on every document whether he approved of it or not, this statement was less than candid. He had been in agreement with his principal officers about the march on London; he had not only subscribed to the Remonstrance but written a covering letter of some emphasis to go with it to the House of Commons. It was not until the violent purging of Parliament, an action arranged by Ireton and reported to him too late for him to prevent it, that he seems to have fallen into real, but still tacit, disagreement with his Council of Officers. But he probably continued to deceive himself that the projected trial of the King was intended only as a threat to compel him to make the kind of peace that the Army wanted. At any rate, he acquiesced in the preparations and the strict guarding of the King. Uninformed Royalist and Presbyterian criticism of him was abusive. His name was coupled with that of Cromwell as the arch-enemy of the monarchy and established order. "Black Tom" and "King Noll" shared the honours as the heirs of John of Leiden, the wild leader of the Munster Anabaptists who had introduced community of women and of property and whose name, for the last century, had been synonymous with unbridled licence and social anarchy. This kind of slander was most unwelcome to the conventional and conservative Fairfax whose actions had been guided, if by anything, then by the desire to keep control of his Army and prevent the wilder elements from breaking all bounds. But abuse from the ignorant tormented him less than the knowledge that many of the better informed looked to him for some decisive statement or action, believing that he could and should stem the course of events. From Paris the unhappy Queen addressed a piteous appeal to him in person, but her pleading can hardly have disturbed him as much as the letters of protest that he received from men of goodwill in London. She was a Papist and an enemy, guilty in part of her husband's downfall; they were godly men whose views he respected. The mystical fanatic William Sedgwick in an open letter fervently adjured him to set a term to the vainglorious wickedness of the Army, guided now by nothing but ambition and sensual appetite. Edward Stephens, a secluded member, vehemently implored him to save the nation from the inexpiable guilt of murdering their sovereign. In a printed appeal he declared that Fairfax alone could prevent the catastrophe: "the power is now yours . . . rouse yourself, my lord, to suppress these blasphemies."[54]

He did not rouse himself. He remained passive, apparently acquiescent, while the Army (of which he was General) and the House of Commons (in which he had a seat) went forward unhindered towards the trial of the King.

The King, it was reported, still appeared confident of rescue, spoke of armed intervention from Ireland, and had given orders for the planting of melons at his royal manor of Wimbledon.[55] But nothing short of some brilliant and improbable plan of escape backed by armed intervention could now save him.

The House of Commons would no longer even consider representations in his favour, whatever their source. The French resident in London presented a letter from the Queen, written at the same time as her appeal to Fairfax. She begged with unaffected anguish and in the humblest terms for leave to come to her husband in his distress. The Speaker accepted the letter, but the House would not allow him to read it.[56]

This was something of a snub to the French resident. The King of Spain's representative was more cautious. Although he was pressed to intervene by Royalists and Presbyterians alike, he told them he had no authority to do so without his King's express command, and he continued—as he had done throughout the war—to maintain a careful neutrality designed to propitiate the winning party.[57]

The Scots Commissioners in London, acting on orders urgently despatched from their Parliament in Edinburgh, presented a strong protest against the trial of the King. The two nations, they argued, had fought against the King's evil policies as brethren and allies, but their avowed purpose had been to maintain the laws, to reform religion and to achieve "the honour and happiness of the King." It had always been understood that there would be "no harm, injury or violence offered to his Majesty's person, the very thought whereof the Kingdom of Scotland hath always abhorred."

The Scots were at the door of the House early on 6th January, with their protest, but had to wait some time before they could present it as there was no quorum until noon—a difficulty that frequently arose since the purging of the House. When the required forty members had at length arrived, the Scots sent in their paper, but "it was laid aside and not read."[58] The House had other and more urgent business.

This was to divest themselves formally of that clog on their action—the powerless, reduced but obstructive House of Lords. They accordingly declared that the Commons alone constituted a true Parliament, and could legislate for the nation. In future they would not issue "Ordinances"—the temporary word which had been in use since the outbreak of the war. They would issue "Acts" of Parliament, as had been done by King, Lords and Commons before the troubles began. They thus arrogated to themselves alone the central right of government. This enabled them to promulgate as an Act of Parliament, on that very day, Saturday, 6th January, their amended plan for setting up a High Court of Justice to try the King.

It was to consist of a hundred and thirty-five Commissioners who were ordered to meet on the following Monday afternoon at two o'clock in the Painted Chamber at Westminster.[59]

The Commons chose Colonel Miles Corbet to inform the King, an unprepossessing man with an ill-reputation among the Royalists—"bull-headed, splay-footed, bacon-faced Corbet."[60] The King received the news with his usual calm. On Sunday he remained for much of the day at his devotions, and when he walked on the terrace he was seen to look fixedly and sadly in the direction of London. He spoke little, and to the point. No-one, he said, had authority to try him. He would recognise no Court, but God and his conscience. He would answer no charge, but would endure and die as a martyr.[61]

CHAPTER FIVE

"THE GREAT BUSINESS"

January 6 - 20, 1649

THE TRIAL of the King of England was no longer the wild threat of fanatics. The unbelievable thing had emerged from the dark region of rumour into full daylight. By an Act of the House of Commons, printed and published for all to read, a High Court of Justice had been called into being for the space of one month to try the King.

Hugh Peter was for quicker work than this. In a sermon to the troops on the following Sunday he promised action within a week. "Honest fellow soldiers, before I come to you again in this place, ye shall see the work done for which you were brought hither."[1] It was indeed widely predicted that the Court would meet at Windsor on Tuesday; if the King refused to plead, he would be sentenced out of hand, and would be given Wednesday to prepare himself for death on Thursday.[2] Windsor would be the place of trial because the King was secured there beyond all chance of escape. In much the same way his grandmother, Mary Stuart, had been tried and executed in the security and privacy of Fotheringhay.

These predictions were wide of the mark. The trial of King Charles was to be wholly different, because those who brought it about believed themselves to be the instruments of God's purpose. Political necessity had long appeared to them in the guise of the Divine Will. Other kings had been deposed, and privately murdered, for reasons more specious than just—Edward II, Richard II, Henry VI; their opponents had no divine mandate. Elizabeth I had sacrificed Mary Stuart under strong political pressure and had strenuously denied her own responsibility.

But those who brought King Charles to trial defended their action on principles of religion and patriotism, and were proud of what they did. For this reason, they chose for the place of his trial, not the enclosed precincts of Windsor but the most famous and public place of the whole kingdom, Westminster Hall; and they built his scaffold in the open street that skirted his palace of Whitehall.

This decision was in keeping with the assured and terrible purpose that inspired the formidable group now at the head of affairs. It would increase the danger, but it would also increase the glory of what they did. It would increase the danger because a trial held in open Court, among a great throng of people, would give opportunities for Royalist attempts to rescue the King and to do violence to his judges. Such risks were also multiplied by the necessity of moving the King from Windsor to Westminster, and by the inevitable postponement of the trial for some days while the Hall was got ready. But the dangers were less important than the impression that would be made, both in England and abroad, when the King himself was arraigned in the place where traitors were usually tried, and where, within the last nine years, his two most faithful servants, Strafford and Laud, had been brought to judgment.

The actions of Cromwell and his associates were not consistent with each other, and measures of superb assurance alternated with awkward and uncertain bungling. They did not need to justify this unprecedented thing to themselves: they knew it to be the will of God. But they wished, none the less, to allay the doubts of weaker men and to ensure the political stability of the nation, by reconciling their proceedings, as best they could, with the known law of the land.

They faced a sea of troubles. The King had already declared that he would neither recognise the Court nor answer the charge. If he persisted in this there could, properly speaking, be no trial at all since there was no means of proceeding to a trial in any English Court if the prisoner would not plead.

The preliminaries too had been unfortunate. It was wholly out of order for the House of Commons to legislate without the House of Lords, and it was doubtful, since Pride's Purge, if the Commons were a free and representative body or had any right to continue in session. Cromwell's attempt to reconcile the leaders of legal opinion to the trial had been unsuccessful, and the wisest, most experienced, most influential of them—Selden, Whitelocke, Widdrington—had gone into the country.

In the first draft of the bill to establish the High Court, the names of the two Chief Justices, Henry Rolle and Oliver St. John, and of Lord Chief Baron Wilde of the Exchequer Court had dominated the list. But all had refused to serve, and in the Act as finally passed their names were quietly omitted. All three had been appointed very recently by Parliament; all were strong opponents of the King. The defection of Rolle may not have been wholly unexpected; he was an old cautious man, with a lifetime's experience in the courts. He had little sympathy for the King who had, in his view, repeatedly infringed the law of the land, but he could not on that account participate in the illegal procedure of bringing him to trial. John Wilde was no loss in any event; rich, pushful and ambitious he had little reputation for learning and was not highly thought of as a judge.[3]

The desertion of Oliver St. John was much more serious. A kinsman and close friend of Cromwell's, he had been an unrelenting opponent of the King for more than ten years. He had made his reputation as counsel for John Hampden in the Ship-money case; he had confirmed it in his speeches against Strafford; during the war he had shared with Vane and Cromwell the leadership of the Independents in the House of Commons. But in this crisis, his respect for law and the constitution as he understood them separated him altogether from the actions of the Army. Like Vane, he could not accept the forcible purging of Parliament, would not recognise the acts of the depleted Commons, and would not make one of the High Court of Justice for the trial of the King.[4] The most that could be expected was that he and the other judges would maintain a non-committal silence about the legal aspects of the matter.

It was an axiom of English law that all justice proceeded from the sovereign. The House of Commons recognising this difficulty had tried to replace this keystone of the system by proclaiming the sovereignty of the people and equating it with their own. Their next care was to order the making of a new Great Seal since there would be obvious difficulties in carrying on the government of the realm without one, and the validity of the seal at present in use, which bore the name and effigy of King Charles, would evidently cease with his life. The Royalists made a bitter jest of this piece of news, declaring that the new seal was to save the rogues the embarrassment of authorising the King's murder in the name of "Charles, by the Grace of God."[5]

The names of the hundred and thirty-five men nominated to the High Court of Justice had meanwhile been published,[6] to be greeted by Royalist and Presbyterian jibes at the squalor and low birth of its members—the dregs of the people, shoemakers, brewers and "other mechanick persons." This was palpably untrue. Even among the officers of the New Model—upwards of thirty of them—most of those nominated were country gentlemen and some were substantial landowners. The men of obscure origin were a minority—Harrison, who had been a lawyer's clerk, Hewson who had been a shoemaker, Pride and Okey who were alleged to have been brewers' draymen but had more probably been brewers.

Apart from Army members, the names of the men selected to be the King's judges suggested not so much a popular or "democratic" Court (the current term of abuse) as a Court chosen as far as possible to represent the most respectable and substantial elements in the country. It had been necessary to remove the names of all English peers when the House of Lords rejected the bill, but the list could still be headed by the noble name of Lord Fairfax, whose title was a *Scottish* not an English barony. Lord Mounson, the holder of an Irish title, was included, and two eldest sons of English peers, Lord Grey of Groby and Lord Lisle. One Knight of the Bath and eleven baronets were also named.

For the rest there had been an evident attempt to bring in the landed gentry of as many counties as possible, and citizens of the principal towns. The list contained Mayors, or one time Mayors, of York, Newcastle, Hull, Liverpool, Cambridge and Dorchester, and several London Aldermen two of whom had held office as Lord Mayor. Reading, Bridport and Great Yarmouth were represented by their Recorders. Norwich, Gloucester, Shrewsbury, Nottingham, Ipswich, Canterbury, Winchester and others by their respective members of Parliament. But the compilers of the list seem to have found no one connected with Bristol, the second largest town in the realm.[7]

The Committee which drew up the Act had worked in the hope, rather than the expectation, that those named would be willing to serve. Their consent had not always been asked—a deliberate omission, for it would have been impossible to include a man who had positively refused while there was much to be gained by swelling out the list with names which were impressive if not wholly convincing. Over a hundred members of Parliament were, for instance, included although the average attendance at the House was now far below that number, and members who no longer attended the ordinary sessions would be most unlikely to accept responsibility for the King's trial. More understandably, the Committee set down the names of several officers in the Army who were at present occupied in the remoter parts of the kingdom—Cromwell's brother-in-law, Desborough, Colonel Lambert, Colonel Overton, Colonel

Rigby, and that active Parliament man, Sir Arthur Haslerig, who was busy persecuting Royalist delinquents and quarrelling with John Lilburne in Durham. These men were in favour of the trial and would have played their part had time and distance permitted.[8]

Fully aware that much of their impressive list was only for show, the Committee allowed a wide margin for absentees, and fixed the quorum at twenty. This was to prove too cautious. The number of Commissioners who confronted the King in Westminster Hall was never less than sixty-seven, and in the end fifty-nine of them signed his death warrant. On the other hand forty-seven of those named never at any time attended the Court, and eight more came only to the preliminary meetings and not to the trial.[9]

One famous name was not on the list: that of Sir Harry Vane who had been, for the last four years, the effective leader of the Independents in the House of Commons. He had despaired of the Newport Treaty and had done all in his eloquent power to get the negotiations broken off by a vote in the House before the Army intervened. Vane had a long record of gaining victories and advantages for the Independent minority by ingenious and sometimes insidious management of the House. But sleight of hand was one thing, and violence another, and the Purge was a breach of Parliamentary privilege which he could not, for some time, bring himself to accept. He had not attended the House since that day. He was still in London; he still zealously attended to his duties as Commissioner of the Admiralty, but he would not take part in the proceedings against the King which he judged to be illegal.[10] Added to his dislike of the Army's action, he had another, more personal, motive for staying away; as the son of a Court official, he felt a genuine compunction about shedding the blood of the King.

The withdrawal of Vane and the judges at least preceded the setting up of the Court. Some unexpected defections came later. Philip Skippon, a Bible-and-sword soldier who, both as a member of Parliament and as commander of the London Trained Bands, had done all in his power to further the interests of the Army in the last weeks, was included in the published list but never took his place in the Court of Justice. Sir William Brereton, a vigorous commander in the war and a strong supporter of the Army in Parliament, was another unexpected absentee. Dennis Bond, a rich merchant, member for Dorchester and one of the most active and assiduous men in the Commons, was not seen during the trial though he emerged immediately after to play his part in the republican government. John Lowry, who had sat for eight years in Parliament as fellow-member with Cromwell for Cambridge, who had fought in the war and supported the Independents throughout, was another who discreetly took cover until the King was dead. The abstentions of these last two probably reflected the uneasiness of the mercantile community. Sir William Allanson, once Mayor of York, also abstained, and two out of four London Aldermen appointed did the same.[11]

One distinguished man withdrew somewhat more noisily. Colonel Algernon Sidney, the clever, arrogant younger son of the Earl of Leicester, had fought bravely in the war and had been wounded at Marston Moor. His father had consistently opposed the King, but did not think it seemly that a son of his should sit on the Court that tried him. Sidney, none the less, attended the preliminary meetings, but only to deride the judicial pretensions of the assembly; the King, he said, could be tried by no Court, and no one could be tried by this Court. Cromwell curtly answered: "We will cut off his head with the crown upon it." Sidney said no more. He withdrew to his father's house at Penshurst until all was over.[12]

Other silent defections were not unexpected. Most of the lawyers appointed to the Court followed the example of their betters and stayed away. Only a few rigid opponents of the King could reconcile his trial with the spirit, if not the letter, of English law. A sovereign who had deliberately attempted to subvert the laws of the land (and this they believed him to have done) was a public danger, and they could therefore invoke against him the natural law of self-preservation, and bring him to justice although they had themselves to invent the machinery to do so.

Of those who attended the trial, not all were fully convinced. If the Royalists were wrong in sneering at the low birth of the judges, they were sometimes nearer the mark in calling them rogues and knaves. The motives and characters of a fair number of those nominated did not bear scrutiny. The influential landowners who had supported Parliament and joined the Independents as their interest dictated were often men of turbulent ambition or rooted grievances: Sir Edward Baynton, the Wiltshire magnate, had been in trouble during his stormy life for duelling, adultery and peculation. Sir Thomas Mauleverer and Sir John Bourchier, both Yorkshire landowners, were a pair of unprincipled, choleric malcontents. Another Yorkshireman, Thomas Chaloner, was widely believed to be inspired by spite because the King had withdrawn the exclusive rights he had at one time enjoyed in a profitable alum works. Sir Michael Livesey, sheriff of Kent, was ambitious, irresponsible and reputed a coward. No one on either side had much to say for Sir John Danvers, who had a long career as a courtier under King James and King Charles, or for Henry Mildmay, the renegade Master of the King's Jewel House. Others—Cornelius Holland, Humphrey Edwards and Gregory Norton—who had been servants of the Crown were viewed doubtfully by their colleagues and execrated by the Royalists.[13]

The necessity to produce an impressively long list took precedence over the consideration of men's characters and personal fitness. The King's trial was to be a public manifestation of God's righteous judgment but the instruments chosen to perform it were by no means all righteous men, and were not even thought to be so by those who selected them. On occasion the choice of names seems to have been both ruthless and casual. "Sir, you must make one in this great business," one of the Committee called out to John Downes, the member for Arundel, who had sat in the Commons for the last eight years without attracting the slightest notice. Downes refused but they would not take no for an answer. "Through weakness and fear I was ensnared," he was to plead when on trial for his life eleven years later. The same story was told, in the same sorry circumstances, by several others. Augustine Garland, a barrister of Lincoln's Inn, said he allowed his name to be put down "for fear of my own destruction. I did not know which way to be safe in anything." Thomas Waite, a Leicestershire squire, asserted he had been brought to London and compelled to sit by a mixture of trickery and force. Simon Mayne said he had risen in the House to protest against the inclusion of his name and been pulled down by a fellow member with a muttered threat of sequestration if he dared to withdraw. Henry Smith, Robert Tichborne and Owen Rowe pleaded bewilderment and weakness—they had not known how to withstand the formidable threats of those in power.[14]

The Committee which drafted the list of judges was certainly formidable—with Oliver Cromwell and Henry Marten, Thomas Scot and Henry Ireton to steer it. But the persuasion they employed to bring in the unwilling seems to have taken effect only on a few irresolute men. Lucy, the wife of Colonel Hutchinson, frankly said that those men lied who later declared that "they were under the awe of the Army, and overpersuaded by Cromwell, and the like." Her version makes too little allowance for human frailty. Like her husband, she was austere and devout, a strong and disciplined character with little understanding and less sympathy for feeble natures. "It is certain that all men herein were left to their free liberty of acting, neither persuaded nor compelled; and as there were some nominated in the commission who never sat, and others who sat at first, but durst not hold on, so all the rest might have declined it if they should, when it is apparent they should have suffered nothing by so doing."[15]

This is strong testimony against the blubbered excuses of Downes: "When those times were . . . how impetuous the soldiers . . . how not a man that durst either disown them or speak against them . . ."; not at any rate a man like Downes, in his own words "a poor, ordinary, mean man."[16] Other poor, ordinary, mean men also convinced themselves in 1660 that they had never wanted the King's death, and stood trembling and stuttering before judges far more terrible to them than Cromwell had been.

The evidence of events supports Lucy Hutchinson. No harm came to the forty-seven appointed members of the Court who never sat, or to the eight who left before the trial, or to the twenty-one who attended the trial but did not sign the death warrant.

Of those fifty-nine who took part in the trial and later set their hands to the warrant, some were weak and unwilling, and some were no better than the Royalists thought them—scoundrels scrambling for the spoils of war and the seats of power. But the majority acted from a sincere conviction that no other course was open to them as God-fearing Christians and lovers of their country. Between thirty and forty men gave character, solidarity, and strength to the High Court of Justice.

Cromwell towered head and shoulders above the rest, taking command at every sign of weakness, refusing to let their purpose slacken. He now, without rival and without question, controlled and inspired the Army. But where, in all this stood the Lord General Fairfax, Commander in Chief of the Army and first named in the High Court of Justice to try the King? Much might depend on the answer to this question. At the first assembly of the Commissioners the answer was still in doubt.

II

The sessions of the High Court of Justice for the trying and judging of Charles Stuart opened on Monday, 8th January, at two o'clock in the Painted Chamber. This majestic room in the ancient Palace of Westminster lay just to the south of Westminster Hall, nearly adjoining the House of Commons. When the Plantagenet kings used Westminster as their residence it had been the royal bedchamber and had become famous as the *Camera Depicta*, the Painted Chamber, in the time of the cultured, aesthetic and politically incompetent Henry III. He had ordered the walls to be decorated with scenes from the Bible and the lives of the Saints. Graceful figures of the Virtues flanked the elegant gothic windows, while Kings, Queens, Prophets and Saints with crowns of burnished gold, and knights in silver armour on horses caparisoned in crimson covered the walls; at the centre of all was the Coronation of Edward the Confessor, King and Saint. This once gorgeous pageant in scarlet and blue, saffron, green, purple and orange-tawny had grown dim and dirty after four hundred years. Much was hidden under tapestry—seven fine pieces of the Labours of Hercules, the property of the King. Some of it had been damaged by careless alterations. Windows had been bricked up, and others had been inserted; a fireplace had been knocked out of one of the massive walls. The glorious Camera Depicta of Henry III was by now only a shadow of what it had once been.[18]

Tables and chairs were set for the Commissioners, and in the wintry season the room was illumined by the huge fire on the hearth and the flickering light of candles. Messengers, clerks and attendants, official or unofficial, came and went. Hugh Peter bustled in and out, full of importance, enthusiasm and advice. The public were admitted for a part, but not all, of the deliberations. It was, however, easy to slip in at any time under cover of so much coming and going. John Evelyn, disapproving, but still irrepressibly bent on seeing all he could, got in one morning and heard Hugh Peter (or so he said) inciting the Commissioners to murder the King.[19]

The first session was not well attended. Only fifty-three Commissioners answered the roll-call. First among them was Thomas, Lord Fairfax. They discussed only the preliminaries, gave orders for the King's trial to be publicly proclaimed and appointed the officials of the Court. John Phelps, who had succeeded Henry Elsyng as Clerk of the House of Commons, was appointed along with one Greaves to be clerks to the Court. Next, they chose lawyers to frame the charge: John Cook, John Aske, Anthony Steele, and Isaac Dorislaus. This was not a very impressive group. Steele had recently been appointed Attorney General by Parliament. He had attracted notice by his vicious prosecution of Captain Burley, a gallant if misguided Cavalier, who had tried to make a one-man rising in the Isle of Wight, and had been hanged for it.[20] Isaac Dorislaus a distinguished Dutch scholar, had once been Professor of Ancient History at Cambridge, where he had been silenced for expressing opinions that were thought subversive of monarchy;[21] since the beginning of the war he had given the benefit of his excellent brain and profound classical and legal knowledge to the King's enemies. Of John Aske nothing whatever is known, and he remained throughout the consultations and the trial a silent presence. The most vigorous of the four was John Cook.[22] He was a barrister of Gray's Inn, a man of considerable education, who had travelled in his youth in the Protestant centres of France and Switzerland, living for some time in Geneva. Later he had gone to Ireland where he seems to have fallen foul of Strafford, though whether for his opinions, or—as the Royalists averred—for his corruption, is doubtful. A man of rabid and sometimes eccentric opinions, he combined fervent religious faith with convinced republicanism and an unusual interest in moral and social reforms. Earlier in the year he had published a book entitled *Unum Necessarium* in which he argued that restrictions on the sale of alcoholic liquor together with free medical and legal services for the poor were the essential foundations of a reformed Christian state.[23]

Next morning, 9th January, the sergeant at arms, Edward Dendy, rode into Westminster Hall attended by six trumpeters and two troops of horse. There he formally proclaimed that Charles Stuart, King of England, was to be tried and the Court of Justice for that purpose would be in session from 10th January in the Painted Chamber. He repeated the proclamation, trumpeters and all, in Cheapside and at the Old Exchange. Crowds turned out to listen but there was neither interruption nor protest which, in view of the armed guard surrounding Sergeant Dendy, was not surprising.[24]

The Commissioners met for the second time on Wednesday, 10th January. Fairfax was no longer there. Though he had come to the first meeting he had taken no part; he had not signed the order issued by his fellow Commissioners for proclaiming the trial, an abstention which at once aroused notice and speculation among the Royalists.[25] It is conceivable that he was, until that moment, in doubt as to the nature of the trial, but his subsequent conduct is hardly to his credit. The Army, of which he was General, had asked for justice on the King; the most active members of the Court were soldiers under his command. All their actions up to that time had been authorised by him, not formally (as he later pretended) but with deliberation. He had agreed to be included among the Commissioners for the trial, though Sir Harry Vane had refused and the Chief Justices had ostentatiously withdrawn. Fairfax cannot have been ignorant that his name headed the list, and his willingness to attend the first meeting indicates something more than an unseasonable curiosity.

Had he, until that day, refused to believe that Cromwell, Ireton and those grim Colonels who made up their following were in earnest? It seems the only explanation. As a responsible landowner, and honest believer in the rights and obligations of the gentry, he disliked and feared the innovations of the Levellers. Did he believe that the trial was a ruse of Cromwell's to discredit the Levellers and make way for the Restoration of the King on the Army's terms? He may have done so. Or he may have thought that the threat of trial and deposition (but surely not of death?) was to be used to compel the King to make the concessions that the Independents wanted.

Fairfax, in his bewildered way, might have agreed to go so far—by implication, he *had* agreed to go so far. He loved his Army and wanted to see his men paid and their good service vindicated against the ingratitude of the Presbyterians in Parliament. Also, he wanted peace and settled government once again in England.

Fearing the Levellers, hating the Presbyterians, he had supported with some warmth his Army's demand for justice on the King. He had led the troops into London. He had acquiesced in Pride's Purge. He had not refused to have his name on the list of Commissioners for the King's trial. But at that first session, in the Painted Chamber he realised at last that the trial was not a political ruse, or if it ever had been intended as such it was so no more. Without any public statement, without any recorded protest, he withdrew from the Court.

Was this enough? Should he not have acted—this gifted soldier, this conscientious commander, this puzzled man who never understood politics? He did nothing. He had, it is true, the day to day affairs of his Army to see to. He had not very much time to himself. It was natural, though it was also noticeable, that Cromwell, Ireton and the "creature Colonels" were constantly in his company. Royalist observers described him as being "baited" by them, and in relays: "baited with fresh dogs all night"[26] runs one comment. They certainly watched him, respectfully, but continually.

But is the excuse good enough? Could he not have spoken out in the Painted Chamber, as Algernon Sidney did? Later, when the murder of the King (for such he thought it) was imminent, Fairfax would excuse himself by saying that, on the eve of the execution, a protest from him would have split the Army and caused Civil War. But at the very outset of the business he might surely have sounded out the mood of the Commissioners, have put at least his case for saving the King's life? Instead he withdrew, tacitly abdicating his authority and prestige into the hands of Cromwell.

The Commissioners met for the second time on 10th January, forty-five of them being present. The insignificant barrister, Augustine Garland, seems to have taken the chair. The major business of the day was to choose a lawyer of sufficient standing to preside at future meetings and at the King's trial. The law was so weakly represented among the Commissioners that the strongest candidate for the office of President was John Bradshaw who had been a judge of the Sheriffs Court in London for some years, and had recently been appointed chief justice of Chester and a judge in Wales.

As an understudy for Lord Chief Justice St. John, Bradshaw was an undistinguished choice, but he was the best man available. He was not however present in the Painted Chamber and he had failed to come to the earlier meeting. Would he, like his betters, refuse the great office thrust upon him? To the relief of his fellow Commissioners he made his appearance at their third meeting, on Friday, 12th January, offered the inevitable (and in this case justified) excuses for his insufficiency for so great a task, was persuaded to take the chair and to accept the title of "Lord President."[27]

The lesser offices of the Court were by now also appointed, not without difficulty. The clerk chosen to assist Phelps, a Mr. Greaves, had pleaded that the pressure of other business made it impossible for him to attend. His excuses were accepted—the Commissioners were evidently anxious to stir up as little trouble as possible—and another clerk, Andrew Broughton, was appointed in his place.[28]

Much more serious than the defection of Greaves was the

last minute defection of the Attorney General Anthony Steele. He may have been as ill as he said he was, and as the Commissioners were willing to believe, but a failure of nerve at the eleventh hour seems more probable. The responsibility for presenting the case against the King thus devolved on John Cook who lacked neither courage nor conviction for the task, and believed that he had been singled out to do this noble work of liberation for the people of England. Indeed he went to it all too eagerly, seeing in King Charles a murderer more evil than Cain (who had not the advantage of being a Christian) and more unpardonable than the plotters who contrived the Sicilian Vespers, the Massacre of Saint Bartholomew, and the Gunpowder Plot—for they, poor wretches, had been Papists who knew no better. His unconcealed vindictiveness against the prisoner would, in the long run, do more service to the King's memory than to his own. But Cook was not conscious of these finer shades; he was not indeed aware that his actions were coloured by personal feeling at all as he planned out withering speeches to hurl at the head of "Charles Stuart whom God in his wrath gave to be a King to this nation."[29]

III

While Cook and Dorislaus were drafting the charge against the King, a group of the Commissioners were inspecting Westminster Hall. A major trial involved considerable disturbance. The Hall was the general meeting place and clearing house for English justice. During the term a number of Courts sat there, in partitions roughly boarded off one from another. Round the walls huddled the temporary booths and shops of tradesmen selling pens, paper, wax, ink, spectacles and other relevant wares. All these would have to be moved. Much demolition, carpentry and upholstering would have to be done before the trial of the King could, in the words of

the Commissioners "be performed in a solemn manner."
It would also have to be performed with due care for security,
a fact which was tacitly recognised when Cromwell, with
Harrison, Ludlow and other soldiers were added to the
Committee charged with planning the arrangements.[30]

On Saturday, 13th January, when they made their report,
a whiff of fear was in the air. The sergeant at arms had orders
to search and close the vaults under the Painted Chamber.
Only after this precaution had been taken did the Commissioners settle to business, and the ubiquitous Augustine Garland
reported the decision of Cromwell and his Committee. The
King, they recommended, should be tried at the South end of
Westminster Hall, where a sufficient space could be cleared
by removing the partitions between the Court of King's
Bench and the Court of Chancery which were situated there.[31]
The rest of the Hall was to be cleared of obstructions to
accommodate the public.

On the face of it this was to try the King in full view of
his people, but the arrangements differed from those which
had been made for other prisoners, and the difference betrayed
the anxieties which tormented the Commissioners. It was
usual to hold a public trial nearer to the centre of the Hall, so
that the accused could be seen from all sides. This necessitated
bringing the prisoner into the Hall by the main door and
conveying him through the crowd of spectators to his
appointed place. But they could not risk bringing the King
through the Hall. By holding the trial at the extreme South
end it would be possible to bring him in through the network
of buildings which lay beyond the Hall, between it and the
river. If he came this way, the King would pass through rooms
and along corridors from which the public could be excluded,
and which could be well-lined with soldiers.

There was another advantage in their choice of site. The
great mass of spectators in the body of the Hall would be
able to see and hear very little of what went on, so that the
gesture of giving the King an open trial would have been

made at a minimum of risk. For better security the public part of the Hall was to be divided from the judges and the prisoner by two parallel barriers—a wooden partition running from wall to wall and, a few feet behind it, a strong railing to hold back spectators. The main body of the Hall was to have another railing set up down its entire length along which soldiers were to be stationed to control the crowd.

There would none the less be galleries for rich spectators overlooking the place of trial itself. These were mostly to be reached from private houses abutting on the Hall, and the Commissioners presumably felt that they could not risk the opprobrium of forbidding the erection of such galleries and the sale of seats. They did not even have any effective plan for investigating the character or checking the names of those who occupied them. Yet the danger of some desperate Royalist firing from this vantage point on the King's judges— on Cromwell himself, or Bradshaw, or Cook—was evident. Cromwell does not seem to have troubled himself about it, but Cook referred with a certain nervous elation to threats against his life and Bradshaw took the precaution of having his hat lined with steel plates.[32] It was not, of course, possible for anyone in the galleries to reach the King, nor would it have been possible for a Royalist assassin to escape, since every approach was guarded by soldiers.

All the same, in view of the horror and despair now prevalent among the Cavaliers, the King's judges exposed themselves to some danger. It was perhaps typical of Cromwell and his fellow soldiers who planned the arrangements in Westminster Hall, that they took every possible precaution to secure the person of the King, but were prepared, as in the day of battle, to take a risk on their own lives.

IV

Meanwhile from most of the London pulpits the Presbyterian ministers continued to denounce the Army, the servile Commons, Cromwell, and all their works. They also, to his considerable distress, denounced Fairfax. He received on 18th January, an appeal signed by forty-seven of the London ministers which, in true Presbyterian style, was couched as a reprimand. Reproaching him for having allowed the Army to seize power, they urged him to undo the evil before it was too late.[33]

A forty-eighth minister, John Geree, preferred to act independently; he sent a pamphlet with a Greek name to Lady Fairfax, denouncing the Army for Jesuitical King-murderers who were a disgrace to the Protestant religion, and arguing that "the generality of the people of the land" abhorred the very idea of trying the King. In a fervent dedication to Lady Fairfax and her mother he implored the two ladies to use their influence with the General.[34]

Lady Fairfax was a woman of character; so was her mother, the venerable widow of the most famous English soldier of his time, Lord Vere. Pursued by the public protests of the Presbyterian ministers, and the private disapproval of his wife and mother-in-law, hectored by Ireton, hypnotised by Cromwell, the Lord General preserved an unhappy silence.

These protests, which were of course widely circulated, together with the reiterated denunciations of the Army by eloquent preachers and the manifestos of Prynne and the more vocal secluded members could not but have an effect on the citizens of London. The situation was the more dangerous because of the Royalist sympathies of the Lord Mayor, Abraham Reynardson. It was imperative to arrange a demonstration of an opposite kind and Robert Tichborne, a London linen-draper by profession and now one of Cromwell's younger colonels, was selected to do it. Some weeks before he had been selected by Cromwell and Ireton to negotiate with the Levellers;[35] he knew London, was closely associated with the Independent preachers, and was in sympathy, not indeed with the Levellers, but with the various malcontents in the City who resented the oligarchic government of the Aldermen. He had no difficulty in organising a strongly worded petition from the London citizens which echoed the formula of the Army petitions for the King's death in demanding impartial justice on "all the Grand and Capital Authors and Contrivers of, and Actors in, the late Wars." This was to go forward not as the unauthorised petition of individual citizens but as an official message from the City to Parliament, and Tichborne expected to do this by means of the Common Council whose members were overwhelmingly in sympathy with the Army.

He had reckoned without the stubborn loyalty of the Lord Mayor, who confronted the Common Council with a categorical refusal to accept or pass on their petition. The angry meeting lasted from eleven in the morning until late in the afternoon, when Reynardson withdrew amid a din of protest. Independent action by the Council should have been impossible, but taking as their example the treatment recently accorded to the House of Lords by the House of Commons, they declared that they could act without the consent of the Lord Mayor and Aldermen. On 15th January, Tichborne presented the London petition to Parliament together with a denunciation of Reynardson for his attempt to thwart the will of the citizens.[36]

It was not so much the petition that Cromwell and his associates valued as the proof it gave them that Reynardson's authority and the influence of the Presbyterian ministers were alike powerless against the organised action of their friends. One other anxiety was still with them. The discussions about the future plan for the nation, the *Agreement of the People*, still went on, in a calmer atmosphere than when Lilburne had been present. The plea for a fundamental reform of government was however eloquently made, in his absence, by the sectarian minister William Erbury. The essential, he argued, was not to destroy the King, but to destroy the oppressive powers that he and others had wielded; to destroy his person and not to remedy "those oppressive principles both in powers and persons" which existed in the country was to leave undone the great work which God had called upon the Army to do. His opinions were echoed by Captain George Joyce, who appealed to Fairfax as one "whom the Lord hath clearly called unto the greatest work of righteousness that ever was amongst men." Fairfax was in the chair but, as usual, a silent presence. Joyce reproached him for "a spirit of fear upon Your Excellency" and warned him "not to shift off that work which the Lord hath called you to."

The spirit of fear was certainly present, a fear lest the fabric of society be shaken by these formidable demands for alterations in the power of the civil magistrates, reform of the laws, curtailment of privilege. But in the end Ireton got his way and the Agreement of the People as it finally worked out did precisely what Captain Joyce had suspected: it enabled the Grandees to shift off the work to which they had been called. For all future plans were dependent on the voluntary termination of the Parliament at present in session and the choosing of a new one with a more realistic territorial distribution of seats and a somewhat enlarged franchise. The first essential being the agreement of Parliament to this scheme, its realisation might be indefinitely postponed.[37]

V

By this time Westminster Hall had been cleared, and the partitions, galleries and benches were fast going up. Orders had gone to the Tower armouries for additional halberds for the guards, and seemly black gowns had been ordered for the lesser officials and messengers of the Court. Colonel

Hutchinson submitted a report from the Committee in charge of the security measures recommending that the King be lodged in Sir Robert Cotton's house during his trial. This handsome mansion with a garden running down to the Thames was conveniently situated between the river and Westminster Hall and could easily be cordoned off by soldiers. A special Court of Guard was hurriedly built in the garden to accommodate two hundred men. Ten companies of infantry were to be constantly on duty about the house and its surrounding buildings. As a further precaution a general order went out that no soldier was to absent himself from his quarters during the trial, and troopers were to keep their horses saddled and their arms ready against any sudden alarm.[38]

But the days went by and the lawyers were still wrestling with the charge. The immense learning of Dorislaus and the ferocious zeal of Cook made neither for brevity nor clarity. The first draft evidently would not do, and a number of Commissioners including Ireton, Scot, and Marten were appointed to assist and advise. Even with their help, the lawyers still failed to made the charge effective, clear and reasonably brief, and on 17th January, Cromwell was added to the group. By the 19th the harassed Commissioners at last produced something acceptable, though the final amendments and corrections were not complete until the morning of 20th January. The trial was to begin that afternoon, none too early; already fourteen days had gone by out of the bare month allotted under the act for trying and condemning the King.

The weather was bitterly cold, adding physical discomfort to the prevailing atmosphere of anxiety, bitterness, and fear. There was ice on the Thames, and in the grey gloom of the sunless winter no one had the heart to demonstrate against the proceedings though there was writing and preaching in plenty. The Presbyterian clergy spoke from the security of their pulpits; protests came off the illicit printing presses and passed from hand to hand. William Prynne and Clement

Walker, the two irrepressible publicists of the excluded members, succeeded in distributing from their place of confinement, an official-looking single sheet in which they pronounced that the Army and all its officers were rebels and traitors, subverters of the laws and liberties of the people, and Jesuitical murderers.[40] This cry of "Jesuit"—based on the widespread belief that the Jesuits advocated King-murder to serve their sinister ends—was to cause great annoyance to the devout anti-Popish republicans, against whom it was, from now on, a continual jibe.

Leveller sympathisers, meanwhile, chose this moment to petition the House of Commons for a free Press, complaining that the Army, under an order from Fairfax, were tracking down secret presses, breaking into private houses and taking citizens into custody under martial law. The House of Commons thanked the honest citizens politely for the petition and promised it "speedy consideration", which in the circumstances meant nothing at all. The King's trial would begin within twenty-four hours, and what thoughts could they have for anything else? Beyond the outcome of that "great business" they dared not look.

During the last week they had issued a Declaration condemning the peace policy of the autumn and defending their present conduct. The King, they argued, would undoubtedly have violated any treaty made while he was under restraint; to treat with him was therefore useless and dangerous, and not to be thought of "unless we should deny the goodness of our Cause, which God hath adjudged on our side, by the gracious Blessings of so many signal Victories; unless we should betray our friends, who have engaged with us . . . to the hazard of their lives and fortunes; unless we should value this one man, the King, above so many millions of people, whom we represent; and prefer his honour, safety and freedom before the honour, safety and freedom of the whole nation." This was the high rhetorical close to an otherwise closely argued condemnation of all previous attempts to reach a settlement with the King. But it was a strangely negative and defensive statement to come from a group of men who had claimed for themselves, contrary to all precedent, supreme power in the nation, and who were about to bring their legal and anointed King to trial for treason. No defiant theories were enunciated, no programme was laid down. The only reference to the future was contained in a concluding sentence that indicated the King's fate by implication only.

"We are resolved, by God's assistance, and that speedily, so to settle the peace of the kingdom, by the authority of Parliament, in a more happy way, than can be expected from the best of Kings."[42]

Such, on the eve of the trial, was the last official utterance of the House of Commons.

VI

All this time the King had been at Windsor, spending his days in meditation and prayer, varied only by walking on the terrace, making constrained conversation with the governor, Colonel Whichcot. Herbert was in constant attendance. Once the King kept this tedious watch-dog occupied for the best part of a day in looking for a diamond seal that had dropped off his watch chain. On another occasion he overslept and the King, who had asked to be called early, promised him a gold alarm-clock for a present, ordering it from a watch maker in Fleet Street through the Earl of Pembroke.

The weather was bitter, and Herbert, who felt the cold, laid down his pallet bed too near the open hearth, where at dead of night it began to smoulder. Waking suddenly, he ran in alarm to the King's adjoining room, and his cries of "Fire" alerted the soldiers on guard outside the door. But the King would not let them in, and the flames were quickly extinguished.

On Sunday the King attended St. George's Chapel and heard the garrison chaplain preach. The soldiers behaved respectfully; the governor was formally courteous. But the Chapel itself, which before the war had been fitted according to the King's conception of dignity, beauty and ritual, had been stripped bare. In the scarred and scoured interior, under the luxuriant gothic vaulting, the Puritan soldiers prayed standing and intoned the metrical psalms, while the King sat impassive. He had expressed one vehement, negative wish: he had refused to hear a sermon from Hugh Peter.[43]

Since he had received formal notice of his trial he had heard no more. Newspapers and pamphlets were kept from him. He received no letters. On or about 19th January, he was informed by Whichcot that he was to be moved to St. James's. "His Majesty made little reply, seeming nothing so delighted with this remove, as he was with the former," writes the ineffable Herbert. The King faced his fast approaching doom with serenity, and, "turning him about, said, God is everywhere alike in wisdom, power and goodness."[44]

He travelled on Friday, 19th January. His coach, drawn by six horses, was brought right in to the castle, just below the keep; the way to the outer gate was lined with musketeers and pikemen, and as the coach rolled out into the town, a troop of horse immediately surrounded it. Thus guarded, the King made his last journey to his capital. He spoke with no one as the closed coach travelled over the frost-bound iron-hard roads through Brentford, Hammersmith and Kensington. Harrison was in command of the troops. Hugh Peter, still officiously hoping to convert the King, made one of the party; but he got no word with Charles, and had to content himself with riding at the head of the procession, an air of undisguised triumph on his coarse round face.[45]

Only a few isolated spectators saw the King's coach go by. It was too cold for crowds to gather, and his movements were not widely known. One Royalist gentleman who rode out to salute him, later averred that the King, seeing him raise his hat, had graciously acknowledged his salute, but the surrounding troopers justled him and his horse into the ditch.[46] By nightfall, Charles was at St. James's, and had gone to his prayers. Beyond the fact that he was to be tried on the morrow, he knew very little. He had not seen the Act which set up the Court; he did not know the names or the numbers of his appointed judges. He was still uncertain of the meaning of this sacrilegious Act. He did not fear death. He had grown familiar over the last seven years with the idea of a violent end, either in battle, or by an assassin's blow. He had long since declared his willingness to die a martyr rather than yield up the rights of the Crown. Yet he still thought it possible that his enemies were preparing for him a last unspeakable act of pressure to break down his resistance.

What would they do, what *could* they do, if he still refused to yield?

CHAPTER SIX

THE KING ON TRIAL

January 20 - 23, 1649

THE MEMBERS of the High Court of Justice assembled in the Painted Chamber at nine o'clock on Saturday, 20th January, to make the final arrangements for the trial which was to begin that afternoon. They had hardly settled down to work before an urgent message from the House of Commons called all members to attend forthwith. There was business to transact and—as usual—no quorum. The High Court perforce adjourned until noon.[1]

There was not, fortunately, very much before the House that morning. The King had requested the attendance of Dr. Juxon, Bishop of London, during his time of trial, and this was granted. Since he left the Isle of Wight Charles had had no chaplain of his own choosing, but now that his end was imminent few in the Commons or the Army wished to continue the futile effort to shake his religious convictions. Juxon was given order to attend on the King, on the understanding that, for reasons of security, he did not come and go from his own house, but surrendered himself for the time being as a voluntary prisoner to share the King's captivity.

A matter of more general importance was the postponement of the law term for a fortnight—for the obvious reason that, until the King's trial was over, no other court could sit in Westminster Hall. This matter being arranged, the House received, with every appearance of interest and gratitude, the amended Agreement of the People—the innocuous plan for a new Parliament and the reform of the government which had been hammered out between the Grandees and the Levellers during eight weeks of debate at Whitehall. The House, to signify its approval in principle, gave order that the document be printed, and promised to consider the implementation of the plan as soon as "the necessity of affairs will permit." The last, hurried piece of business was an order to provide two thousand extra coats for the soldiers, sorely needed replacements in this exceptionally cold winter.[2]

It was now close upon noonday and the Commissioners for the King's trial were restive. The House rose. As for the Agreement, "the necessity of affairs" would certainly not allow of its being considered until after the King was tried, condemned, and dead. And by then there would be other, more urgent matters before the House. In "the first year of freedom by God's blessing restored" neither Parliament nor government would have time for any Agreement of the People.[3] The lethal timing of its presentation to the House of Commons could have been an accident; it could also have been a final twist of Ireton's cold ingenuity.

While the Commissioners reassembled in the Painted Chamber to make the final adjustments to the charge, the King was on his way from St. James's. Colonel Tomlinson, who was responsible for his safety, took no avoidable risk. Charles was conveyed in a closed sedan chair, lent for the occasion by the Earl of Pembroke.[4] He was surrounded on all sides by foot soldiers marching in close formation. He could neither be seen nor approached. Tomlinson avoided as far as possible narrow or built-up places where an obstruction or an ambush might facilitate a rescue. The King was carried across the Park from St. James's into the rambling precincts of his palace of Whitehall, and straight to the river at the garden stairs where a barge awaited him. An old palace servant, John Henry, a Welshman, lived in the house adjoining the stairs and had charge of them. He was at his door, with his seventeen year old son, to watch the King go by, and as he walked from his chair to the barge, Charles called a friendly recognition: "Art thou alive yet?"[5]   This was the only daylight moment of his journey, between the enclosed sedan chair and the curtained barge on the river.

He was carried up the Thames for half a mile, beyond Westminster stairs and the usual landing-place for Westminster Hall, as far as the private landing-place of Sir Robert Cotton's house. All the way along the banks boats filled with curious spectators watched his covered barge go by, preceded and followed by soldiers closely packed in open boats.[6] Disembarking, he walked between rows of soldiers across the frost-bound garden into the well-secured and well-appointed house which was to be his prison during the trial. Colonel Tomlinson's authority extended as far as Cotton House. Here the responsibility for the King's person during the trial devolved upon Colonel Francis Hacker and the oddly named Colonel Hercules Hunks. The King was still accompanied by his servants; Thomas Herbert, the gentleman in attendance, and three or four lower servants including John Joiner, the chief cook, who had been in his service before the war, but had since then fought in the Parliamentary forces and risen to the rank of Captain.

In Cotton House large rooms selected for the royal bedchamber and dining-room had been hurriedly got ready. Once more, as on so many other occasions, members of the King's peace-time household were willing to perform whatever maimed rites Parliament ordained. Clement Kinnersley, a gentleman of the Wardrobe who had not followed the King to the wars, had prepared both Holmby and Hampton Court to receive the royal prisoner and was now in charge of the arrangements at Cotton House. The King was more zealously guarded here than at St. James's or at Windsor. Neither Hunks nor Hacker had the education and good manners which distinguished Tomlinson; they permitted noisy and inconsiderate conduct to the troops under their command, several of whom were always just outside the King's room, with licence to open the door and keep watch on him at any time. They smoked and talked unchecked while on duty and had no orders to remove their hats in his presence or show any mark of respect.[7]

In the Painted Chamber, meanwhile, fifty-eight Commissioners with Bradshaw in the chair held a last private sitting to discuss the final arrangements. Many years later a Royalist gentleman was to claim that he had hidden in the room and had observed Cromwell's face go "as white as a wall" when he saw, from the window, the King as he came through the garden of Cotton House. He had heard Cromwell ask what they were to say if the King demanded by what authority they brought him to judgment, and Henry Marten had answered: "In the name of the Commons in Parliament assembled and all the good people of England."[8]

Nothing so dramatic is recorded in the minutes of John Phelps the assiduous clerk, though the Commissioners discussed the method of procedure that they proposed to adopt. First they would publicly read the "Act of the Commons of England assembled in Parliament" which gave them their authority; then they would send for the King who would be charged, as they had already decided, "in the name and on the behalf of the people of England." They expected the King to deny their authority—his intention to do so had been published in the Press. By common consent they left it to Lord President Bradshaw to handle this situation as best he could, by reprehending and admonishing him, or if all else failed by ordering his removal. If his unwillingness to recognise them took the obvious form of refusing to take off his hat in their presence, they decided to overlook the affront.

John Cook then presented the charge, in its final form engrossed on a scroll of parchment. They read it over with approbation. It was by now close on two o'clock and they adjourned to Westminster Hall.[9]

Some coming and going of Commissioners had taken place during this two hours' meeting. The deplorable Henry Mildmay had lost his nerve and slipped away; so had a more

obscure Commissioner, the Welshman, Thomas Wogan.[10]
Late arrivals had however swelled their numbers and by about
two o'clock sixty-eight of them formed up in procession
ready to enter Westminster Hall.

Spectators already filled the lower part of the Hall. The
galleries directly above the judges' seats were crammed and
some enterprising people had scrambled up into the embrasures
of the high gothic windows. There seems to have been no
system of checking the identity of spectators even in the
galleries which overlooked the judges, though Colonel
Axtell, in command of the soldiers in the Hall, was seen to let
in some favoured persons and to push out others.[11] Outside,
on the leads, soldiers were on guard; otherwise the inquisitive
would have clambered on to the sloping roofs below the
windows and broken the thick glazed panes to see into the
Hall. Whatever hesitations and fears disturbed the Commissioners as individuals or as a body, the face which they
presented to the public was one of righteous confidence.
The tremors of anxiety and doubt which shook the lesser
men, and would occasionally come to the surface in a manner
which could not be disregarded, were at first masked by the
resolute bearing of Bradshaw as President, of Cromwell and
his supporting colonels, and of the smaller but no less convinced group of civilian republicans.

There is no direct evidence about the arrangements for
reporting the trial. It was not one of the questions discussed
by the Commissioners. Presumably they had left it all to their
principal licenser of the Press, Gilbert Mabbott.

No Royalist reporting of the trial was likely. The order
prohibiting the presence of Cavaliers in London did not
in effect keep them out of London, but—by putting them in
danger of arrest—it kept them out of public places. In a
small society, the chances of recognition were large, and few
active Cavaliers ventured to Westminster Hall. The editors
of the three clandestine Royalist news-sheets were all marked
men, leading the harassed lives of fugitives. Yet it would

still have been possible for them to collect information from eye witnesses of the trial and to publish what was favourable to the King. They made no attempt to do this apparently feeling that to report the trial in any way was to condone it. They preferred merely to publish scurrilous attacks on the members of the Court and angry denunciations of the whole business.

There remained the licensed Press—six regular newspapers, to which in the last week of January three more would be added to gratify the immense public curiosity about the trial. Gilbert Mabbott, the son of a Nottingham shoemaker, once secretary to Fairfax and himself of Leveller sympathies, had a democratic and republican pride in the trial. Rightly gauging the extent of public interest, he arranged not only to print the fullest possible day to day information in his own paper *The Moderate*, but to issue, as occasion demanded, supplementary pamphlets devoted to the trial alone, under the quietly confident title of *"A Perfect Narrative of the Proceedings of the High Court of Justice in the Tryal of the King."*

During the last month Mabbott had shared his heavy work as licenser with an assistant named Theodore Jennings, an Independent who had served in the Army as a Scout Master. Jennings took advantage of the trial to start a newspaper of his own towards the end of January. It was called *A Perfect Summary* and made a third with Mabbott's *The Moderate* and *Perfect Occurrences* of the sectarian Henry Walker, all alike in favour of the Army and bitterly opposed to the King. Two more papers were licensed at the end of January. The editor of one, *The Army's Modest Intelligencer*, made up his editions by pirating at random from his colleagues, and the venture collapsed after five weeks. The second, *The Kingdom's Faithful Scout*, was a subsidiary venture by Daniel Border, the competent editor of an already existing paper, and lasted rather longer.[12]

A further series of supplementary pamphlets describing the occasion were issued by Henry Walker under the title

"*Collections of Notes taken at the King's Tryal by Henry Walker who was present at the Tryal.*" In spite of his insistence on this personal touch, Walker's report was less full and lively than either of Mabbott's publications.

Of the four editors who had no close links with Army, Parliament or the sects, three—John Dillingham of *The Moderate Intelligencer*, Daniel Border of *The Perfect Weekly Account*, and Richard Collings of *The Kingdom's Weekly Intelligencer*—show signs of independent observation. Samuel Pecke, the veteran editor of *A Perfect Diurnall* gave the fullest report but kept most closely to the lines lad down by Mabbott. Not one of the four wrote anything that was likely to endanger his livelihood.

An anonymous journalist, with a cautious Royalist slant, procured a licence for a special account of which one number only was published. *The King's Tryal* covered the first day and then disappeared possibly because Mabbott, who saw no objection to using his powers as licenser for his own advantage as a journalist, wanted no more competitors in the field.[13]

How far did Mabbott actually control the reporting of the trial? The Presbyterian polemicist, Clement Walker, who was still in prison and could not attend himself, reported furiously that "much of the King's argument is omitted and much depraved, none but licensed men being suffered to take notes."[14] Since anyone wishing to take notes would have to be in an expensive and prominent seat, the licensing of those who took them would have presented no serious difficulty, but it did not follow that their reports were heavily censored, nor do they seem to have been. Nearly a dozen of them were still alive eleven years later to give evidence against the Regicides, and none suggested that there had been interference with their work.[15] Some must have been working directly for Mabbott; others for other editors. Seventeenth century methods of shorthand varied considerably, but it was possible with the best type of stenography (or tachygraphy —both words were used) to make a verbatim record. The printed texts suggest that only one full verbatim record was actually made, very probably by collating the notes of several shorthand writers in different parts of the Court.

This record, which Mabbott used for his account of the trial in the *Moderate*, and printed in full in his *Perfect Narrative* was evidently made available to any journalist who cared to use it, and was used at one time or another by nearly all of them, including Mabbott's colleague Theodore Jennings for his *Perfect Summary*, and even the self-sufficient Henry Walker for his *Perfect Occurrences*. But it was not compulsory to use it for Mabbott licensed the single issue of *The King's Tryal*, a much less full account which does not attempt verbatim reporting and appears to be written up from independent observation. On several occasions John Dillingham in his *Moderate Intelligencer* was clearly using a summary of the trial made from notes independent of Mabbott's version, and signs of the same independent observation occur though much less frequently in Daniel Border's *Perfect Weekly Account* and in Richard Collings' *Kingdom's Weekly Intelligencer*.

There is evidence of friendship or hostility to the King in the descriptions of his bearing provided by each editor; but there is no evidence of suppression of his words, for it is hard to see (in despite of Clement Walker's accusation) how he could have spoken at greater length or more effectively than in the existing reports.

The censors were not apparently afraid of the impression likely to be made on the public by anything that the King said. But there are suppressions and omissions of a different kind. Thus none of the newspapers emphasises, and few make any mention at all of, interruptions from spectators or disturbances among the members of the High Court.

This suppression may have been entirely the work of the censors, who were naturally anxious to withhold any information which would reveal the weakness, divisions and extreme unpopularity of the Court. But it is also possible that the shorthand reports were themselves indistinct, inadequate, or silent on these points. Interruptions which became famous eleven years later when, at the trials of the Regicides, everything was done to emphasise the strength of the sympathy for the King, may not at the time have been so dramatically noticeable as they were afterwards said to have been.[16]

II

Shortly after two o'clock, the Commissioners entered the Hall, preceded by twenty halberdiers and by officers solemnly carrying the sword and mace, the rear brought up by a further party of guards. They took their places on the tiered benches covered with red baize that had been set up for them below the great south window. Bradshaw's chair was somewhat raised in the middle of the front row. He had a reading desk and scarlet cushion in front of him. On either side sat the two Commissioners he had chosen to assist him in points of law, William Say and John Lisle. These three were all attired in their black barristers' gowns. The rest of the Commissioners were in whatever sober raiment suited their calling. It is uncertain where Cromwell sat. The guards took up their stations on either side of the Court, below the public galleries. The two clerks, Phelps and Broughton, were a few feet below and in front of Bradshaw at a table handsomely covered with a Turkey carpet.[17]

Phelps now rose to his feet and read out the preamble of the Commission empowering the Court to act. Bradshaw then ordered the prisoner to be brought, and twelve of the halberdiers marched off to fetch him.

While the King was on his way, Phelps read the roll-call, the Commissioners who were present rising to their names. As he called on Lord Fairfax a masked lady in one of the nearer galleries briefly raised her voice in protest, but her words were quickly submerged by the clerk's continued reading of the list and the movements along the benches as the Commissioners rose to their names. Not until much later would it be known that the speaker was Lady Fairfax and that she had cried out: "He has more wit than to be here," or, at somewhat greater length, that "the Lord Fairfax was not there in person, that he never would sit among them and they did him wrong to name him."[18]

During the reading of the roll-call there had been some last-minute fidgeting with the arrangements of the Court. The arm-chair, covered with red velvet, which had been set for the King had been moved nearer to his judges, then back again.[19] Now the King himself appeared, preceded and followed by soldiers who took up their stations on either side of the Court. He was dressed in black, wearing round his neck his blue ribbon and jewelled George, and on his black cloak the great irradiating silver star of the Garter. He walked quickly without looking to right or left and sat down in the red velvet chair. He now had his back to the people gathered in the Hall. All that any of them could see, above the wooden barrier which marked off the Court, and between the heads and pikes of the soldiers who guarded it, was his tall black hat, and his grey hair falling on to his shoulders. Only those in the galleries had any view of his face. He was impassive, showing no flicker of recognition or curiosity.

At his side a small table with pen and ink had been placed, to enable him to make notes for his defence. He was attended by three domestic servants, of whom John Joiner was one; but they had been halted a few feet away from him, and seem to have been standing behind the guard of soldiers who accompanied him.[20] Those who were nearest to him—and they were within arm's length of him on his right—were the three lawyers in charge of the prosecution: Cook in high excitement, Aske silent and unobtrusive, Dorislaus ready with a mass of learned information if it should be needed. The King did not look at them.

There cannot have been silence in that enormous crowded

room. Yet above the shuffling, rustling murmur, the breathing, the coughing, the footfalls, there must have been in the railed-off enclosure where the King faced his judges, a moment of tenseness, of at least a limited silence, before Bradshaw began. "Charles Stuart, King of England, the Commons of England, assembled in Parliament, being sensible of the great calamities that have been brought upon this nation, and of the innocent blood that hath been shed in this nation, which are referred to you as the author of it; and according to that duty which they owe to God, to the Nation, and to themselves, and according to that power and fundamental trust that is reposed in them by the people, have constituted this High Court of Justice before which you are now brought, and you are to hear your charge upon which the Court will proceed."[21]

He stopped, and John Cook instantly followed on his cue: "My Lord, in behalf of the Commons of England and of all the people thereof, I do accuse"—and here he swung round and glared at the prisoner—[22] "Charles Stuart here present, of high treason and high misdemeanours, and I do, in the name of the Commons of England, desire the charge may be read unto him."

He had it in his hand, the heavy scroll of parchment, half unrolled.

"Hold a little," said the King, but Cook continued to unroll the indictment. Charles lifted the silver-headed cane that he habitually carried and tapped Cook two or three times on the arm to attract his attention; Cook did not turn but the head of the cane fell off. There was no one near enough to retrieve it and the King, after a second's pause, stooped for it himself.[23]

"Sir," said Bradshaw, "the Court commands the charge to be read; if you have anything to say afterwards, you may be heard."

Charles remained silent, and Cook launched into the charge with evident enjoyment. It was the first time that the King knew precisely what the accusation was. He must have listened attentively, though he assumed a contemptuous indifference.

In its final form the charge was of no overwhelming length; it would have taken less than ten minutes to read. It went direct to the heart of the matter. As King of England, Charles had been "trusted with a limited power to govern by, and according to the laws of the land, and not otherwise." He had however conceived "a wicked design to erect and uphold in himself an unlimited and tyrannical power to rule according to his Will, and to overthrow the Rights and Liberties of the People." In pursuit of this design he had "traitorously and maliciously levied war against the present Parliament and the people therein represented." After this accusation came a list of those places at which the King had been present at the head of his troops during the First Civil War. Next he was accused of endeavouring to gain help for his designs by procuring "invasions from foreign parts." Then, after his defeat, he had "renewed or caused to be renewed the said war against the Parliament and good people of this nation in this present year," and given commissions to his son and to others to do so. These wars, wicked, murderous and destructive in themselves had as their sole objective the "upholding of a personal interest of Will, power and pretended prerogative to himself and his family against the public interest, common right, liberty, justice and peace of the people of this nation." He was thus responsible for "all the treasons, murders, rapines, burnings, spoils, desolations, damages and mischiefs to this nation, acted and committed in the said Wars, or occasioned thereby." For these reasons, Cook concluded, on behalf of the people of England, he impeached "the said Charles Stuart as a Tyrant, Traitor and Murderer, and a public and implacable Enemy to the Commonwealth of England."[24]

During the reading the King had looked up at the galleries, scanned the faces of the Commissioners, and turned about to take stock of the crowd behind him in the Hall.[25] His countenance betrayed no emotion at all until Cook pronounced the words "tyrant, traitor and murderer" whereupon "he laughed as he sat, in the face of the Court."

His bearing impressed spectators differently according to their political attitudes. A Royalist described with admiration the "undaunted courage and calmness of his carriage as if he had been surrounded with his friends." But Colonel Ludlow, watching him from his seat among the Commissioners, commented indignantly that "he looked with as impudent a face as if he had not been guilty of the blood that hath been shed in this war."[26]

Cook had done, and now Bradshaw faced the haughty prisoner with the first and vital question. "Sir, you have now heard your charge . . . the Court expects your answer."

The King had never, in the whole course of his life, been a good speaker. He had a reasonably quick wit but it was notorious that he had an impediment of the tongue. His accusers may have counted on this to help them; he would not be difficult to interrupt and silence if he challenged their authority. But the intensity of the ordeal worked on the King with the incalculable power of shock, and he was, almost throughout his trial, fluent, strong and clear.

"I would know by what power I am called hither," he began, with cold amazement, "I would know by what authority, I mean *lawful*." He emphasised the word and threw in scornfully—"There are many unlawful authorities in the world, thieves and robbers by the highway. . . ." It was, he implied, by some such unlawful violence that he had been brought from the Isle of Wight. "Remember I am your King," he continued, "your *lawful* King, and what sins you bring upon your heads, and the judgment of God upon this land; think well upon it, I say, think well upon it, before you go from one sin to a greater. . . . I have a trust committed to me by God, by old and lawful descent; I will not betray it to answer a new unlawful authority; therefore resolve me that and you shall hear more of me."

The King's opening challenge was audible to Bradshaw and to those near at hand, but much of it was lost even to those in the galleries owing to a sudden noisy influx of spectators at the lower end of the Hall.[27] Its substance was however clear from Bradshaw's somewhat irritable repetition of the phrases which had been already so much emphasised by John Cook; he exhorted the King to answer "in the name of the people of England, of which you are *elected* King."

This was altogether too wide of the facts and Charles came back with conviction: "England was never an elective Kingdom, but a hereditary Kingdom for near these thousand years." In the face of such total disregard for law and precedent he went on vigorously: "I do stand more for the liberty of my people, than any here that come to be my pretended judges."

Bradshaw, thwarted by these quick and pregnant replies, decided that the moment had come to admonish the King. "Your way of answer is to interrogate the Court, which beseems not you in this condition. You have been told of it twice or thrice."

But nothing would stop the King. He went serenely on: "I do not come here as submitting to the Court: I will stand as much for the privilege of the House of Commons, rightly understood, as any man here whatsoever. I see no House of Lords here that may constitute a Parliament. . . . Let me see a legal authority warranted by the Word of God, the Scriptures, or warranted by the constitution of the Kingdom and I will answer."

To stop this continued and all too eloquent defiance, Bradshaw decided to cut short the proceedings and ordered the King to be removed. The words were a cue for a demonstration which had evidently been planned in advance, and some of the soldiers in the body of the Hall began to cry out "Justice! Justice!" The King was momentarily startled at the sudden shouts behind him and turned to look round. Bradshaw took this for a weakening of his resolve, and with a sudden change of tactics again asked if he would answer the charge.

Charles recovered himself at once, and as the shouting subsided, began another lengthy speech. "Let me tell you it is not a slight thing you are about," he admonished Bradshaw. "I am sworn to keep the peace, by that duty I owe to God and my country, and I will do it to the last breath of my body; and therefore ye shall do well to satisfy first God, and then the country, by what authority you do it; if you do it by an usurped authority, you cannot answer. There is a God in Heaven, that will call you, and all that give you power to account. . . ."

Bradshaw could not, for some further sentences, break into his discourse, and was not altogether successful when he did so. The Court would adjourn, he declared, until Monday when they would expect the King's answer. As for their right to try him, "we are satisfied with our authority."

"You have shown no lawful authority to satisfy any reasonable man," said the King and Bradshaw was ill-advised enough to snap back at him: "That is in your apprehension; we are satisfied that are your judges."

"It is not my apprehension, nor yours neither, that ought to decide it," said the King. This time Bradshaw desisted from further argument and ordered the removal of the prisoner. Charles rose, and looked towards the table where the charge now lay, along with the sword and mace. "I do not fear that," he said.[28]

On all sides of him as he left the Hall, the soldiers broke out with their cries of "Justice! Justice!" which were taken up by some of the spectators, but others shouted "God save the King."[29] Charles went back to his room in Cotton House. The rest of the evening he spent in thinking over the events of the afternoon and writing out with a fine mixture of clarity and passion his reasons for refusing to admit the authority of the Court and some rather more brief reflections on the character of the charge.[30] Somewhat to the embarrassment of his captors, he refused to take off his clothes or go to bed that night because of the soldiers in the room. Next day, being Sunday, was wholly given over to prayer and meditation with Juxon.[31]

Meanwhile the Regicides considered the happenings of the day and planned for the immediate future. Only a few can have been, like John Cook and Hugh Peter, so deeply convinced of the grandeur of what they were doing that nothing could shake them. Hugh Peter was seen in Westminster Hall as the crowds dispersed, holding up his hands and saying "This is a most glorious beginning of the work." John Cook, going home to Gray's Inn in the winter darkness, was stopped by an acquaintance who, with lugubrious curiosity, began: "I hear you are up to the ears in this business."

"I am serving the people," said Cook with dignity.

"There's a thousand to one will not give you thanks," answered his neighbour. But Cook was not to be put down. "He must die," he said, "and monarchy must die with him."[32]

III

The next day being Sunday the Commissioners kept it as a fast and heard three sermons. The preachers were not happily chosen. Joshua Sprigge, chaplain to Fairfax, showed his participation in the doubts of the Lord General by his elucidation of the ambivalent text "He that sheds blood, by man shall his blood be shed." Another Army chaplain skirted on an equally critical theme: "Judge not that ye be not judged." Only Hugh Peter pleased the principal Commissioners by the enthusiasm with which he preached on the text: "I will bind their Kings in chains."[33]

Next morning sixty-two Commissioners met in private session in the Painted Chamber to consider what should be done now that they understood the King's intention of refusing to acknowledge the Court. This, they agreed, was not to be permitted since thereby the prisoner sought to wound the supreme authority of the people, through their representatives the Commons, who had set up the Court. But how were they to prevent his repeated onslaughts—onslaughts which the most fanatical among them could not fail to recognise as remarkably convincing in law? For this was the insoluble problem which they had set themselves: to reconcile their wholly unprecedented action with the English Common Law, a law rooted in the practice and precedents of centuries.

They might have done better to assert, even to boast of, the novelty of their procedure. In that case Bradshaw could have elucidated their intentions in the most stirring language at his command instead of trying in vain to proceed correctly according to the Common Law which was evidently not applicable. But this would have been foreign to his own conceptions and those of his colleagues; they were determined to act as though there was nothing irregular in their conduct.

If the prisoner would not plead, in a case of treason, the law laid down that he should be treated as though he had pleaded guilty.[34] This hardly solved their problem, for they had wanted to demonstrate the King's guilt by calling witnesses, and allowing John Cook to condemn his policies and his conduct in a stirring speech for the prosecution. But it was not possible either to examine witnesses or to make out a public case for the prosecution if the accused stood mute or pleaded guilty, for in that case—logically enough—no such demonstrations were required by English law. Therefore the silence of the King destroyed a principal purpose of the trial. Certainly he could be taken as guilty and sentenced to death; but he could not be *proved* guilty for all the world to see.

What were they to do?

Since the Court resembled no other Court that had ever sat in England it is remarkable that they did not carry the difference further, allow Cook to call his witnesses, make out his case, and utter the ferocious speech for the prosecution that he had planned.

The laconic minutes of John Phelps throw no light on the discussion in the Painted Chamber, but it seems unlikely that such a course was even suggested. They decided instead that Bradshaw was to prevent any further protests from the King by tersely telling him that the Court was constituted by " the Commons of England assembled in Parliament . . . whose power may not, nor should not be permitted to be disputed by him." More than this, Bradshaw was not empowered to do; he could only draw the prisoner's attention to the fact that, if he would not answer the charge his silence would be treated as a plea of guilty.

They must have hoped that the King, moved by this threat, would reconsider his refusal. If he did so without reservation, he was to be given a copy of the charge to study overnight so that he could make out his defence next day. They decided to hold at least two more sessions, on Monday and Tuesday afternoons. If Charles continued in his refusal to plead he would be treated as guilty and summoned before them once more, on Wednesday, to receive sentence.[35] Execution would follow on Friday or Saturday and the whole painful and dangerous business would be over before the end of the week.

On Monday afternoon therefore they proceeded to Westminster Hall and sent for the prisoner. This time seventy Commissioners were present, the proceedings opened with a proclamation that anyone who caused a disturbance would be instantly arrested—an admission that the protest of Lady Fairfax had perturbed the judges, though her identity was still unknown. Rumour had named the interrupter as the notorious Royalist, Lady Newburgh.[36]

Charles had not persisted in his refusal to go to bed. He had slept on Sunday night regardless of the soldiers, and he entered the Hall this Monday afternoon with his usual dignity, taking his seat once again in his crimson velvet chair. He saw

Bradshaw look towards Cook to open the session, but Cook was taking last-minute advice from Dorislaus, the two black-robed men conferring in whispers, their backs to the King. Charles saw no reason why he should be kept waiting. This time he did not—as he had done before—tap Cook lightly on the wing of his gown; he gave him a sharp admonitory poke with his cane. Cook swung round, furious, glared at him, then caught Bradshaw's eye, and began.[37] "May it please your lordship, my Lord President, I did at the last Court in the behalf of the Commons of England exhibit and give in to this Court a charge of high treason and other high crimes against the prisoner at the bar. . . . My lord, he was not then pleased to give an answer, but instead of answering did there dispute the authority of this High Court. My humble motion . . . is that the prisoner may be directed to make a positive answer either by way of confession or negation; which if he shall refuse to do, that the matter of the charge may be taken *pro confesso*, and the Court may proceed according to justice."

The cards were on the table. If the King did not plead he would be regarded as having admitted his guilt. Bradshaw now followed with an emphatic but still wholly unconvincing statement that the Court was "fully satisfied with their own authority" and that the whole kingdom, the King included, must therefore be satisfied with it too.

The King had now heard one threatening speech and one feeble one. He struck in, as cool and fluent as on the first day but even more deadly, for he knew more exactly the weakness of his opponents and he had cleared his mind by writing out his ideas on paper. But he did not speak from notes. "If it were only my own particular case," he said, "I would have satisfied myself with the protestation I made the last time I was here against the legality of the Court, and that a King cannot be tried by any superior jurisdiction on earth. But it is not my case alone, it is the freedom and the liberty of the people of England; and do you pretend what you will, I stand more for their liberties. For if power without law may make laws, may alter the fundamental laws of the Kingdom, I do not know what subject he is in England, that can be sure of his life, or anything that he calls his own."

He would now, he said, explain in greater detail his reasons for refusing to answer them. Bradshaw interrupted precipitately. The Court could not listen to arguments and disputes from a delinquent, he said. The King must submit, and give them "a punctual and direct answer."

But Charles was not to be bullied. He knew not only his inalienable rights as a King, but also his rights as an Englishman.

"Sir, by your favour," he said, with ironical courtesy, "I do not know the forms of law; I do know law and reason, though I am no lawyer professed; but I know as much law as any gentleman in England; and therefore (under favour) I do plead for the liberties of the people of England more than you do: and therefore if I should impose a belief upon any man, without reasons given for it, it were unreasonable."

Bradshaw found his voice again to interrupt him. "Sir, you speak of law and reason; it is fit there should be law and reason, and there is both against you." They were not against him, as Bradshaw must have been uncomfortably aware. What was against the King was his own abuse of law in the past, his appeal seven years ago not to reason but to arms. But this case could never be proved if he would not answer the charge. "Sir, you are not to dispute our authority," commanded Bradshaw, with no remaining hope that the King would obey. "Sir, it will be taken notice of, that you stand in contempt of the Court, and your contempt will be recorded accordingly."

It sounded a little weak to threaten a man for contempt of Court who was already accused of treason and murder.

"I do not know how a King can be a delinquent," the prisoner reflected aloud, referring to a term used earlier by the Lord President, and he went on to argue that delinquent or no, every man was allowed to demur if he could show reason for questioning the capacity of a Court.

Bradshaw had not expected this. No one, he blustered, would be permitted to question the capacity of *this* Court. "They sit here by the authority of the Commons of England, and all your predecessors and you are responsible to them."

That the sovereign was responsible to the Commons, not the Commons to the sovereign, was a doctrine that none of the King's predecessors would have recognised. He was on to it at once: "Show me one precedent."

Bradshaw was incensed: "Sir, you ought not to interrupt while the Court is speaking to you." But the King was not to be silenced. He certainly knew as much law as any gentleman in England and more than most.

"The Commons of England was never a Court of Judicature," he said, "I would know how they came to be so."

It was a very palpable hit. Parliament was indeed a Court, but not the House of Commons. Bradshaw in desperation ordered the clerk, Andrew Broughton, to call on the prisoner to answer the charge.

If he hoped this formality would divert the flow of the King's eloquence he was wrong. He merely took up his refrain: "I will answer so soon as I know by what authority you do this."

Bradshaw could only bring the session to a close by ordering the guards to remove the King. But he was not to solve his problem so easily for Charles would not go. "I do require that I may give in my reasons why I do not answer, and give me time for that."

"It is not for prisoners to require," Bradshaw reproved him.

"Sir," said the King, "I am not an ordinary prisoner."

They stopped short of violence; the soldiers did not surround and forcibly remove him. So he spoke on, demanding that they should listen to his reasons. "Show me that jurisdiction where reason is not to be heard," he challenged them.

Bradshaw lost his head and his temper. "We show it you here," he exploded, "the Commons of England." Then, realising that he had slipped, he hurried on to threaten the King that the next session would be the final one.

Charles still did not rise to go. "Well, sir," he said, "remember that the King is not suffered to give his reasons for the liberty and freedom of all his subjects."

At last Bradshaw saw the opportunity for a rejoinder: "How great a friend you have been to the laws and liberties of the people, let all England and the world judge!" The King was shaken, or it may be that the guards were closing in, and the necessity for speed made his speech for the first time hesitant: "Sir, under favour," he began, "it was the liberty, freedom, and laws of the subject, that ever I took—defended myself with arms—I never took up arms against the people, but for the laws."

In this uncertain fashion the second day ended and the King left the Hall, to the usual shouts of "Justice". But in the narrow corridors between the Hall and Cotton House— so at least Herbert wrote some years later—one of the soldiers on guard, said aloud as he passed, "God bless you, Sir," The King thanked him, but his officer struck him on the head with his cane. "The punishment exceeds the offence," said the King, and later according to Herbert, reflected that the soldiers bore him no malice; they cried out for "Justice" because they had been ordered to do so, and would do the same for their own leaders when the occasion arose.[38]

The illusion was consoling to the King, but it was an illusion. Some of the soldiers were indeed deserters or renegades from his own army, but may not have loved him any the better for that. Some were good-natured, decent men who felt a natural pity when they saw him in distress, and a respect for the dignity and calm with which he met his ordeal; enough pity and enough respect to prompt an occasional

"God bless you, Sir." But the majority of the soldiers hated him, for making war on his people not once but twice, for trying to bring in foreign troops, or even the wild Irish; hated him for abandoning the Protestant cause in Europe, for persecuting godly ministers in England, for favouring Papists and encouraging the friends of his French Popish wife.

If they believed all the slanderous rumours and pamphlets now circulating, they hated him also for corresponding with the Pope, for betraying the Protestants of La Rochelle, and for conniving at the murder of his father. More crudely, many of them hated him simply for being a King with soft white hands, fine linen and a velvet cloak who had ordered his poor subjects to be shot and cut down in battle, who had had prisoners beaten and starved, and had condemned honest John Lilburne to be whipped at the cart's tail.[39]

In his room at Cotton House the King—Herbert later recorded—asked about the composition of the so-called Court of Justice. Herbert told him that they were a mixed body of members of Parliament, officers and London citizens. The King does not seem to have pursued the inquiry, merely stating that he had looked carefully at them all, and did not recognise more than eight of their faces.[40] It was true he would have known Cromwell, Harrison, Ireton and the principal officers; he would have known Harry Marten, whom he detested, and the dwarfish Lord Grey and the one-time courtier John Danvers. But Bradshaw and his two assistants, Lisle and Say, with most of the other Commissioners, were wholly strange to him—men who to his knowledge had played hitherto no noticeable part in the affairs of the nation.

IV

Next day, Tuesday, 23rd January, at noon, a brief consultation was held in the Painted Chamber. The Commissioners decided to repeat their methods of the previous day. Nothing in the unrevealing minutes kept by John Phelps indicate who spoke or what was said, but their intentions had not changed since the week-end; they would give the King one more chance of answering the charge, before proceeding to the sentence on the morning of Wednesday 24th.[41]

The session in Westminster Hall began in the early afternoon. Seventy-one Commissioners were present, the largest attendance so far, although still only a little more than half the total number appointed. A shield bearing the national symbol, the Cross of St. George, had been set up in the centre of the wall above the Commissioners, apparently an innovation on this day.[42]

The King came in with his habitual calm, looked for a moment at his judges "with an austere countenance" as Mabbott expressed it, and sat down in his chair. Once again Cook opened the proceedings by recapitulating, briefly and strongly, the charge that the King had attempted to destroy the laws and introduce tyrannical government by means of war. As for his repeated refusal to answer, Cook argued that "according to the known rules of the law of the land," a prisoner who would not put in a plea of guilty or not guilty should be regarded as having pleaded guilty by implication. There was, in any case, no possibility of doubt as to his guilt. "The House of Commons, the supreme authority and jurisdiction of the Kingdom, they have declared, that it is notorious, that the matter of the charge is true, as it is in truth, my lord, as clear as crystal and as the sun that shines at noonday: which if your lordship and the Court be not satisfied in, I have notwithstanding, on the people of England's behalf, several witnesses to produce. . . . And therefore I do humbly pray that speedy judgment be pronounced against the prisoner at the bar."

Bradshaw now addressed himself once again to Charles. He had informed him "over and over again," he said, in the manner of a schoolmaster reasoning with a wilful pupil, "that the Court did affirm their own jurisdiction; that it was not for you, nor any other man, to dispute the jurisdiction of the supreme and highest authority in England." The Court, he must understand, would not be trifled with, and they might very well assert their authority by sentencing him out of hand. They would however allow him one more chance "to give your positive and final answer in plain English, whether you be guilty or not guilty of these treasons laid to your charge."

He concluded, and for a moment there was silence in the Court. When the King spoke it was with greater deliberation than on the two previous days. "When I was here yesterday I did desire to speak for the liberties of the people of England; I was interrupted; I desire to know yet whether I may speak freely or not."

Bradshaw replied that the Court would hear him "make the best defence you can", but only after he had "given a positive answer concerning the matter that is charged upon you."

The King swept the conditions aside. "For the charge, I value it not a rush," he said, "it is the liberty of the people of England that I stand for. For me to acknowledge a new Court that I never heard of before, I that am your King, that should be an example to all the people of England, for to uphold justice, to maintain the old laws; indeed I do not know how to do it."

Asserting his authority, he offered a patronising word of praise to Bradshaw: "You spoke very well the first day that I came here of the obligations that I had laid upon me by God, to the maintenance of the liberties of my people; the same obligation you spake of, I do acknowledge to God that I owe him, and to my people, to defend as much as in me lies the ancient laws of the Kingdom: therefore until that I may know that this is not against the fundamental laws of the Kingdom, by your favour I can put in no particular charge." The last word should have been "answer"—not "charge"—but the slip of the tongue was revealing since, in the King's opinion, he should have been in a position to charge his "pretended judges" with treason.

He went on once again to offer to give his reasons for refusing to acknowledge them, and again Bradshaw interrupted, but the King would not be silenced. "By your favour, you ought not to interrupt me. How I came here I know not; there's no law for it to make your King your prisoner."

Once or twice Bradshaw tried to force his way in, before he at length stopped the King's flow of words,[43] by calling on Broughton, the clerk, to read out once more, and for the last time, the formal demand for the King's answer. Andrew Broughton must already have been on his feet.

"Clerk, do your duty," said Bradshaw.

"Duty, Sir!" said the King, with ringing scorn.

Broughton hurriedly read out the words, requiring "Charles Stuart, King of England" to give his positive answer "by way of confession or denial of the charge," and Charles, for his only response, again denied the legality of the Court, in the interests, as he firmly said, of the privileges of the people of England.

Bradshaw, for the first time that day, saw an opportunity for counter-attack. "How far you have preserved the privileges of the people, your actions have spoke it, but truly, Sir, men's intentions ought to be known by their actions; you have written your meaning in bloody characters throughout the whole Kingdom."

Charles did not flinch before the onslaught, which meant nothing to him since he did not think it true. He made one more attempt to speak, but was again prevented by Bradshaw.

"Sir, you have heard the pleasure of the Court, and you are (notwithstanding you will not understand it) to find you are before a court of justice."

"I see I am before a power," said the King dryly, and rose to go.[44]

One journalist, the sympathetic John Dillingham of *The Moderate Intelligencer*, unable to hear the phrase, caught the meaning by tone and gesture and printed it as "Pish, Sir! I care not a straw for you!"[45]

Something of a disturbance must by now have occurred, though none of the journalists ventured to describe it. But several of them reported without explanation that the Crier loudly called out, "God bless the Kingdom of England!" This unprecedented shout may well have been prompted by the need to drown, or to disguise, shouts less welcome to the ears of the Commissioners, shouts of "God save the King" or "God bless you, Sir,"[46] as the King walked away between his guards.

CHAPTER SEVEN

THE KING CONDEMNED

January 24 - 27, 1649

THE KING went back to Cotton House; the crowds dispersed from the Hall into the discouraging dusk of an English winter. But the Commissioners who had hitherto separated at the end of each session, now went together to the Painted Chamber.[1]

The situation was grave. The progress of the trial was little short of disastrous, and only those whose blind hatred of the King prevented them from seeing the weakness of their own position can have imagined otherwise. The leaders—Cromwell, Ireton, Marten and the rest—had been prepared for the King's refusal to recognise them. But they had not been prepared for his persistence in that refusal, nor for his claim to stand for the laws and liberties of his people, still less for his eloquence, or for that authority of his presence and his words by which he dominated the proceedings.

A judge of stronger personality and more experience than Bradshaw might have prevented him from doing so; the Lord President had not failed to assert the power of the Court, but three times in succession he had ordered the removal of the prisoner by the soldiers because he could wring from him no submission whatever, not even a momentary weakening. On every occasion, therefore, he had drawn attention to precisely that element in the proceedings which should least have been emphasised—the overriding power of the Army, and the rule of force not of law. Each indication of the Army's power and presence served to underline the truth of the King's claim, that the freedom of his people was threatened—and not by him. The power of the Army was a present reality. The King's persecution of Puritan ministers, his Star Chamber sentences on his critics, his attempt to overawe Parliament by force, even his war—seemed now to many of his civilian subjects a long way off. Already the time before the outbreak of the Civil War had become a hazy and happy recollection, much to be preferred to this era of " plunder, excise and blood "[2] for which they blamed the Army. Against this background the King's public claim to stand for the liberty of his people could be dangerous.

If he had pleaded not guilty, if witnesses had been called, it would have been possible to contradict his assertion to stand for his people by evidence of his violence and ill-will towards them. Could this effect be achieved by other means?

That evening in the Painted Chamber the final session was postponed, and next morning the Commissioners appointed a committee to hear the witnesses.[3] By this process they hoped to satisfy the waverers in their midst—of whom there were now many—and to indicate to the public that they did not lack evidence for the charge against the King. Renewed efforts were also made to persuade Fairfax to countenance the trial by coming to Westminster Hall for the next session.[4] But the Lord General was harried no less vigorously by those on the other side. He had received an open letter from an officer in the Army, one Francis White, who had on earlier occasions taken it upon himself to offer advice to the leaders of the Army. Major White was no lover of the King; he felt, with the Levellers, that his destruction was less important than the elevation of the people: " The King and his party being conquered by the Sword, I believe the Sword may justly remove the power from him, and settle it in its original fountain, next under God, the people."

But as for the King, though it might be—as Major White conceded—" a just thing " to kill him, yet " I know not how it may justly be done." More practically, he suggested that the King be kept in prison, because once he was dead, his son would claim the crown and be infinitely more dangerous, being young and free, than his imprisoned father. All in all, it was for the Lord General Fairfax " to use the Sword with as much tenderness as may be to preserve the lives of men and especially the King."[5]

Almost simultaneously with Major White's public letter came further printed protests from the Presbyterian clergy, both in London and in the country. The Scots Commissioners published the vigorous remonstrance that they had addressed in vain to the House of Commons, and William Prynne issued, in an amended and enlarged form, the denunciation of the Army that he had spoken in Parliament on the eve of the Purge.[6]

Fairfax did not move in response to this hail-storm of pamphlet persuasion, but he still refused to attend the High Court of Justice. An inspired paragraph in Henry Walker's *Perfect Occurrences* stated that the Lord General had been unable to sit with the judges in Westminster Hall owing to the pressure of other business.[7] In his *Perfect Summary* Theodore Jennings went even further, and suggested that Fairfax had refrained from sitting in the Court because malicious Cavaliers had accused him of wanting to be king, and he had therefore thought it better to give no countenance to the slander by taking no part in the condemnation of Charles.[8]

Meanwhile the witnesses against the King, thirty-three of them, were heard by the appointed Committee (of which Cromwell was not a member) on the 24th, and on the 25th their depositions were read out at a public session of the High Court in the Painted Chamber.

Several citizens of Nottingham had been found to give evidence about the King's setting up of his standard at the beginning of the war; one of them was the painter who had painted the standard pole. Other witnesses were veterans who had fought through the war. Richard Blomfield, a London weaver, who had been in the Army of the Earl of Essex when it surrendered to the King at Fowey gave evidence that he had seen his comrades plundered in the presence of the King contrary to the articles of surrender. Another, a husbandman from Rutland, swore that at the capture of Leicester the King had not only permitted the prisoners to be stripped and cut about by his men, but when a Royalist officer had tried to stop this barbarity had said: " I do not care if they cut them three times more, for they are mine enemies," the King being all this while " on horseback, in bright armour, in the said town of Leicester." Numerous others merely testified to having seen the King armed and in battle, encouraging his troops. Some of these witnesses were evidently soldiers who had at one time served in the Royalist ranks, and later joined the victorious Army—a process not unusual at this time where loyalty and honour were expensive luxuries, and the foot-soldiers, who were often pressed men in the first place, preferred enlisting with the victors to the alternative of walking, or begging, their way back to their distant homes.

One civilian witness, Henry Gooch, gave evidence that he had communicated privately with the King in the Isle of Wight during the Newport Treaty and had received instructions to get into touch with the Prince of Wales about authorising the raising of troops. Little is known to indicate whether Gooch was a Royalist who had been frightened into making these admissions, or an *agent provocateur*, but what he said was borne out by some of the King's private correspondence intercepted during the Treaty, which was also exhibited as evidence.[9]

The depositions of the witnesses put beyond doubt the King's personal participation in the war and his intention of continuing it, even during the recent Treaty negotiations. They may have helped a little to strengthen the wavering resolution of the more doubtful Commissioners and to impress any members of the public who found their way into the Painted Chamber. At any rate some of the newspapers printed the evidence in whole or in part.[10]

Meanwhile the High Court was embarrassed by two minor but awkward incidents. The officer chosen to command the special guard which attended Lord President Bradshaw, a certain Major Fox, was arrested for debt and committed to prison, whence he had to be rescued by special command of the Court. This naturally gave all Royalists and Presbyterians a further opportunity of sneering at the disreputable character of the Court and all its officers.[11]

The second incident was more troublesome as it revealed the lack of unity among the Commissioners. Two of the least of them, John Downes and John Fry had fallen into an argument about the Trinity which had ended with Downes openly stating in the House of Commons that Fry had denied the divinity of Christ. This heresy, which had gained some ground among the sects, shocked the more conventional Puritans, and its propagation was a capital offence. When Downes accused Fry of holding it, the charge had to be treated seriously. Fry naturally denied it, though in terms confused enough to suggest that he had given occasion for the misapprehension. He was suspended from sitting in the House of Commons until a full inquiry could be made, and it followed logically that he could no longer be one of the King's judges. This was unfortunate as Fry was one of the most resolute and assiduous members of the Court. But it was still more regrettable that, during the solemn business of trying the King, one Commissioner should publicly accuse another of a scandalous and capital blasphemy.[12]

In London and Westminster meanwhile pamphlets against the King's trial were freely circulated, ranging from the printed versions of the official Scottish protest to the House of Commons, and the representations of the Presbyterian ministers to Fairfax, to the confused ramblings of Mrs. Mary Pope, a salter's widow, who had once or twice already denounced the politics of the Army in print. Quite apart from the rather ill-phrased leaflet, sold for her by " Mrs. Edwards, the bookbinder's widow in the Old Bailey ", this voluble lady had announced her intention of intervening in person at the trial, and had—if all rumours were to be credited—declared that the King's condemnation was quite impossible and she would wager £15 (a large sum for her, no doubt) that Charles would be restored to his throne within the next six weeks.[13]

To counteract the more serious manifestations of disapproval, a petition of a different kind was handed in to the High Court of Justice, in which three troopers warmly asserted their faith in the authority of the King's judges and exhorted them not to falter in taking "vengeance against our grand tyrant Charles Stuart and all such inhuman murderers who have destroyed their fellow creatures without cause."[14]

The Royalists had once believed that every Sovereign in Europe would hasten to help King Charles as soon as his life was threatened. But by this time their expectations were blighted. They had put about a rumour that the Queen of Sweden was preparing an Army of ten thousand in " fourteen tall ships ", with equivalent help from France and Holland.[15] The story was taller than the ships, and no more had been heard of them. The only hope on the Royalist horizon came from the King's nephew Prince Rupert. After commanding the Royalist cavalry in the war, he had more recently linked his fortunes to those of the Prince of Wales in Holland. Here he had been given command of half a dozen ships, revolted from the English fleet which were in poor condition and with mutinous crews. Displaying his usual resourcefulness and energy, he had restored order in the ships, and by a little well thought-out piracy in the Narrow Seas had increased their number. About this time his fleet had left the shelter of the Dutch coast, fourteen sail in all " bending towards Ireland, driving the whole Channel before them."[16] But there was nothing that he could do to give direct help to the King; a landing was out of the question.

The King of France—or rather his regents—when the trial was first foreshadowed, had issued a manifesto denouncing the murderous rebels of England[17] but since then a revolt in Paris had caused the Queen-regent to flee from the capital with the child King. The French Government was in no condition to make any further gesture. According to the English newspapers the rebels of the Paris *Parlement* had set up their banners, inscribed *Salus populi suprema lex* in the heart of the capital. They had at all events taken control, and Paris, besieged by the royal forces, was cut off from news and supplies from the outer world. It was bitterly cold and firewood was almost unprocurable. The exiled Queen of England in the cold and half-deserted Louvre, waited for news of her husband in numb despair.[18]

In Holland the Prince of Wales, coming in person to the meeting of the Dutch Estates at the Hague, implored them to send help to his father. They responded after a fashion; two envoys were despatched, who actually arrived in England late in January bearing a solemn appeal from the Dutch to delay the trial of the King and submit the whole matter to arbitration.[19]

But the formalities of diplomacy would take time, and while the Dutch envoys were being formally received at Gravesend, the Court of Justice had come to a final decision. After hearing the witnesses on 25th January, the forty-six Commissioners present (it was the smallest attendance yet recorded) resolved that they could now proceed to sentence the King to death. There was some discussion of the propriety of deposing him first, but this was in the end set aside, and a small sub-committee was appointed to draw up the sentence. Cromwell was not on this committee which consisted of only seven members—Alderman Scot, Harry Marten, Ireton, Harrison and three lawyers, William Say, John Lisle and Nicholas Love.

Next day, 26th January, when the Commissioners reassembled in the afternoon, sixty-two were present which was a slight improvement on the very poor attendances of the previous day. The draft sentence was produced, condemning the King as " a tyrant, traitor, murderer and a public enemy to be put to death by the severing of his head from his body." The public were not admitted to the discussions which continued throughout the afternoon. John Phelps reported them very briefly as " several readings, debates and amendments ". It does not appear that any vote was taken among the Commissioners, but if they were unanimous, it was only because those of stronger wills and stronger voices bore down the weaker members. At any rate, the form of the sentence was agreed by nightfall, and the King was to be brought to Westminster Hall next day to hear it pronounced.[20]

It was during this interlude in the Trial that an offer came from the King's most devoted friends—the four who had waited on him at Newport—Richmond, Hertford, Southampton and Lindsey. These four noblemen undertook to guarantee with their estates and their lives any terms whatsoever on which Army and Parliament would restore his freedom and his royal title. The offer, made with a desperate sincerity, was set aside without consideration.[21]

At ten o'clock on 27th January the Commissioners reassembled—sixty-eight of them this time. The sentence was produced on its scroll of parchment, and final arrangements made for the proceedings of the day. If the King were to make a last-minute submission to the jurisdiction of the Court, they agreed to adjourn and consider what should be done. Such an action of his at this stage could only cause a dangerous delay but they might none the less feel bound to accept it and begin the trial again. It was more likely that, rather than submit, he would make some other suggestion which they ought in justice to consider—or appear to consider. They left the management of this to Bradshaw's discretion.

But on the whole they thought it more probable that the King would continue silent, in which case the Lord President had only to give sentence after permitting him to speak first if he wished to do so. Further, they agreed that, to show that the death sentence was the judgment of the whole Court, they would all stand up when it was pronounced in token of their consent.[22]

Nothing now remained to be done before the last session of the trial opened, and they broke up until the afternoon.

II

It was known to most of those present, and certainly to the prisoner, that the purpose of the Court was to pass sentence. To indicate the solemnity of the occasion Bradshaw was, for the first time, robed in red. As the King came in the soldiers and some of the spectators shouted for Justice! and Execution![23] Charles was calm and purposeful. He had, in the interval, thought of a proposition to lay before the Court, not so much to save his life, which he had never feared to lose, but to save the monarchy for his son: or it may be merely to create delay in the hope of some new revolution in the unsteady affairs of the nation.

Instead of waiting until the Lord President opened the proceedings, he began at once: " I shall desire a word to be heard a little, and I hope I shall give no occasion for interruption."

Bradshaw was taken aback, but was determined that the prisoner should not be allowed to make the opening speech; there was a brief tussle before the King gave way, on the understanding that he would be heard later, and Bradshaw addressed the Court:

" Gentlemen, it is well known to all, or most of you here present, that the prisoner at the bar hath been several times convened and brought before the Court to make answer to a charge of treason and other high crimes exhibited against him in the name of the people of England——"

At this moment there was a stir in one of the galleries where two masked ladies sat side by side, and one of them called out: " Not half, not a quarter of the people of England. Oliver

Cromwell is a traitor." Colonel Axtell, who was in charge of security in the Hall, ordered his men to level their muskets at her. Some said that they heard him shout "Down with the whores." Her companions in the gallery were as anxious to silence her as Colonel Axtell was, and within seconds she was hustled out, and Bradshaw resumed his interrupted speech.

Not very many people can have heard the exact words which had been hurled at the heads of Bradshaw and Cromwell, though there was of course no doubt of their general bearing. The identity of the speaker was even more obscure; it was unknown to the man who had sold her the seat, and her face was visible to no one. Colonel Axtell cannot have recognised her, and the newspapers which briefly commented on the interruption of a " malignant lady " may have thought that she was indeed—as was rumoured—Lady Newburgh or even the voluble Mrs. Pope.

But the masked interrupter was Lady Fairfax, who had come, accompanied by her friend Mrs. Nelson, to relieve her conscience, and perhaps also to relieve her husband's. Who in that crowded Court recognised her voice? Cromwell, very possibly, since he knew her well, and some of the colonels—though evidently not Axtell, for he would hardly have threatened to fire on the wife of his general. Few in the Hall or among the audience can have realised that the significance of the interruption lay not in the words, but in the identity of the speaker. If Fairfax had permitted or authorised his wife to make this disturbance, it could be the signal that he himself was about to intervene. But the caution with which she concealed her identity suggests that this strong-minded lady was acting without her husband's knowledge.[24]

As the noise subsided, Bradshaw had continued speaking. The Court, he said, had fully considered the case: the prisoner, having refused to plead, could be regarded as having confessed. Furthermore, the things with which he was charged were notorious. They had therefore agreed upon the sentence, but were none the less willing to hear him speak in his defence before it was pronounced, provided he did not " offer any debate " concerning the jurisdiction of the Court.

Charles did not offer any debate, but he took care to reaffirm his attitude to the Court: " Since that I see that you will not hear anything of debate concerning that which I confess I thought most material for the peace of the Kingdom and for the liberty of the subject, I shall waive it; I shall speak nothing to it, but only I must tell you, that this many a day all things have been taken away from me, but that, that I call more dear to me than my life, which is my conscience and my honour: and if I had respect to my life more than the peace of the Kingdom and the liberty of the subject, certainly I should have made a particular defence for myself; for by that at leastwise I might have delayed an ugly sentence, which I believe will pass upon me. . . . Now, sir, I conceive, that an hasty sentence once passed, may sooner be repented than recalled; and truly, the self-same desire that I have for the peace of the Kingdom, and the liberty of the subject, more than my own particular, does make me now at last desire, that, having something to say that concerns both, I desire before sentence be given, that I may be heard in the Painted Chamber before the Lords and Commons. . . . I do conjure you, as you love that which you pretend (I hope it is real) the liberty of the subject and the peace of the Kingdom, that you will grant me the hearing, before any sentence be passed. . . . If I cannot get this liberty, I do here protest that so fair shows of liberty and peace, are pure shows and not otherwise, since you will not hear your King."

The King's request was not wholly unexpected. It was none the less embarrassing for, though Bradshaw would have preferred to refuse it outright as merely an excuse for further delay, Charles had spoken so reasonably and with so much feeling that he had undoubtedly made an impression on his hearers. Bradshaw made things no better by trying to prove that the King's request was only another way of declining the jurisdiction of the Court. Charles interrupted with ironic forbearance: " Pray excuse me, Sir, for my interruption, because you mistake me; it is not a declining of it, you do judge me before you hear me speak. . . ." Once again he emphasised his concern for the peace and liberty of his people.

Bradshaw could only reiterate that the King had already delayed justice for many days by refusing to plead, and ought not to be permitted to delay it any further, but as he warmed to his ungrateful task, he was aware of a barely suppressed disturbance among the Commissioners on his left.

It was the excitable John Downes. His neighbours to the right and left were convinced Regicides, the resolute sectary William Cawley and Cromwell's brother-in-law Colonel Valentine Walton who had lost a son in the war. These two had listened unmoved to the King's words; not so Downes. " Have we hearts of stone? " he appealed to them, " Are we men? " Annoyed, they tried to quieten him, even to pull him down for he showed signs of trying to get up to protest aloud. " If I die for it, I must do it," he gasped. At this Cromwell, who sat immediately in front of him, turned round: " What ails thee? Art thou mad? Canst thou not sit still and be quiet? " Then Downes got out something like, " Sir, no, I cannot be quiet," struggled to his feet and in his loudest voice declared that he was not satisfied.

This whispering and fidgeting was intelligible to Bradshaw as a danger signal. There may have been other whisperers and fidgeters among the weak, uneasy, frightened men. Certainly eleven years later Thomas Waite was to claim that he too had risen to protest; and others, too, would say that they had been on the point of doing so.

Bradshaw therefore suddenly swerved away from his argument against further delay, and concluded weakly that the Court would withdraw for consideration.

Unseemly arguments broke out once they had left Westminster Hall, but John Phelps set down none of this in his discreet minutes of the Court. What happened in that half hour we know only from the accounts given by some of the survivors in 1660. Downes, according to himself, stood up to Cromwell with all his puny strength and implored his colleagues to hear the King who surely now was about to make offers on which they could settle the peace of the nation. Cromwell sneered and raged, called Charles " the hardest hearted man on earth ", and Downes a peevish, troublesome fellow. All alone (for—according to his account—no one else would speak) poor Downes endured the threats and arguments of the Commissioners, until at last he gave up in tears and they went back to the Hall and left him. So, in his own defence, he told the tale eleven years later.

Others, however, averred that they too had spoken up for the King: Thomas Waite, Edward Harvey, even one of the lawyers who had drawn up the sentence, Nicholas Love. They all agreed that Cromwell, formidable in his impatient wrath, had scornfully overruled all their protests.

It seems probable that there was indeed a movement of genuine, anxious protest among the Commissioners and that some of them besides Downes vocally expressed their doubts. Cromwell—his nagging anxiety about Fairfax sharpened by the interruption in Court twenty minutes before—would have been in no mood to tolerate delay. He could easily have spoken of Charles in the way Downes later remembered; he certainly felt no trust at all in any offers he might make. He had experienced the King's advances, withdrawals and evasions far too often. (" Good? By this man against whom the Lord hath witnessed. . . .") His impatient anger rallied his supporters and drove the waverers back into line. Half an hour later the Commissioners, resolute or ruffled, re-entered the Hall, leaving John Downes to seek refuge in the Speaker's room and ease his heart with tears.[25]

When the King had been once again brought back to his chair, Bradshaw addressed him with renewed resolution. He accused him of attempting to delay judgment, refused to call a meeting of Lords and Commons to hear what he had to say, and announced that the Court would now proceed to the sentence.

Charles answered with a resigned irony: " Sir, I know it is in vain for me to dispute. I am no sceptic for to deny the power that you have; I know you have power enough. . . ." Skirting lightly on the unlawfulness of their power, he went on to ask once again that he might be given opportunity to propound a new plan for the peace of the Kingdom to the Lords and Commons of his Parliament. Naturally it would cause a delay, " but a little delay of a day or two further may give peace, whereas an hasty judgment may bring on that trouble and perpetual inconveniency to the Kingdom, that the child that is unborn may repent it."

It was thought by some at the time that what he intended to propose was his abdication in favour of his son.[26] But no one was to know for certain because Bradshaw continued immovable in his rejection of the offer, although Charles made one last, vehement appeal: " If you will hear me, if you will give but this delay, I doubt not but I shall give some satisfaction to you all here, and to my people after that; and therefore I so require you, as you will answer it at the dreadful day of Judgment, that you will consider it once again."

Bradshaw was unperturbed by the prospect of the Last Judgment; his conscience was clear. If the King had nothing more to say, he declared, the Court would proceed to sentence.

" Sir," said the King, " I have nothing more to say, but I shall desire that this may be entered, what I have said."

The moment had now come for Bradshaw's address to the prisoner, an oration which lasted about forty minutes and on the preparation of which he had evidently spent much pains. It was a creditable performance, garnished with a good deal of learning and presented with some dignity. He began by asserting the principle for which the war had been fought: that the King was subject to the law, and that the law proceeded from Parliament. Rather more uncertainly he added that it also proceeded from the people.

With some citing of Bracton and other ancient authorities he proceeded to take a cursory glance at the Barons' War " when the nobility of the land did stand out for the liberty and property of the subject." The duty once so happily performed by the Barons had, he suggested, now devolved upon the Commons. The King—he hurried on—" is but an officer in trust and he ought to discharge that trust. . . . This is not law of yesterday, Sir, (since the time of division betwixt you and your people) but it is law of old." He went on to expound the significance of Parliament as the ultimate court of justice for the realm, and the duty of the King, as elected King and by his coronation oath to see that Parliaments were frequently called for the protection of the people. From this he demonstrated the truth of the charge that the King had tried " to subvert the fundamental laws of the land: for the great bulwark of the liberties of the people is the Parliament of England; and to subvert and root up that, which your aim hath been to do, certainly at one blow . . . had confounded the liberties and the property of England."

He went on to a rather far-fetched comparison of Charles to Caligula, and then proceeded to give examples of the manner in which kings, both in ancient and more recent times, had been accounted answerable for their crimes. As for the alleged hereditary right of the sovereign, Bradshaw had no difficulty in pointing out that this had frequently been passed over both in Scotland and in England. There were also precedents for calling kings to account: Edward II and Richard II had been deposed for their misdeeds, though these did not " come near to that height and capitalness of crimes that are laid to your charge."

He put it together deftly enough, but it was not convincing. Neither of the depositions he cited were generally regarded as legal; they had been acts of force by powerful interests in the State. Although it was true that the line of inheritance had often deviated in England and in Scotland, no one really doubted that the monarchy was by law hereditary. And although the legal antiquarians of an earlier generation had largely misinterpreted the actions of medieval barons, the purpose of their revolts, and most of all the meaning of *Magna Carta*, not one of them would have considered the present Court or the manner of the King's trial as in any way justifiable by medieval (or any other) precedent.

But when he left the hopeless task of legal and historical justification and entered upon theory, he made a crucial point, and made it well.

" There is a contract and a bargain made between the King and his people, and your oath is taken: and certainly, Sir, the bond is reciprocal: for as you are the liege lord, so they liege subjects. . . . This we know now, the one tie, the one bond, is the bond of protection that is due from the sovereign; the other is the bond of subjection that is due from the subject. Sir, if this bond be once broken, farewell sovereignty!

" These things may not be denied, Sir. . . .

" Whether you have been, as by your office you ought to be, a protector of England, or the destroyer of England, let all England judge, or all the world that hath look'd upon it."

Here he touched the central core of government, and it was here that Charles had failed. The authority of a ruler is valid only so long as he can offer protection in return. The idea of social contract, here in Bradshaw's thoughts, corresponded to no existing contract, but this convenient figment of theory did undoubtedly correspond to the practical experience of Western Europe over the last seven hundred years. Feudal society had been built on this principle: the overlord gave protection and the vassal paid with allegiance. English law and the English crown had grown from these beginnings. And it was a matter of practical experience that the ruler who failed in his primary task of protection could no longer expect to exact allegiance.

The King's friends might argue that the King had made war only in defence of his rights. But, rightly or wrongly, *he had made war on his subjects*, and in the crudest possible manner this was a violation of the fundamental bond between him and his people.

Bradshaw went on to reiterate the charge: "Sir, the charge hath called you a Tyrant, a Traitor, a Murderer, and a public enemy to the Commonwealth of England. Sir, it had been well if that any of all these terms might rightly and justly have been spared, if any one of them at all."

The violence of the insult startled the King, who uttered an angry exclamation, unlike the contemptuous smile with which he had greeted these words a week before. They were indeed bitterly wounding to his dignity and his pride, since no more telling accusations could be made against a king. He knew himself to be innocent but was aware of the damage which was now being wrought on the outward appearances of his kingship and his mind worked towards an answer, as Bradshaw went on.[27]

The Lord President at some length explained why the words Tyrant, Traitor and Murderer had to be used, and went on to assert yet again the legal standing and the especial righteousness of the Court, and the dauntless resolution of all who sat in it: "Though we should not be delivered from those bloody hands and hearts that conspire the overthrow of the Kingdom in general, and of us in particular for acting in this great work of justice, though we should perish in the work, yet by God's grace and by God's strength, we will go on with it."

He now, as the rabid sectary Henry Walker approvingly reported, "pressed the King in a sweet manner to repent of his sins."[28] He urged him to recognise his sin and implore the forgiveness of God for blood-guiltiness, as David did for the death of Uriah.

The parallel of David and Uriah was painful, for the King, who felt no blood-guiltiness for the war, had suffered a long agony of conscience over Strafford's death—his subject and servant to whose death he had unjustly consented. Unable to endure longer the stream of accusation, he interrupted. "I would desire only one word before you give sentence; and that is that you would hear me concerning those great imputations that you have laid to my charge."

It was far too late now for the King to answer the charge, and Bradshaw irritably told him so. "Truly, Sir, I would not willingly, at this time especially, interrupt you in anything you have to say that is proper for us to admit of. But, Sir, you have not owned us as a Court, and you look upon us as a sort of people met together; and we knew what language we receive from your party."

"I know nothing of that," said the King.

But Bradshaw went on, silencing the prisoner: "You disavow us as a Court: and therefore for you to address yourself to us, not acknowledging us as a Court to judge of what you say, it is not to be permitted. And the truth is, all along, from the first time you were pleased to disavow and disown us, the Court needed not to have heard you one word."

Over-justifying himself, determined now at all costs to stop the King from speaking again, he hurried on to the end, declared the King guilty and commanded that the sentence be read. The Clerk—it was probably Andrew Broughton—read out the formula on which the Commissioners had agreed, briefly recapitulating, the appointment of the Court, the charge and the course of the trial, and concluding with the sentence: "that the said Charles Stuart, as a Tyrant, Traitor, Murderer and a public enemy, shall be put to death, by the severing his head from his body." At the conclusion of the reading the Commissioners rose to their feet to signify their agreement.

The King who had listened calmly to the last, now spoke, "Will you hear me a word, Sir?"

Bradshaw had not expected this request. A prisoner condemned to death was already dead in law and could not speak in Court. The fact was so familiar to him that it had not occurred to him that the prisoner did not know it. But the King, as he himself had said, was no ordinary prisoner. " You are not to be heard after the sentence," said Bradshaw, and ordered the guard to take him away.

The curt refusal dismayed the King. He had not believed that his trial would end with such abrupt brutality. He had been, all along, convinced that after the sentence he would be allowed to speak again. Now, suddenly, he saw that his last chance had gone, leaving him recorded and condemned as guilty simply by his silence. He could not believe the monstrous injustice.

" I may speak after the sentence——" he began; " by your favour, Sir, I may speak after the sentence ever." Then in growing agitation as the guards closed in, " By your favour, hold! The sentence, Sir—I say, Sir, I do——"

The guards were all round him, ready to take him away by force. Then he found his voice for one last word: " I am not suffered for to speak: expect what justice other people will have."

As he went out his servant John Joiner heard Colonel Axtell give his men the signal to cry out, so that he left the Hall to shouts of " Execution! Justice! Execution! " " Poor creatures," he said with a smile, " for sixpence they will say as much of their own commanders."

This time he did not return to Cotton House but was hurriedly conveyed to Whitehall in a sedan chair, by way of King Street. Troops lined the route but crowds of people at the windows watched the closed chair go by. As he came in to his palace, on foot through the Privy Garden, between his guards, he saw a faithful old servant weeping: " You may forbid their attendance, but not their tears," he said.[30]

Meanwhile the spectators dispersed from the Hall and the Commissioners went back into the Painted Chamber. John Downes, under what compulsion of curiosity or fear, had rejoined them.[31] But their present business was short—merely to appoint some of their number to " consider of the time and place for the execution of the sentence against the King." Five of the soldiers were chosen—Sir Hardress Waller, Colonels Harrison, Deane and Okey, and Commissary General Ireton. After that, they adjourned until Monday morning, having the intervening Sabbath for their thankful and anxious prayers.

The King too would be at prayer. He had no quiet and no privacy. The soldiers had been removed from his bedroom at the request of Herbert who now slept there himself. As a guard he was certainly preferable to a couple of ordinary halberdiers, and in these last unhappy days he seems to have shown, within the limits of his loyalty to the Army, a genuine sympathy and human concern for the unfortunate King. For greater comfort Charles had the kindly Bishop Juxon. He had ordered his dogs to be removed.[32] The greyhound Gypsy, the spaniel Rogue, his companions at Newport and at Hurst—these he found disturbing to his composure. His mind must now be turned to God alone. He did not know how long he had to prepare for death, but he knew that the time would be short.

CHAPTER EIGHT

KING CHARLES THE MARTYR

January 28 - 30, 1649

SUNDAY had come round once more and the sabbatarian truce fell on Westminster. Hugh Peter preached before the soldiers quartered at St. James's on a fearful text from Isaiah:

All the kings of the nations, even all of them, lie in glory, every one in his own house.

But thou art cast out of thy grave like an abominable branch, and as the raiment of those that are slain, thrust through with a sword. . . .

Thou shalt not be joined to them in burial, because thou hast destroyed thy land and slain thy people.

He was disappointed because the King was not there to hear. He believed it would have done him good.[1]

At Whitehall on Sunday morning, Charles received offers of spiritual help from the leading Presbyterian ministers of London, and also from the popular Independent preacher, John Goodwin. He thanked but refused them all, and listened instead to Bishop Juxon who preached consolingly on a text from Romans: " When God shall judge the secrets of all hearts. . . ."[2] About five in the afternoon his captors moved him from Whitehall back to St. James's.[3] The purpose of this repeated shifting of his place of imprisonment is obscure; it may have been to spare him the noise of the builders at work on the scaffold, but more probably it was to foil any attempt at rescue which might have been plotted had he stayed for

166

long in one place. In other ways his captors were reasonably considerate. The soldiers under Tomlinson's command were less unruly, and his request for a transcript of what had been said in Court was granted.[4]

He seems to have been spared the company of Thomas Herbert for at least a part of Sunday, for Herbert records about this time a walk in the park and a meeting with his wealthy cousin and patron the Earl of Pembroke. The Earl asked after the King and expressed surprise that the gold alarm-clock that he had ordered for him some weeks earlier had not been delivered. The eve of his execution hardly seemed an appropriate time to be discussing the whereabouts of a missing alarm-clock, but Herbert duly delivered Pembroke's fatuous message, and the King, after remarking that he would not have enjoyed the use of the clock for long, sent Herbert out on a further errand. He drew a ring from his finger, an emerald set between diamonds, and told him to take it to Lady Wheeler, at her house in Westminster, there to exchange it for a casket she would give him.[5]

The King's mind was much on his children. Four of them were abroad, safe from the power of his enemies—his two elder sons and his eldest daughter were in the Low Countries, where the Princess was wife to the young Prince of Orange. The Queen, in Paris, had with her the little Princess Henrietta, born at Exeter during the war; this was a child almost unknown to the King who had seen her once as a month-old baby and approvingly called her " my youngest and prettiest daughter."[6] But two of his children were in England, in the care of the Duke of Northumberland: Elizabeth who was thirteen and the Duke of Gloucester, five years younger. These two he hoped to see before he died.

He refused to see a group of courtiers who came to bid farewell—the loyalists who had waited on him at Newport, his cousin Richmond, the Earls of Hertford, Lindsay and Southampton. They came in the company of his nephew, the German prince, Charles Louis Elector Palatine, who may have used his influence to gain permission for them all to visit the King. This calculating, thick-skinned young man had lived in England as the guest of Parliament for the past four years. While his two younger brothers, Rupert and Maurice, were leading the Royalist forces, he had hovered about Westminster cherishing the unspoken hope that, in the event of his uncle's defeat and deposition, he might be offered the Crown. The King had no intention of giving any of his few remaining moments to his disloyal nephew. He would, perhaps, have received the others had they come without him, but as it was he sent word that his time was all too short to prepare for death, and he would talk with no one except his children, or those who brought him news of them.[7]

His captors permitted him to see a messenger from the Prince of Wales. This was Henry Seymour who had been page and courtier to King Charles during his time of prosperity. Seymour had not seen him for some years, and when Colonel Hacker admitted him to the presence he was overcome by extravagant grief, fell on his knees, kissed the King's hand with tears, and "clasped about his legs, lamentably mourning." Recovering himself he gave Charles a letter from his eldest son. The Prince's words were few and poignant. He had no news of his father except from conflicting rumours and the printed news-sheets, and he could do no more than express his anxiety and his filial obedience: "I do not only pray for Your Majesty according to my duty, but shall always be ready to do all which shall be in my power to deserve that blessing which I now humbly beg of Your Majesty."[8]

The King did not speak to Seymour alone. Colonel Hacker stood at the door, and Herbert was constantly in the room. He said nothing, therefore, of any great moment. He sent verbal messages to the Prince and entrusted to Seymour his letter of farewell to his Queen, the beloved wife who, in this world, he would never see again.

He also added a word of commendation for Colonel Tomlinson, as a civil and considerate man. He may have done this so that Seymour would reassure the Queen and Prince that he had received no physical violence; he may have done it as an oblique reproof to Hacker, standing within earshot and showing neither civility nor consideration; or he may simply have answered some anxious inquiry of Seymour's. It is not very important, but Colonel Tomlinson was a man who looked ahead, and the use that he later made of this testimonial suggests that he had taken steps to procure it. As the officer responsible for the King's security, he may have overruled Hacker in authorising the admission of Seymour to his presence, and he may well have insinuated that he required some such recognition of his courtesy.[9]

When Seymour had gone, the King returned again to his meditations with Bishop Juxon.

It was said, within a short time of the King's death, that a last offer from Cromwell and the Independents had reached him that Sunday night. They would spare his life and restore him to his throne if he would relinquish all power into their hands. To this it was alleged that the King replied that " he would rather become a sacrifice for his people than betray their laws and liberties, lives and estates, together with the Church and Commonwealth, and the honour of the Crown, to so intolerable a bondage."[10]

There is little foundation for this story which was first circulated by Clement Walker in his polemical attacks on Cromwell and the Independents, and seems to have grown from the stubborn conviction of many, both Royalists and Presbyterians, that the purpose of the trial was merely to terrify the King. Holding to this belief, they would logically imagine that such an offer must be made and—since the King was executed—that he had refused it. It is possible also that Fairfax, after seeing the Dutch ambassadors, discussed such an offer with his Council, and contemplated making it. But it seems unlikely that, even if it was discussed, it ever reached the King. The resolute men of the Army had made their last offer to Charles in November when they sent him their terms in the

Isle of Wight. Cromwell had spoken his bitter and convinced opinion to Downes when he refused to hear anything more from the King in the last day of the trial and called Charles " the hardest-hearted man on earth ". No renewed offer to the King would have been made with Cromwell's consent, and none could have been made without it.

II

The Prince of Wales had done all that was in his power to save his father. He had sent Fairfax a letter imploring him and Cromwell " to raise lasting monuments to yourselves of loyalty and piety by restoring your sovereign to his just rights and your country to peace and happiness." This letter they received but set aside without an answer. Later it was said that he had sent a blank sheet of paper, signed and sealed, on which they were to inscribe whatever terms they pleased for the preservation of his father's life. But in view of the King's specific instructions to his son never on any account to allow considerations of his own or his father's safety to wring from him concessions that compromised the Crown or the Church, this seems improbable, and there is no hint of such an appeal in the account given by Clarendon, at this time the close adviser of the Prince in Holland.[11]

He was on the other hand responsible for the only foreign intervention to be made on his father's behalf, that of the Dutch, whose two ambassadors had been despatched entirely as a result of his personal appeal to them. They had arrived in London on the 26th, a distinguished pair of veteran—even venerable—diplomats. The elder of them, Albert Joachimi, who had represented his country in England on previous occasions, was nearly ninety years old; his colleague, Adriaen Pauw was considerably younger, and had recently guided the negotiations for peace between his country and Spain to a successful conclusion.

They had wished to make their representations to Parliament on the 27th but had been told that, owing to the King's trial, it could not be arranged until Monday 29th. They had at first accepted this, but when sentence was pronounced on the King they had made a half-hearted attempt at more immediate action. On Sunday they had insisted on seeing both Speaker Lenthall and Fairfax. Neither interview had any effect. Fairfax received them formally, with Cromwell and his Council of Officers about him. The conversation was in French, through interpreters. When they asked the Lord General to use his influence to save the King's life, he and his officers made evasive comments and after some discussion they had to be content with a disingenuous official answer: the Army could not act except by order of Parliament. Nothing could be done until the Commons reassembled on Monday.[12]

On Monday at last the envoys were received though not until two in the afternoon. The formalities were correctly observed and they were accommodated on chairs draped in cloth of silver. They went first to the House of Lords, where the half dozen peers listened attentively to their plea and promised to confer with the Commons on the matter. An hour later they were received in the Lower House on two chairs set on a handsome Turkey carpet. They noticed that the Commons politely removed their hats at every reference to the Dutch government, but remained with their heads covered when the name of King Charles was mentioned. But no serious discussion took place, for when Adriaen Pauw had read out the official protest of his government, he was told that the Commons could not consider it until it was translated into English. Having thus postponed their answer, the House instantly and rather hurriedly rose, the members so far forgetting the reverence due to the ambassadors as not even to wait for them to withdraw first.[13] Their haste was probably in order to cut off all possibility of a conference with the peers. The Dutch envoys could do no more than prepare the translation of their protest and send it, later that evening, to the

Speaker. They were uncertain when the King would die. The general opinion was that it would be some time on the following day, Tuesday, January 30th.

While the Dutch ambassadors and their suite drove to and fro in Westminster in their stately coaches, workmen were busy setting up railings and erecting a scaffold. The Commissioners responsible for deciding on the place of execution had made their choice already. The King was to die outside the royal Banqueting House, completed for him by Inigo Jones about twenty years before. *The Moderate* hailed the decision with appropriate comment. This was the very place, they said, where Charles had first drawn the sword against his people: "The King's party, the day the citizens came down to cry for justice against Strafford, killed one of the citizens and wounded many, being the first blood spilt in this quarrel."[14]

The Moderate's history (or memory) was at fault. When the London apprentices stormed outside Whitehall for justice on Strafford, the King's party had not retaliated. It was during the Christmas revels seven months later that some of the royal guards had had a clash with Puritan citizens; the words "Roundhead" and "Cavalier" had then first been used in anger. A few of the citizens had been wounded; none had been killed.

The choice of site for the King's execution had nothing to do with such considerations. The open space before the Banqueting House was a great deal more easily guarded than the usual places of public execution, like Tower Hill or Tyburn. It was a relatively small square, overlooked on three sides by the buildings of Whitehall.

The palace of Whitehall extended about two hundred yards inland from its gardens and frontage on the river. The ancient thoroughfare called King Street that linked Westminster to Charing Cross was older than the palace, and no attempt had been made to close or divert this public way. It ran right through the precincts of the palace. Henry VIII had built the

Holbein Gate over the street to carry a corridor linking the residential part of the palace on the riverside to the Tilt-yard, Cockpit and other additional galleries and outbuildings on the side of St. James's Park. The new Banqueting House, with its stone façade in the classical Italian manner, was at right angles to the mellowed red and black chequered brick of the graceful, turreted Holbein Gate. Opposite the Banqueting House, on the farther side of King Street, ran the blank wall of the Tilt-yard. The street was broad here, about a hundred and twenty feet, but every building that abutted on it was part of the Army Headquarters. Furthermore, during the war several windows of the Banqueting Hall had been bricked up, and a battery of guns had been mounted on a platform in the angle between the Holbein Gate and the Banqueting House.[15] A better guarded part of the public street could not have been found.

While the carpenters got to work on the necessary preparations, the Commissioners met once more in the Painted Chamber. Only forty-eight came. According to the record of John Phelps, the clerk, they agreed to the place of execution for the King and ordered that the death warrant be drawn up accordingly. This was quickly done and the document brought back for signature.

So the minutes read in the form in which Phelps finally authenticated them on the great roll of parchment that was transmitted into Chancery in December 1650 as a perpetual record.[16] But he was evidently not telling the whole story in this version, for the King's death warrant had certainly been drawn up and may have been partly signed before the meeting on 29th January

The document which was spread out for signing on that day was blemished by a number of erasures as though reflecting the second thoughts of some incompetent clerk. The date, 29th January, had evidently been altered. The phrase " upon Saturday last was sentenced" had been crammed in over another erasure and the word " was " had been added above the line. Farther down the date of the execution, the "thirtieth", was spaced widely out over an erasure.

From all this it would appear that the warrant had been drawn up in advance, probably on the previous Friday 26th, the day on which it had first been assumed that sentence would be pronounced. The date of sentence would then have read " upon Friday " and not " upon Saturday last "; and the date of execution would have been the " twenty-seventh ", not the " thirtieth ". The only explanation for erasing and altering these dates, instead of drawing up a new warrant, would be that something of value existed on that particular warrant which would be lost if it were destroyed. What could this be except the signatures of the judges? Some of these, therefore, had been written as early as the twenty-sixth or twenty-seventh. After the protest of John Downes and the other untoward incidents of the day on which Charles was sentenced it was possible that several who had already signed might not be willing to repeat their signatures on a new death warrant.[17]

It is probable (if not absolutely beyond question) that Cromwell with Ireton, Marten and the others who were fully resolved had been, ever since the previous Friday or Saturday, gathering signatures, and that the document which was laid on the table in the Painted Chamber on the 29th was already at least half signed. The minutes of John Phelps are designed to indicate that the Commissioners signed the warrant in the Painted Chamber on that day and no other. But he did not tamper with the roll-call, and fifteen out of the fifty-nine who signed the warrant are not recorded as present on 29th January.[18]

Some fragmentary and confused evidence about the way in which the warrant was signed came out eleven years later when the survivors of the fifty-nine were on trial for the murder of the King. It was then that stories were told of the unseemly and violent behaviour of Cromwell—how he had dragged Richard Ingoldsby to the table, held his unwilling hand and forced him to write his name.[19] (Ingoldsby had been helpful at the Restoration and it suited the government in 1660 to believe this unlikely tale in spite of the flowing signature on the warrant which visibly contradicted it.) Another witness had seen Cromwell dip his pen in the ink and scrawl a mark on Harry Marten's cheek, and Marten after signing his name had done the same for Cromwell.[20]

Fear of Cromwell was evidently one reason why some men signed the warrant. Several members of the Court urged in their own defence, in 1660, that they had bravely resisted him, and one described how he had kept away from Westminster altogether when the warrant was signing, as the only sure way of avoiding his alarming pressure.

Cromwell's pressure was more effectively avoided by such calm assurance as that which Colonel Tomlinson displayed. As the officer in charge of the King he made his duties an excuse for absenting himself whenever possible from the meetings of the Commissioners, and no one appears to have noticed that he did not sign the warrant.[21] Cromwell's persuasion was directed chiefly to the tremulous members of the Commons. At about eleven in the morning on the 29th he was standing with others at the doors of the House to intercept Commissioners on their way in; later, when most of them were in their places, he rounded up any who had slipped past him, by coming into the House, saying " Those that are gone in shall set their hands, I will have their hands now."[22]

One way and another, by the evening of that day, there were fifty-nine names in seven irregular, parallel columns at the foot of the warrant. Of that number at least two thirds, and probably more, had signed willingly. It was natural enough that those who hoped for mercy after the Restoration of Charles II should make much of the force and fear which dominated the proceedings, but by far the majority signed their names without any persuasion. Bradshaw's name stood first; next came that of Lord Grey, taking the precedence due to his rank; then O. Cromwell, in his clear, bold hand. Henry Ireton was the ninth to sign, John Hutchinson thirteenth, Thomas Harrison seventeenth. The quorum of the Commissioners had been fixed at twenty, a figure which was remembered when the more timorous Commissioners began to hold back. Valentine Walton, Cromwell's brother-in-law signed his name thirty-ninth. Was it he who said to the next signatory Simon Mayne, "What have you to fear? The quorum is twenty, and there is forty here before you." Mayne, whose small nervous handwriting stands at the top of the sixth column, remembered the speech when at his trial in 1660, but not the speaker.[23] The last twenty names contain a number of doubtful men—John Downes and Thomas Waite among others—but also some of the most resolute—Colonel Jones, Colonel Moore, Thomas Scot, and John Carew. The greater the number of signatories, the more impressive the warrant would appear to be; it would certainly be noticed that the number of Commissioners who set their hands to it was smaller than the number who had acquiesced in the sentence in Westminster Hall. Hence the prolonged and determined effort to secure additional signatures, beyond the essential quorum and beyond the number of those who willingly gave them.

An idea still persisted that the trial and sentence were for show—a means of compelling the King to abandon his authority. Those who took part in them might still claim that they had not intended the King's death. But those who signed the warrant made themselves responsible for his execution. It was directed to three officers of the Army, Colonel Hacker, Colonel Hunks and Colonel Phayre, and it required them to see that the King was put to death by the severing of his head from his body between the hours of ten in the morning and five in the afternoon on Tuesday, January 30th.

III

The King had been early at his devotions on the 29th with the help of Bishop Juxon. After prayers he took the casket which Herbert had fetched on the previous evening, broke the seals, and turned over the contents, which consisted for the most part of broken insignia of the Garter. " You see," he said to the curious Herbert, " all the wealth now in my power to give my two children."[24]

The House of Commons had granted his request to see them, and in the afternoon they were brought up from Sion House to St. James's. Princess Elizabeth was a plain, serious girl of thirteen, old enough to understand her father's wrongs and sensitive enough to feel them acutely. The Duke of Gloucester was a lively little boy of eight whose public appearances in London or Hyde Park were usually greeted with popular interest and applause. It had been rumoured repeatedly that the King's enemies would put him on the throne in his father's place as a puppet king.[25]

Charles had come to know these two children only at the end of the Civil War. Both had been in the hands of Parliament throughout the conflict. But during his imprisonment at Hampton Court in the autumn of 1647 they had visited him often and he had taken great comfort in their company, though it was now fifteen months since he had seen them.

Both children immediately fell on their knees, Elizabeth crying bitterly. The King raised them to their feet, and drawing them aside—for they were not alone—spoke first to his daughter. He had much of importance to say to her that he could say to no one else. He was anxious, not without cause, about the relations between his two eldest sons between whom there was much adolescent jealousy. She was to tell " her brother James, whenever she should see him, that it was his father's last desire, that he should no more look upon Charles as his eldest brother only, but be obedient unto him as his sovereign." The Princess was crying so much that he could not be sure that she was taking it in. " Sweet heart, you will forget this," he said. She shook her head. " I shall never forget it whilst I live," and she promised to write it down.

It is thus from the account that she set down that night that we know what passed between them:

> He told me he was glad I was come, and although he had not time to say much, yet somewhat he had to say to me, which he had not to another, or have in writing, because he feared their cruelty was such, as that they would not have permitted him to write to me. He wished me not to grieve and torment myself for him, for that would be a glorious death that he should die, it being for the laws and liberties of this land, and for maintaining the true Protestant Religion. He bid me read Bishop Andrews' *Sermons*, Hooker's *Ecclesiastical Polity* and Bishop Laud's book against Fisher, which would ground me against Popery. He told me, he had forgiven all his enemies, and hoped God would forgive them also, and commanded us, and all the rest of my brothers and sisters to forgive them. He bid me tell my mother that his thoughts had never strayed from her, and that his love should be the same to the last. Withal he commanded me and my brother to be obedient to her, and bid me send his blessing to the rest of my brothers and sisters, with commendation to all his friends.

After reading over what she had written, the Princess noticed an omission and added a postscript:

> Further, he commanded us all to forgive these people, but never to trust them, for they had been most false to him and to those that gave them power, and he feared also to their own souls; and desired me not to grieve for

him, for he should die a martyr; and that he doubted not but the Lord would settle his throne upon his son, and that we should be all happier than we could have expected to have been if he had lived.[26]

He said less to the Duke of Gloucester, and in the simplest possible language for it was important the child should understand. The unity of the family and the legal descent of the Crown might depend on this:

"Mark, child, what I say," said the King, taking his son on his knee, "they will cut off my head, and perhaps make thee a king: but mark what I say, you must not be a king so long as your brothers Charles and James do live; for they will cut off your brothers' heads (when they can catch them) and cut off thy head too, at last; and therefore I charge you, do not be made a king by them."

The child who, all the time his father spoke, had "looked very steadfastly upon him", now said with great firmness: "I will be torn in pieces first."

This answer greatly pleased the King. He had little more to say and every reason, both for his own and the children's sake, not to prolong the interview. He gave them the casket and most of his remaining jewels to take away, keeping back only a few personal things and the George, cut in a single onyx, that he intended to wear on the scaffold. Then he kissed and blessed them both and sent them away.[27]

Soldiers on guard, and spectators outside the gates of St. James's who saw the children leave, predicted that the Princess would die of grief, and within a day or two the newspapers were reporting that she had actually done so.

Later that afternoon the King sent for Colonel Tomlinson to ask him to accompany him on the following day. In Tomlinson's phrase—"desired me that I would not leave him." This Tomlinson promised to do, so that the King would be certain in his last hours of more considerate treatment than he expected from Hacker. In thanks for this last civility Charles gave him the small gold toothpick case that he usually carried in his pocket.[28]

The King spent what was left of the evening in further prayer and meditation with Bishop Juxon, and some hours after dark gave him leave to go, saying that he would want him early on the following morning. He himself sat up reading and praying until nearly midnight before going to bed in his accustomed fashion, with a wax-light burning in a silver basin, and Herbert lying on a pallet at his bedside. He slept peacefully for several hours.[29]

Between five and six o'clock he awoke, drew back the bed curtain and called to Herbert who had fallen into an uneasy and restless sleep. "I will get up," said the King, "I have a great work to do this day." As he was dressing he made conversation with Herbert who admitted that he had been dreaming and at the King's request proceeded to recount what he had dreamt. He had heard a knock at the door and on opening it had found Archbishop Laud—who had died on the scaffold in January, four years earlier—asking to speak with the King. The Archbishop had talked privately with the King, then kissed his hand and taken his leave, first however bowing so low that he fell prostrate. Herbert had hastened to help him and had at that moment been awakened by the King's call to him.

Charles expressed a courteous interest in this not very auspicious dream, and turned to other things. "Herbert," he said, "this is my second marriage day; I would be as trim to-day as may be, for before to-night I hope to be espoused to my blessed Jesus."

The bitter January frost was still unbroken and the King, anxious that he might not feel the cold, put on two shirts so that he would not shiver when he came to prepare for the block and so give an impression of fear. "I fear not death. Death is not terrible to me. I bless my God I am prepared."

Bishop Juxon was at his door as soon as Charles was dressed, but before they proceeded to prayers together, the

King entrusted his remaining books and possessions to Herbert for distribution after his death. The Bible which he had studied daily during his imprisonment, with marginal annotations in his clear, careful hand, was to be given to the Prince of Wales, with " a last and earnest request that he would frequently read it." Princess Elizabeth was to have the three books he had recommended to her for her religious instruction. The Duke of Gloucester was to have the *Works* of his grandfather, King James—a volume which Charles himself had studied many times with filial duty and respect. He was also to have the *Practical Catechism* compiled by good Dr. Hammond whose sermons, during all the war years, had been a comfort and inspiration to the King. There was one book of a lighter kind to dispose of, the fashionable French romance, *Cassandre*, by Gautier de la Calprenède, which Charles sent to the Earl of Lindsey, who had served him in his bedchamber during the war at Oxford and again in that brief interlude at Newport.[30] For his son the Duke of York he had kept back an ingenious toy, a large double ring of silver with figures engraved on it, which could be used as a sundial and a slide-rule " resolving many questions in arithmetick." It was the invention of Richard Delamaine who, long ago, had taught mathematics to King Charles.[31] One last present, his gold watch, he sent to the Duchess of Richmond, wife of his cousin and daughter of that Duke of Buckingham who had been his close friend throughout his youth and whose dear memory he always cherished.

These few gifts disposed of, the King spoke privately with Juxon for an hour, and then received the Sacrament. The Gospel was the 27th Chapter of St. Matthew, the Passion of Our Lord. Charles thought that the Bishop had chosen it for the occasion, but it was the lesson ordained for the day in the Prayer Book, a chance which much impressed the King, as it was later to impress devout Royalists meditating on his martyrdom.[32]

Between nine and ten Colonel Hacker knocked lightly on

the door, but at first got no answer. He knocked a second time more firmly and was admitted. He was visibly trembling as he told the King that it was time to go to Whitehall. Charles said he would come "presently", and after a brief further prayer with Juxon, he took the Bishop's hand saying, "Come, let us go." Herbert followed, carrying the small silver time-piece that habitually hung at the King's bedside. Just as they went out into the Park he asked Herbert the time (it was ten) and then told him to keep the clock in memory of him.[33]

Colonel Tomlinson was waiting for the King. It was a sunless morning, the ground hard with frost, the Park colour-less and bare. Tomlinson went on one side of the King, his hat in his hand, Juxon on the other, Herbert followed behind. The small group was immediately surrounded on every side by the two companies of infantry who were drawn up ready. The procession marched off, with drums beating. An intrusive and ill-mannered spectator who somehow got through the soldiers and stared offensively at the King was removed at Juxon's request. Conversation was not easy against so much noise, but Charles exchanged a few words with Tomlinson, telling him that he hoped the Duke of Richmond would be permitted to take care of his burial, and then, as an after-thought, that he hoped it would not be too hasty, lest his son should come over to bury him. A strange injunction, if Tomlinson recorded it truly, as if Charles had been confident as he went to his death that this was the certain prelude to his son's immediate restoration. He was later reported to have asked that a quicker pace be set for the troops because "he now went before them to strive for a Heavenly Crown with less solicitude than he had often encouraged his soldiers to fight for an earthly diadem."[34] He may have said something of the kind and it would be natural for him to want the men to march briskly; he was himself a fast walker and the day was cold.

An open wooden staircase led at that time from the Park

into the adjoining buildings of Whitehall. On the King's left, as he climbed it, was the Tilt-yard, on his right the cluster of houses and galleries in the region known as The Cockpit. Here the Earl of Pembroke, old courtier and false friend, still occupied the rooms which had been his when the King was in residence in the days of his power. He stood at his window, with the Earl of Salisbury at his side, and together the two turncoat peers watched the King as he came into Whitehall for the last time. It was something, at least, that they did not also watch the execution. Indifferent to public contempt, both would accept the Republican government within days of the King's death, and seek election to the House of Commons when the House of Lords was abolished.[35]

From the staircase the King passed along the gallery above the Tilt-yard. It was hung with the pictures of his family, his father, his mother in her green hunting dress with five little dogs round her feet, several portraits by Van Dyck, the luscious allegory of Peace and War painted for him by Rubens, and the great Titian he had brought back from Spain, the Emperor Charles V, standing, full-length, with his Irish wolf-hound beside him.[36]

The King walked quickly on. Crossing the street by the upper floor of the Holbein Gate he may have seen, through the window, the black-draped scaffold, the mounted troops drawn up near to it, the close-packed crowd that filled the open space. He was taken to the room in which he had recently slept, and there left with Herbert and Juxon. It was about half past ten in the morning and he had not expected more than a few moments to rest and speak with the Bishop. But the moments lengthened into hours and still he did not hear the last awaited knock at the door.[37]

IV

Had something gone wrong? Later, rumour-mongers and Royalists were full of sinister stories. The public executioner and his assistant, they whispered, had refused to kill the King. There had been a frantic search for two men to take their places. Volunteers had been called for from Hewson's regiment, and two troopers, Hulet and Walker, had finally agreed to do it in disguise. Others said that Hugh Peter, in false wig and beard, had played the part of executioner; or Captain Joyce, or even Oliver Cromwell. An ill-informed French account confidently averred that "Fairfax et Cromwell" personally beheaded their King.[38] But there seems to be no adequate reason to think that "young Gregory" as the Londoners called the City's principal hangman had refused to perform his task. His real name was Richard Brandon and he had succeeded his father Gregory Brandon in his office, hence his familiar nickname. He lived in Rosemary Lane, near the Tower of London, and he had, in the last eight years beheaded the Earl of Strafford and the Archbishop of Canterbury, Sir John Hotham and his son and Sir Alexander Carew. He prided himself on his dexterity with the axe, had an accurate eye and a steady hand, and never needed to strike more than once. Furthermore, the payment was high for such a skilled operation and would be especially high for the King. If "young Gregory" was nervous at what was now required of him—and he could hardly fail to be—both self-interest and pride in his skill would be strong arguments to overcome his fear.

It is however possible that he either could not find an assistant (it was usual for the executioner to work with an assistant) or thought it more discreet not to bring his own man with him. The execution was not popular with the humbler sort of people to whom Brandon belonged. Fearing the black looks of his neighbours, or some Royalist's dagger, he may have made it a condition that he should work disguised and with an assistant provided by his employers. This would explain why volunteers were called for from Hewson's regiment, and one of them may have been the second disguised figure who appeared on the scaffold later that day.[39]

There had been difficulties too among the officers in charge of the proceedings some hours before the King reached Whitehall. The three to whom the death-warrant had been directed Hacker, Hunks and Phayre, had to sign the order for the execution itself, and over this, on the morning of the 30th, trouble had arisen. At the time it was concealed, but after the Restoration Hunks, giving evidence against his old comrades in arms, called up the wrangling scene.

In a small room in Whitehall Ireton and Harrison lie in bed together (very early in the morning, therefore?); close to the door is a table with pen and ink, and the order lying upon it. Cromwell, Hacker, Phayre, Hunks make a crowd in the room. Voices are raised in argument: Hunks—the mistakenly named Hercules Hunks—has lost his nerve. No, he will not sign. Cromwell shouts at him; he is " a froward, peevish fellow." Colonel Axtell appears in the doorway, and speaks: " Colonel Hunks, I am ashamed of you; the ship is now coming in to harbour and will you strike sail before we come to anchor?"

Hunks did not sign, and eleven years later he would stand, obsequiously voluble, in the witness box while Francis Hacker listened in stubborn resignation and Daniel Axtell in a cold sweat denied that any such thing had happened.[40]

But all this must have taken place before Hacker went to St. James's to fetch the King. The scaffold was by now ready, the soldiers drawn up in every room through which the King would pass, the spectators crowded and waiting, in the street, at windows, on balconies, even on the roofs as far as eye could see. It was something else that caused the long delay.

Down at Westminster, a piece of vital legislation was being hurried through the House of Commons. It had been forgotten, apparently until that morning, that on the death of the King his son could, and undoubtedly would, be proclaimed as his successor by the Royalists, or even the Presbyterians. Since the Lord Mayor, Reynardson, was notoriously for the King, the danger that something of this kind might be instantly done even in London, with some semblance of authority, was a real one. Such a proclamation might be awkward for the Army and the Commons who had indeed tried and condemned the King, but had not deposed him, had not proclaimed a republic, and had not so far made any official statement about the fate of the monarchy.

In the tense anxiety of the last days, no one had had time to work out any plan for the future, and there was certainly no time on the morning of 30th January to draft, present and pass an act making England a republic. Yet action of some kind must be taken before the King's head was off. They did the only essential thing; they made it illegal for anyone to proclaim a new king. And to make sure that the public, especially in London, fully understood the authority of the present House of Commons they ordered that the resolutions by which they had proclaimed themselves to be the true representatives of the people and thus the source of all just power should be instantly printed.

In this way they could not indeed prevent the proclamation of King Charles II, but they could prevent its being done in any authoritative way, and they could instantly arrest and prosecute anyone who ventured to do it.

The brief emergency bill was read twice in the morning, engrossed hurriedly while the Commons broke up at midday, read a third time and passed the moment they got back to their seats.[41] By then it was nearly two o'clock, and the King was still waiting at Whitehall.

A few ill-planned efforts were still being made to help him. The two Dutch ambassadors after spending the early part of the morning in consultation with the Scots Commissioners, had decided to approach Fairfax once again.[42] They found him at his house in King Street within a hundred yards of the scaffold where the King was to die. For once Cromwell was not with him. Fairfax looked as worried as usual and was probably also short of sleep. Later he would assert that he had spent much of that night in consultation with those who wanted to save the King. They had urged him to declare for the King and prevent the execution. After a long struggle he had rejected the suggestion because it could only precipitate immediate bloodshed; he was willing to risk his life, he argued, but not the lives of others.[43]

Something of this kind may indeed have happened in the night, and Fairfax was probably wise not to attempt the King's rescue in this way. Whether or not he could count on a personal following in the Army if he turned on Cromwell, it must have been clear to him that the King, as a prisoner, was at the mercy of his immediate captors. In the event of a split in the Army, he would be murdered before his friends could reach him.

Now he listened sympathetically to the Dutch and the Scots and agreed that he would go with some of his principal officers to the House of Commons and ask for a postponement of the execution. On this promise, they left him, but were dismayed to find as they emerged from the house, no less than two hundred cavalry on guard outside. While they conversed with the Lord General all the adjoining streets had been lined with soldiers, standing so thick that they had great difficulty in driving back to their own quarters. In mournful consultation, the Dutch and the Scots agreed that no earthly power could now save the King; it was useless to attempt anything more.[44]

Fairfax still deceived himself, or tried to do so. Whatever the purpose of the guard outside his door, it was not to prevent his leaving the house, for he seems to have been present in the vicinity of the Banqueting House about midday or a little later, and here to have met Cromwell, Harrison and others. He knew the King was awaiting execution in the palace and knew that no precise hour had been set for it. (At the time of his arrival the bill against proclaiming a new king was not yet through Parliament.) Deluded as to the time still available for argument, he was closeted with someone (perhaps Harrison? perhaps Cromwell?) for the next two hours. Talking? Praying? Afterwards many stories would be told of how he had been decoyed and deceived. But he seems to have been a willing dupe. He did not wish to be held personally responsible for the King's death; beyond this he no longer greatly cared.

V

It was nearly two o'clock in the afternoon before Hacker knocked for the last time on the King's door. Charles had waited calmly, sometimes in silence, sometimes talking with Bishop Juxon. He had eaten nothing since the previous night, intending that no food should pass his lips, on his last day, except the Sacrament. The kindly sensible Bishop dissuaded him from this plan, and Herbert fetched a small loaf of white bread and a glass of claret. The King drank the wine and ate a small piece of the bread.

At the last summons he rose calmly, although Juxon and Herbert immediately fell on their knees, tearfully kissing his hands. He helped Juxon to his feet and asked Herbert to open the door and tell Hacker to lead the way. He followed along the corridors of his palace and through the great Banqueting Hall, going all the way between two lines of soldiers, shoulder to shoulder. In the last hours, the people had crowded into the palace, and behind the soldiers they pressed and struggled to get a sight of the King, some of them loudly calling out prayers and blessings as he passed. No one stopped them. The soldiers were themselves silent and dejected.[45]

It was seven years since Charles had fled from Whitehall and the riots of the London apprentices; during that time his once beautiful palace had stood half-empty, had been used for its own purpose by Parliament and later occupied by the Army. For reasons of defence the seven noble windows of the Banqueting House had been partly blocked by boards or masonry. The light and gorgeous hall that the King remembered was now dark and bare. Far above his head, the great ceiling by Rubens, representing the triumph of wisdom and justice over rebellion and falsehood, can hardly have been visible in the grey light.

The King passed through the hall, and so out to the scaffold which was built against the palace wall and approached through one of the windows which had been enlarged for the purpose.[46] The scaffold was covered in black and near to the block three or four staples had been driven into the wood so that the King could be bound if he refused to submit. The small platform was already crowded with people—the executioner and his assistant, not only masked, as was usual, but disguised beyond recognition in thick close-fitting frieze-coats with hair and beards that were evidently not their own.[47] Colonel Tomlinson was there and Colonel Hacker, several soldiers on guard (among them John Harris the Leveller journalist), and two or three shorthand writers with note-books and ink-horns. Herbert remained inside the palace but Juxon came with the King.

Charles looked towards the axe and the block, and asked Hacker if no higher one could be provided. It was extremely low, not more than ten inches from the ground. Coming farther on to the scaffold he noticed the mounted troops drawn up between it and the crowds who filled the street. He had probably expected this, but he saw at a glance that it would be impossible and undignified to attempt to speak to the people. He took out of his pocket and unfolded a piece of paper about four inches square on which he had made a few notes, then addressed himself to the group round him on the scaffold, and more especially to Colonel Tomlinson.

"I shall be very little heard of anybody here," he said,

" I shall therefore speak a word unto you here. Indeed I could hold my peace very well, but I think it is my duty, to God first, and to my country, for to clear myself both as an honest man, a good King and a good Christian."

He began by briefly attesting his innocence: " I think it is not very needful for me to insist long upon this, for all the world knows that I never did begin a war first with the two Houses of Parliament. . . ."

He gave his own brief, and convinced, account of how the troubles had begun, with Parliament, as he saw it, the aggressor, but added: " God forbid I should lay it on the two Houses of Parliament. . . . I do believe that ill instruments between them and me have been the chief cause of all this bloodshed."

Yet if, as a King, he denied the justice of the sentence against him, he added that as a Christian he saw his fate as God's judgment on him: " An unjust sentence that I suffered to take effect, is punished now by an unjust sentence on me."

He did not speak the name of Strafford; for most of those who heard, or afterwards read, his words there was no need to be more explicit.

Passing now to his duties as a Christian he declared that he had forgiven all the world, " and even those in particular that have been the chief causers of my death: who they are, God knows, I do not desire to know, I pray God forgive them." It was a strange statement to make, but true. During these last weeks he had never seen or spoken to any of the chief commanders of the Army. Fairfax and Cromwell and Ireton, the three whom he had come to know eighteen months before when he had negotiated with them at Hampton Court had not confronted him since he became their prisoner. He had been a prisoner, cut off from the world, communicating only with lesser men and underlings, Ewer and Rolfe, Harrison and Whichcot, Tomlinson and Hacker. At his trial he had been judged and prosecuted by Bradshaw and Cook, two obscure lawyers neither of whom he had ever heard of before. " The chief causers of my death, who they are, God knows. . . ." He could have made a very good guess, but it was true that he did not, absolutely, *know*. All these men who stood round him now, and would in a few minutes, in cold blood, murder him—they were instruments merely. But the hidden enemies who had finally destroyed him, who and where were they? Fairfax? Cromwell? Ireton?

He went on: " I wish that they may repent, for indeed they have committed a great sin in that particular; I pray God, with St. Stephen, that this be not laid to their charge. Nay, not only so, but that they may take the right way to the peace of the Kingdom: for my charity commands me not only to forgive particular men, but my charity commands me to endeavour to the last gasp the peace of the Kingdom. So, Sirs, I do wish with all my soul, (and I do hope there is some here will carry it further) that they may endeavour the peace of the Kingdom."

He looked towards the clerks who were busy taking notes, then went on with great composure to instruct his enemies in politics. They would achieve nothing by unjust conquest; they must learn to know their duty to God, the King—" that is, my successors "—and the people. They should call a national council to settle the affairs of the Church. As for the King—— He broke off short, for one of the officers on the scaffold, happened by accident to touch the axe. " Hurt not the axe," said the King, " that may hurt me."

He resumed. Their duty to the king was clearly laid down in the known laws of the land. Then he came to the people: " Truly I desire their liberty and freedom as much as anybody whomsoever; but I must tell you their liberty and freedom consists in having of government, those laws by which their life and their goods may be most their own. It is not for having a share in government, Sir, that is nothing pertaining to them. A subject and a sovereign are clear different things. . . . Sirs, it was for this that now I am come here. If I would have given way to an arbitrary way, for to have all laws changed according to the power of the sword, I needed not to have come here;

and therefore I tell you (and I pray God it be not laid to your charge) that I am the Martyr of the people."

He added a regret that he had had so little time to put his thoughts into better order, and would have concluded there, had not Juxon reminded him that " for the world's satisfaction " he should make some statement about his religion. It was true that in putting forward this last eloquent claim that he died for the liberties of his people, he had " almost forgotten" (his own words) to vindicate himself and his Church from the accusation of Popery. He now solemnly attested " that I die a Christian according to the profession of the Church of England, as I found it left me by my father. . . . I have a good Cause and I have a gracious God; I will say no more."

He turned now to speak to the grotesque figures by the block. For some reason, perhaps out of nervous forgetfulness, the executioner did not go through the usual formula of asking for, and receiving, the forgiveness of his victim.[48] There is, in no account, any indication that these words were said. The King explained that he would pray briefly and then sign for him to strike. He also asked how he should arrange his hair not to impede the axe. Then with the help of Juxon, he put on his cap and pushed his hair underneath it.

" There is but one stage more," said Juxon, " which though turbulent and troublesome, yet it is a very short one; you may consider it will soon carry you a very great way; it will carry you from Earth to Heaven; and there you shall find, to your great joy, the prize you hasten to, a Crown of Glory."

The King replied: " I go from a corruptible to an incorruptible Crown, where no disturbance can be, no disturbance in the world."

He now took off his George, the insignia of the Garter, the last of his jewels and gave it to the Bishop with the one word " Remember."

He took off his doublet, and for a moment resumed his cloak, against the bitter cold. Looking at the block he asked if it was set fast, and again regretted that it was no higher. The reason for the low block was to make the execution easier to perform if he had offered any resistance. The executioner was, naturally, unwilling to explain this. " It can be no higher, Sir," was all he said.

The King stood for a moment raising his hands and eyes to Heaven and praying in silence, then slipped off his cloak and lay down with his neck on the block. The executioner bent down to make sure that his hair was not in the way, and Charles, thinking that he was preparing to strike, said, "Stay for the sign."

" I will, an' it please Your Majesty," said the executioner.

A fearful silence had now fallen on the little knot of people on the scaffold, on the surrounding troops, and on the crowd. Within a few seconds the King stretched out his hands and the executioner on the instant and at one blow severed his head from his body.[49]

A boy of seventeen, standing a long way off in the throng, saw the axe fall. He would remember as long as he lived the sound that broke from the crowd, " such a groan as I never heard before, and desire I may never hear again."[50]

CHAPTER NINE

FREEDOM, BY GOD'S MERCY RESTORED...

February 1649

IMMEDIATELY the King was dead two troops of horse which had been stationed respectively at the north and south ends of the street advanced into the crowd which dispersed before them with remarkable speed saving themselves as well as they could from the horses' hooves by dodging up side lanes and alleys.[1] Within half an hour the place was empty.

Some of the guards and a few of the more determined and dexterous spectators had none the less managed to dip handkerchiefs in the King's blood, or even to scrape up fragments of earth from below the scaffold or tear off pieces of the blood-soaked pall, but the King's body had been reverently carried back into the palace, where it was placed in a coffin and taken under the guidance of Juxon and Herbert to the room where it was to be embalmed.

On the way back from this melancholy errand Herbert met Fairfax in the Long Gallery, and was astonished when the Lord General asked him " how the King did ". On being answered he " seemed much surprised." A few paces farther on Herbert saw Cromwell who merely informed him that he would let him have the necessary orders for the King's burial.[2]

As for the Lord General, he withdrew to his own house and tried to assuage his feelings of inadequacy and guilt by writing verses:

Oh let that day from time be blotted quite,
And let belief of't in next age be waived
In deepest silence th'act concealed might,
So that the Kingdom's credit might be saved.

Thus far the unhappy man, no more gifted for poetry than for politics, expressed only the futile hope that the King's death, together with his part in it, should be expunged from memory. In the last two lines he took courage to shift the blame:

But if the Power Divine permitted this,
His Will's the law and ours must acquiesce.[3]

Had Fairfax been deliberately detained by Cromwell or Harrison in discussion and prayers while—as they well knew—the King was on the scaffold? Later it would be said that he had been tricked,[4] but could he have been so easily deluded unless he had been a willing victim? He had acquiesced, and knew he had done so, concealing his responsibility under the all-covering phrase, the Will of God.

At Whitehall a Mr. Trapham with his assistant had come to embalm the body while Herbert and Juxon returned to their homes. Before the Bishop left he was held up for a time by some of the officers, presumably Hacker and Phayre. The King had been seen to give him the sheet of paper which he had used while speaking, and this they now required of him. They no doubt wished to compare it with the shorthand notes taken on the scaffold before allowing a version of the King's words to be published. The ultimate decision about publication would rest with Jennings and Mabbott, and the shorthand writers had presumably been employed by either or both of them.

Juxon had some difficulty in finding the paper which he had thrust into a deep pocket among other notes and fragments. When at length he disentangled it, his interrogators were suspicious, lest he had tried to substitute something else. But a tall, long-sighted soldier who had stood close behind the

King as he spoke volunteered that he had seen that very paper in the King's hand.[5]

In due course newspapers and pamphlets came out with accounts of the King's death. The Royalists asserted that omissions had been made in his speech[6] but—as with the text of the trial—so much was printed that reflected credit on the King and discredit on his enemies that it is hard to believe that anything vital had been concealed.

Through the Press, the story of the King's last hours would reach his subjects in the farther parts of the kingdom, to be received at first—and in spite of the long weeks of fore-warning—with a kind of stunned incredulity. " There was such a consternation among the common people throughout the nation, that one neighbour durst scarcely speak to another when they met in the streets, not from any abhorrence at the action, but in surprise at the rarity and infrequency of it," wrote a Puritan Yorkshireman. The sense of shock, which was evidently real enough though brief, was differently inter-preted by Royalists.

" None of the Kings, no not one . . . ever left the world with more sorrow: women miscarried, men fell into melan-choly, some with Consternations expired; men women and children then, and yet unborn, suffering in him and for him. . . ."[7]

In Westminster on the day of the King's death there was every sign of sorrow and dismay. In London feelings were mixed; some shops were open as though nothing was the matter, others were closed. Sympathy with the Army was wide spread among the humbler citizens, and naturally in all the substantial congregations of the Independents, but there was no sense of triumph or even relief. Most people of all persuasions were silent and subdued.[8] The Presbyterians, it was said, had come to look on the death of the King as though it were some phenomenon of nature, like an eclipse, which no mortal power could prevent.[9] The Independents and the Army, even, seemed more stunned than elated at what they had done. Even the irrepressible Hugh Peter fell ill and took to his bed.[10] No attempt was made to conceal the general shock and grief; sympathetic comment in the newspapers was not checked. "This Day it did not rain at all" wrote Richard Collings in *The Kingdom's Weekly Intelligencer*, "yet it was a very wet day in and about the City of London by reason of the abundance of affliction that fell from many eyes."[11]

Tears and silence were the rule, not demonstrations hostile to the Army. But at Westminster School under the authority of the redoubtable Dr. Busby, "the King was publicly prayed for an hour or two before his sacred head was struck off."[12]

The atmosphere was different at St. Paul's, where the boys, in their playtime, freely commented on the event of the day and one of them, Samuel Pepys, a zealous Roundhead of fifteen, declared that if he had to preach on the event he would take for his text "And the memory of the wicked shall rot."[13]

A representation of the King's death, frequently engraved both in England and abroad, shows a woman fainting and other spectators turning away in grief. The picture was probably not done from sketches made at the time, for the artist has drawn the Banqueting House with eight windows instead of seven and with other inaccurate architectural details. But it looks like a pictorial reconstruction from eye-witness descriptions of the scene, and may give a very fair impression of the behaviour of the crowd. Some distance away, at Wallingford House, looking down to Whitehall, Archbishop Ussher watched the King on the scaffold; he had not seen him since the days at Newport, where he had preached his birthday sermon predicting a year of jubilee. He fell down unconscious as the axe was raised to strike.[14]

John Evelyn, whose intelligent curiosity had got the better of his Royalist scruples when he made his way into the Painted Chamber to see the King's judges in session, could not endure to witness " the murder of our excellent King ". Instead he stayed at home at Sayes Court and kept the day as a fast. But late in the afternoon his brother George and a friend came to visit him, and were able to give him the sad account of all that had passed.[15]

Private citizens had only their own consciences to satisfy as to their conduct. The situation was much more difficult for the resident representatives of foreign powers in London. The Spaniard, Alonso de Cardeñas had, in the interests of the hard-pressed Spanish monarchy, kept on very good terms with the people in power throughout the Civil War. The present government was in some ways more satisfactory to him than any of its predecessors since the Independents, who claimed to believe in toleration for all religions, were already giving greater freedom to Roman Catholics, especially in London. He had received a letter from the governor of the Spanish Netherlands, urging him to ask for a postponement of the King's trial. But this was only despatched on January 27th and he was able to express suitable regret that it had not reached him until the day after the King's death. No protest would have had any effect, he commented calmly. The Independents of the Army were resolved to kill the King and nothing could have stopped them. He had, however, put his whole household into mourning. The French and the Dutch representatives had done the same. In diplomatic circles " anyone who neglected to do so would be looked upon unfavourably."[16]

The representatives of European powers gauged the feelings of their masters with perfect accuracy. An appearance of disapproval, or at least of regret, must be maintained, but there was no need to break off relations with the effective rulers of England in defence of the monarchical principle or the heirs of the murdered King. The two Dutch envoys, with a touch of kindness, paid a visit to the King's children at Sion House. The Princess and her brother were in deep mourning but the rooms of the house were not, in the customary fashion, draped in black, nor had any of the servants been put into mourning liveries. Their sad task accomplished, Pauw and Joachimi departed for Holland, cleverly avoiding by their haste the gifts which were usually bestowed on ambassadors, gifts which they preferred not to receive from the blood-stained hands of the English government.[17]

The French resident, whose King was the nephew of the murdered Charles, felt that some indication of grief and anger must be given. He let it be known that he intended to leave. The government retaliated by hinting that if he did, they would like him to take the King's children with him. As he had not the slightest idea whether this arrangement would be welcome to the French Court, and it would in any case have involved him in heavy expense, no more was heard about his leaving. Presently he received instructions from Cardinal Mazarin to avoid if he could any formal recognition of the existing government of England, but on no account to do anything to offend them.[18]

The same cautiously double-faced conduct distinguished most European powers. Only the Tsar of Russia ordered English merchants out of his dominions, but he seems to have seized on the excuse of the King's death to complete a policy of exclusion towards which he had already been working for some time.[19] Only the Swiss Confederation welcomed the extinction of the monarchy, giving God " thanks for the establishment of the Republic in many parts of the Swisses country."[20]

The shocking news was slow to reach those who were most deeply concerned in it. The Prince of Wales, at the Hague, had heard nothing but doubtful rumours since he despatched Sir Henry Seymour with the Dutch mission on 23rd January. Not until 4th February, five days after his father's death, did any certain information reach Holland. It came then, not in any despatch or message to the Prince, but in the general news-letters from England. His advisers knew it first and debated how to tell him. In the end, one of his chaplains, Stephen

Goffe, went in to him and, after a preliminary hesitation, addressed him as " Your Majesty ". He needed no further words; overcome with emotion he signed to Goffe to leave him and remained for some hours alone with his grief.[21]

The Queen was still cut off from news by the disturbances in France and the continuing siege of Paris. A false rumour reached her that her husband had been rescued by a sudden rising of the people at the very foot of the scaffold. Tremulous between tears and relief she half believed it.[22] The cruel truth reached her cold and miserable little Court in the Louvre on 9th February. She received the news in frozen silence, and sat for a long time without speech or motion, staring in front of her, until a childhood friend, Madame de Vendôme, embracing her knees and imploring her to speak, released the torrent of her tears.[23]

When at length she was able to think and plan again her thoughts were wholly for her eldest son—" le Roi ", as he was henceforward in all her thoughts and words. Surely every European prince would take action against these execrable murderers and restore the rightful King to his father's throne ?

The same thoughts were expressed with hardly less vigour by a more experienced and less passionate statesman. Edward Hyde, principal adviser to the young King, expected a universal outburst against " those incarnate devils ".[24] It did not come. The Queen and the young King received letters of condolence in their grief from every Court in Europe, but very few—it was said only the King of Portugal—added also the customary words of congratulation and goodwill to the new sovereign of England.[25]

But in the British Isles, in Scotland, in Ireland, and even in England under the threat of the Army, the new King was proclaimed. On 3rd February the act forbidding the proclamation of a new King posted in Guildhall was torn down and replaced by a denunciation of the Regicide Parliament, ending with the words " God save King Charles II."[26] Ten days later the excluded members of Parliament denounced the murder of the King and declared their loyalty to Charles II.[27] At Pontefract, still holding out after eight months' siege, the Royalist governor struck a gold coin for *Carolus Secundus*.[28]

In England such actions were defiant gestures merely. But in Scotland the government in power, the Presbyterian nobility who had first rebelled against King Charles I, now officially proclaimed his son at the Mercat Cross in Edinburgh.[29] In Ireland, the Royalists were still strong. The Marquis of Ormonde proclaimed him in Ireland and Prince Rupert, in command of the Royalist fleet, did the same at Kinsale.[30] At about the same time, the governor of the Scilly Isles, though he was uncertain of the correct formula and had to concoct one of his own, made shift to inaugurate the reign of King Charles II.[31]

The axiom that there can be no vacancy of the Crown was thus demonstrated by the stubborn Royalists in spite of the act of Parliament which on 30th January had prohibited the proclamation of any successor to Charles I, and the additional act which a week later abolished the monarchy. Since the acts were promulgated by the illicit remnant of the House of Commons only, law and precedent were both on the side of King Charles II. Law and precedent, but not the sword.

The popular astrologer, William Lilly, who had that month as usual issued his annual bulletin of what the stars foretold, had uttered one safe prognostication: " Absolutely the soldier or sword is rampant this year."[32]

II

After his execution, the King's body had been embalmed and placed in a coffin lined with lead under a black velvet pall. It was then carried to St. James's where it remained for a week. The surgeon who embalmed it, Mr. Trapham, was beset with requests for locks of hair and other relics but refused to comply with them.[33] Many also clamoured to see the King's body out of reverence or curiosity, but few were admitted. Long after, a story would be told of one mysterious visitor at midnight. As the loyal Earl of Southampton watched by his dead master a muffled figure entered the room, gazed for some time in silence at the body, uttered the words: "Cruel necessity", and turned away. The voice and gait were like those of Oliver Cromwell.[34]

The story was told by Alexander Pope to Joseph Spence early in the eighteenth century. It was supposed to have been told by Southampton in the first place, but he had been dead for twenty years when Pope was born. It is possible that he had told the story and that it had been correctly transmitted. It is possible that he mounted guard over the King's body, although there is no evidence in any contemporary source to suggest that he did so. It is possible that the coffin may at times have been open so that the King's face would be visible, though it appears from Herbert's accounts that it was closed after the embalming. The incident is just possible, but it sounds much more like one of those inventions which seem to spring up almost naturally to supply something missing in the story. Cromwell, more than any other man, had brought King Charles to his death. Cromwell would, in the end, become the ruler of England. Charles and Cromwell would be, in popular memory, inseparably linked. But at no point during the trial or the execution had Cromwell personally confronted the King. When history fails to supply the moment of drama, human invention will often fill the gap.

Some days passed before the House of Commons at length gave order for the King's burial. The nearest place was the vault of Henry VII's chapel where his father and mother were interred with several of their children. But there were obvious objections to burying the King in a place so famous and so accessible. Demonstrators and relic-hunters were alike to be feared, and the new government did not want to see the grave of Charles turned into a place of pilgrimage at their very door.

They decreed that the body was to lie at Windsor in St. George's Chapel and that the Duke of Richmond was to arrange for the burial at a total cost of not more than five hundred pounds.[35]

The sum was adequate but not excessive by the standards of the time, since all the King's servants, and he still had a household of nearly twenty, would expect to be provided with mourning. Ten pounds apiece was allowed for this to the King's principal attendants, seven pounds to the coachman and five to the postillion. Herbert and three others had twenty pounds each.[36]

Richmond was in charge of the funeral. Herbert and Anthony Mildmay, with the assistance of John Joiner, were to convey the body to Windsor on 7th February. Herbert organised this undertaking in such style as to cost no less than two hundred and twenty-nine pounds and five shillings although the journey was made in darkness. The King's coach was hung all in black, and a hundred and thirty pounds was spent, in addition to the allowance already made, on mourning liveries for the servants who followed in four more black-draped coaches. The two troops of horse which accompanied the coach were presumably at the Army's cost, but Herbert spent three pounds on torches—three dozen of them, fifteen shillings in tips for the men who carried the coffin from the coach at Windsor, and another ten shillings on black hangings for the hall of the Dean's house where the body lay briefly before it was carried to the King's own bedchamber.[37]

Richmond arrived in Windsor on the 8th, accompanied by the three other noblemen who had attended the King through the war years—Hertford, Lindsay, and Southampton. Together they visited St. George's Chapel to decide on the place for the burial. Herbert, who would later—when all the others were dead—imply that he had chosen where the King's body should rest, seems to have attended them in a less exalted capacity. It was he who paid the workmen who opened the vault, and was ready with five shillings and sixpence to gratify

Widow Puddifat and Isaac the sexton who unlocked the chapel door.[38]

In the chapel they found that Colonel Whichcot the governor had already had a shallow grave prepared in the chancel on the south side of the Communion table. This was rejected by Richmond and his friends who wished to lay their master in the vault where the bones of earlier kings were known to rest. But it was more than a hundred years since any sovereign had been buried at Windsor and some doubt existed as to the whereabouts of the vault. They found it in the end by stamping on the pavement until they heard a hollow echo. A stone was levered up and on looking into the vault below they saw a large leaden coffin still covered with the rotting fragments of a purple pall. On one side of it was a small coffin, and on the other space for a third. They surmised correctly that here lay King Henry VIII with his third wife Jane Seymour, the mother of his son. There would have been room for Katherine Parr, his sixth wife and surviving widow, on his other side, but she had married again and was buried elsewhere. That left—as their further investigations showed—room for the coffin of King Charles.[39]

It remained now only to decide the inscription which should be attached to it, and Richmond traced on a strip of soft lead the words " King Charles 1648 ", which were accordingly cut out and fixed to the lid.[40] It was said that one of the noblemen wished to look once more at the face of his master, and had the coffin briefly opened before it was soldered down for the last time.[41]

Richmond now saw Colonel Whichcot about the final arrangements for the funeral next day. The governor utterly refused to allow Bishop Juxon to read the service for the dead from the Common Prayer Book because use of the book had been prohibited by Parliament. Richmond argued with some warmth that when Parliament had put the burial arrangements in his hands they had tacitly permitted him to use what service he chose. Whichcot stubbornly refused to interpret their action in this way: he was convinced that Parliament could not have intended to authorise the use " of what so solemnly they had abolished, and therein destroy their own act ". In vain Richmond and his friends tried to persuade him that a dispensation for a single occasion could not be held to " destroy " the act. He would not agree.[42]

The King's body had meanwhile been moved from his bedchamber into St. George's Hall. Shortly before three in the afternoon the sad little procession set out for the chapel. The coffin was carried by soldiers of the garrison, the four corners of the black velvet pall being held by Richmond, Hertford, Southampton and Lindsay. Bishop Juxon came next carrying the Book of Common Prayer, closed. The rest of the King's servants followed. Colonel Whichcot also attended, to make certain that his orders were obeyed. The cold weather had not yet broken. The ground was hard with frost, the air grey and sunless. As they crossed from St. George's Hall to the chapel, snow began to fall on the bare, bowed heads of the mourners, and on the King's black coffin.

Whichcot had suggested that the Bishop should extemporise in the Puritan fashion, but this Juxon would not do. No service was held; no prayers were said aloud. The King's body was lowered in a silence broken only by the muffled movements of the little group about the open vault. There was a momentary hesitation with the rich velvet pall, then Richmond signed that it should be left where it lay over his master's coffin in the darkness.

The Bishop, the King's friends and the King's servants turned away, while Whichcot superintended the replacing of the stones over the burial place,[43] leaving Charles with his strange companion in death: the King who broke the Church of England from the Roman communion to gain political advantage and to satisfy a sensual appetite, and the King who died because he saw in the Anglican faith the best and purest form of the Christian doctrine and the Church militant on earth.

III

On the day of the King's burial a book appeared in London with a title in Greek: Εικὼν Βασιλική. The sub-title explained that it was: *The Pourtraicture of his Sacred Majestie in his Solitudes and Sufferings*. It had not been passed by the censor and it carried no printer's name, though it came from Richard Royston a devoted loyalist who had published several reports and manifestos in the King's favour or purporting to come from him. The book was a series of reflections and religious meditations, interspersed with prayers, on the principal events of the King's reign from the beginning of his troubles to his imprisonment at Carisbrooke. They were accepted instantly as the King's own work by the Royalists, and the little book—in spite of every effort to suppress it—sold in great numbers at a high blackmarket price, and was reprinted thirty times within the year.

Later on a divine named John Gauden would assert that he had composed it, and his elevation to a bishopric by Charles II suggests that the claim was not groundless. Using papers given him by Charles at about the time of the Newport Treaty, he had expanded them to create a remarkably convincing picture of the martyred King. This had been part of a plan known to, and approved by, Charles for countering the many pious books issued by his opponents with something of the same kind written or seeming to be written by him. A first suggested name, *Suspiria Regalia*, The Royal Sighs, was abandoned because it offered too obvious a target to the censors. It seems to have been Jeremy Taylor who suggested that a Greek title, printed in Greek letters, might conceal the character of the book for the first few days of its existence, just long enough for it to capture the public imagination and give the printer time to cover his tracks.[44]

The dispute about the authorship of *Eikon Basilike* is not relevant to its immediate impact at the time of publication.

In 1649 it was accepted with gratitude and reverence by the Royalists as the King's authentic record of his troubles, his patience and his faith. It created the vision of King Charles the Martyr in which they needed to believe.

In *Eikon Basilike* he appears as a man who had made errors and was aware of them, but who sought the guidance of God in leading him through his troubles and would not relinquish his duties and obligations as a Christian King whatever dangers threatened him. The story broke off with the King's imprisonment at Carisbrooke and a series of meditations on death which were remarkably—too remarkably—prophetic of what was ultimately to befall him. He foresaw that he might die " by the hands of my own subjects, a violent, sudden and barbarous death; in the strength of my years; in the midst of my Kingdoms; my friends and loving subjects being helpless spectators; my enemies insolent revilers and triumphers over me, living, dying and dead. . . ." And this was to happen because his enemies, having made a war on him, now tried to wash the blood off their own hands by shedding his. " With them my greatest fault must be, that I would not either destroy myself with the Church and State by my word, or not suffer them to do it unresisted by the Sword; whose covetous ambition no concessions of mine could ever yet, either satisfy, or abate." But he forgave his enemies while condemning the wickedness of their actions, and faced his end with the constancy and serene conviction of a Christian martyr.

The King's Book—as it came to be called—together with the reports of his trial and death still freely circulating created an idea of him which took root, flourished, even made converts. A tearful tribute, *A Handkerchief for Loyale Mourners* was available as early as 2nd February, unlicensed and without the name of author or printer. This " cordial for drooping spirits " frankly compared the King's martyrdom to the Crucifixion.[45] The comparison soon came to be freely made. One devoted Royalist went even further, writing in a private letter on 21st February: " Even the crucifying of our blessed

Saviour, if we consider him only in his human nature, did nothing equal this; His Kingdom not being of this world, and He, although as unjustly condemned, yet judged at a lawful tribunal."[46] The Anglican divine, John Warner, Bishop of Rochester, preaching privately on the Sunday after the King's death, chose for his theme "that most lawless, cruel and hellish murder of God's anointed—Christ the King of the Jews." The real subject of his sermon was very thinly disguised and in the printed version which soon appeared the abbreviation "Ch:" for "Christ" removed any possible doubt.[47]

On all sides stories were circulated, in print and by word of mouth, telling of the miracles wrought by scraps of linen stained with his precious blood. Cures of fits, blindness, and scrofula were freely reported. Some of the miracles were more original. Visitors who had gone to see the caged lions at the Tower—a popular London sight—were astonished at the rage with which the oldest lion roared and bared his teeth at one of their number. The gentleman—not a Royalist—confessed he had bought for a curiosity a piece of rag stained with the royal blood. He offered this to the venerable King of Beasts, who was instantly appeased, fondled the sacred relic with reverent paws, and soon after peacefully passed away.[48]

The comparison of the King's martyrdom to the Passion of Christ led the Royalists to magnify the horrors of his end. He too had to be mocked and spat upon by the brutal soldiery, and stories of these imaginary outrages became articles of faith among the more devoted Cavaliers.[49] Soon even he acquired another Christ-like function and was imagined by Royalist clergy and Royalist poets as an intercessor for his poor deluded people with God the Father.[50]

Pictures of the King were in constant demand, from the cheap woodcuts and engravings to portraits in oils of considerable size. The number of these still in existence after three hundred years indicates the relative freedom with which they were produced and sold. Edward Bower, the painter, had evidently procured himself one of the expensive seats in

Westminster Hall whence he had a good view of the King; from sketches made during the trial he painted—several times and for different patrons—a dignified and moving picture of the King, in his black cloak, with his silver-headed cane, seated in the red chair. This is the last authentic likeness we have of Charles.[51]

Other artists painted or engraved pictures of the King on the scaffold, sometimes bare-headed, holding his cap in his hands and preparing for the final blow; sometimes with his hair already covered, raising his hands and eyes to Heaven in his last prayer. Almost all these pictures are ugly and even grotesque, since the skill of the available artists did not serve to convey the emotions that they, and their patrons, undoubtedly felt.

Some patrons preferred a more allegorical treatment. The frontispiece of *Eikon Basilike* showed the King in royal robes in prayer, with various emblems about him—his own crown and a crown of thorns—while a beam of light from Heaven shines full upon him. This was the type for many engraved—and a few painted—commemorations of the King. Commemorative medals were also struck, some of them abroad, but some apparently in England. The best known had the King's head on one side, and on the other a hammer striking a diamond with the inscription "Inexpugnabilis".[52] Occasionally patrons commissioned trick portraits of the King—so painted that they appeared to represent something different, but revealed the face of King Charles when viewed from some unusual angle. It is a little hard to understand the purpose of this concealment, since no serious attempt seems to have been made to prevent the display of the King's portrait in private houses.

Statues and pictures of the King in public places were a different matter. The King's statue at the New Exchange, the elegant shopping centre of London, was removed. The statue in bronze by Le Sueur in the gardens at Whitehall was sold to a contractor to melt down. He had the forethought to bury it, though he offered to a gullible public a large number of pocket knives said to be hafted in metal from it. When Charles II returned, he was able triumphantly to produce the statue intact.[53] It stands to-day at the top of Whitehall.

The party in power were much more concerned to prevent the circulation of Royalist literature, but although the "resistance" news-sheets along with nearly all the other existing papers were stifled by a new and ferocious censorship act in the autumn,[54] *Eikon Basilike* defied the efforts of the government watchdogs. So did a number of lesser books, ballads, and broad-sheets. Most of these took the form of lamentation over the King's death, sometimes in verse. A few produced coherent political arguments. *The Charge against the King discharged or the King cleared by the People of England* appeared in mid-February without the name of author or printer, but dated "in the first year of England's thralldom".[55] It was a competent and on the whole temperate defence of the King. The equally anonymous *Inquisition after Blood* was a more curious production. The author was concerned to deal with the widely disseminated slander that the King had connived at Buckingham's alleged murder of his father. While he of course denied that Charles had had anything to do with his father's death, he argued that even if it had been so, he had ceased to be answerable to the law as soon as he became King "for the Crown washeth away all spots".[56]

But the most effective propaganda for the King had been permitted by the government itself—the publication of the text of the trial. Before the end of February they had altogether repented of this rash action, and further publication of the trial was forbidden on the lame excuse that imperfect and unauthorised versions were being circulated[57]—though there is no evidence that any of the pamphlets available differed from the texts already authorised by the censor. Very much later in the year, in November, a printer was arrested for defying the ordinance. But he had only re-printed the *Perfect Narrative* originally issued with Mabbott's approval.[58]

Prohibition of further publication came too late to change the impression which the first reports had made on all except the most convinced opponents of the King. These did however launch almost immediately a strong counter-attack. On the same day as *Eikon Basilike*, appeared John Cook's *King Charles his Case or an Appeal to all Rational Men*. This was the substance of the speech for the prosecution which he had not been able to make in Westminster Hall, prefaced by a violent attack on the King and on all who were foolish or wicked enough to defend him. "Blessed God, what ugly sins lodge in their bosoms, that would have had this man to live!"

He rehearsed the political sins that Charles had committed, his "prevarications and bloodguiltiness", and dismissed the theory that the King can do no wrong as "blasphemy against the great God of truth and love, for only God cannot err." As for the courage displayed on the scaffold, both by the King and other Royalists, this was no evidence of virtue, but rather the reverse since it showed that they were concerned to the last with the outward appearances of this sinful world. In conclusion he uttered the unrealistic hope that the mis-guided Cavaliers would change their opinions "and join with honest men in settling the nation upon noble principles of justice, freedom and mercy to the poor."[59]

The theory of popular sovereignty was more lucidly defended by John Milton whose *Tenure of Kings and Magistrates* appeared four days later on 13th February, though it was not until the following October that he completed the answer to *Eikon Basilike* commissioned from him by the government. This was a point by point demolition of the pious thoughts attributed to the King with some scathing comments on the text—including the scornful discovery that one of the prayers had been copied not from a work of piety but from Sir Philip Sidney's *Arcadia*.[60]

But neither the eloquent pamphlets of Milton, the zealous

preaching of Goodwin, Dell, Peter and other Independent ministers, nor the political arguments of numerous republican pamphleteers made much difference to the state of public opinion. Yet the government need not have been greatly troubled by the manifestations of grief and respect for the King; they were not indications of militant Royalism. The general wish for peace led the majority to acquiesce in whatever government was strong enough to maintain itself with the minimum of disturbance. The militant Royalist minority could often count on the sympathy but rarely on the co-operation of their neighbours. Admiring the constancy of the late King, hailing him as a martyr, treasuring pictures and relics of him, propagating tales of his sufferings and of the miracles wrought by his blood, these were not the prelude to action; they were a substitute for it. In spite of the indignation and the widespread sense of outrage, the King's death had exactly the effect that Cromwell and his more perceptive associates had hoped. It destroyed the active centre of Royalism in England. The King had refused to conclude a peace. Peace could now be imposed without him. There was still fighting in Ireland. There might be—there would be—invasion from Scotland. But from the King's death until the bloodless Restoration of his son eleven years later the English Royalists never achieved more than ineffective local conspiracies.[61] Contrary to all predictions King Charles II, abroad and out of the power of his enemies, proved far less dangerous than King Charles I had done as their prisoner at home.

IV

The King's death had been preceded by a hurried Act of Parliament prohibiting the proclamation of a successor. A week later an Act was passed abolishing the monarchy. The Lord Mayor, Abraham Reynardson, refused to publish it in the City. He held out for eight days before he was arrested and taken to the Tower; a few weeks later he was deprived of his office by the Council of State, fined two thousand pounds—to pay which his goods were put up for sale—and sentenced to remain in prison at the pleasure of the government. His gesture was noble though useless, but many of his wealthy fellow citizens had reason to feel grateful to him for one practical precaution he took before his arrest. He burnt all the papers relating to discussion in November about the Newport Treaty when a majority of Aldermen had voted in favour of the negotiations with the King; no one searching his house would find any record of their names.[62]

In various parts of the country it was rumoured that Justices of the Peace would refuse to act because they had always held office under the Crown and now no longer knew by what authority to proceed. But this was mostly talk. In the interests of law and order—in the interests of the Justices themselves, their friends, tenants, and neighbours—the day to day life of the country had to go on. If the greater number of them deplored and in their hearts repudiated the death of the King, few were prepared to take any positive action to dissociate themselves from the new government.

The same was true of more important men than the country Justices. The two Chief Justices had withdrawn during the King's trial, but they had not resigned. They came back, with their lesser colleagues, to administer justice in the interests of the nation as soon as the King was dead. Members of Parliament, too, who had withdrawn in protest at the Purge, or absented themselves during the trial, now began to drift back to their seats.

There was face-saving and hair-splitting of different kinds. A Council of State was appointed by Parliament, consisting of the ablest men in Army, Parliament and the Law. Cromwell was often in the chair. Some of those appointed objected to the oath imposed on them and were permitted to take it in an amended form.[63] Everything, in fact, was done to reassemble the component parts of government and to prevent further changes. If the Royalists had no chance against a régime founded on the strength of the Army, neither had the Levellers. Their strength in the Army itself had dwindled, and their last attempt to gain power by a mutiny in May was rapidly stifled. Lilburne, tried for treason in July, was acquitted amid popular acclaim; nothing could kill his personal popularity but his cause was dead.

Abroad, denunciations of the King-murderers multiplied, while relations with them were maintained. Accounts of the trial, based on the official English versions, appeared in French, Dutch and German, Latin, Italian and even Polish. Controversy about the King's death, at a high intellectual level, raged in Latin between Claude de Saumaise and John Milton. German, Dutch and French pamphleteers published considered and sometimes trenchant denunciations of the English Parricides.[64] Andreas Gryphius, the most distinguished poet in Germany, wrote several epigrams and a tragedy on the subject.[65] In France, St. Amant exhorted the princes of Europe to cease fighting each other and unite to crush the English:

> *Irritez vous, mortels, liguez vous potentats,*
> *Fondez sur cet état avec tous vos états,*
> *Faites partout la paix pour lui faire la guerre!*[66]

In France, itself shaken with civil wars, some of which had an element of popular revolt, a few pamphlets of a different sort appeared, praising "Fairfax et Cromwell" and criticising the King and his friends.[67] But in general feeling in France against the English murderers ran very high. Royalist exiles were frequently insulted in the streets because they were English, and thought therefore to be responsible for the murder of their King.[68]

Yet it was soon clear to any of the King's friends who had hoped for a European rising against the English Republic that no such thing would happen. Cautious attempts of foreign powers to retain contact with the new government for the time being developed insensibly into new diplomatic commitments, the Spaniards being the first to give full recognition.[69] Within a few years European rulers would be exchanging letters of compliment and family portraits with Oliver Cromwell.

Violent action did occur—but it was always that of Royalist exiles. In May 1649 Isaac Dorislaus who had assisted John Cook to draw up the charge against the King, was savagely murdered in The Hague by a party of young Royalist soldiers. A year later Anthony Ascham, sent by the English government as ambassador to Spain, was tracked down and killed by vengeful Royalists.[70] Neither the Dutch nor the Spaniards made much attempt to punish the murderers; in this slackness they revealed their latent sympathy with the Royalists, but for practical purposes they pretended more concern than they felt and maintained their relations with the English government.

The wars which some years later broke out first with Holland and then with Spain had nothing to do with the murder of the King and were no help to the forlorn cause of his son.

Both in England and in Europe the trial and death of Charles provoked expressions of anger, indignation, and horror followed by feeble action, apathetic acquiescence or shamefaced diplomatic approaches to the murderers. Only in Ireland and Scotland was an active struggle carried on against the English Republic for the restoration of Charles II, and in both countries Cromwell's Army triumphed.

Elsewhere, the astonishing thing that had happened, act of heroism, unspeakable crime, or both, had to be faced and dealt with in terms of day-to-day politics. It was the long, inevitable anti-climax.

CHAPTER TEN

EPILOGUE: THE REGICIDES

THE RESTORATION of King Charles II in 1660 brought the day of reckoning for the men who had killed his father. Cromwell, Ireton, and Bradshaw were dead and their bodies had been interred with formal honours in Westminster Abbey, where they had denied burial to the King.

Their coffins were removed under the new government, and on 30th January, 1661, their three corpses were exposed all day on the gallows at Tyburn, a grisly spectacle which pleased the populace and caused even the civilised John Evelyn to praise "the stupendious and inscrutable judgments of God." At sunset the bodies were taken down and buried in the common pit below the gibbet. The heads were cut off and exposed on the top of Westminster Hall.[1]

But most of those who had been concerned with the death of the King were still alive in 1660. Forty-one out of the fifty-nine who had signed the warrant were living. So were others who had been too close to the King's death to hope for mercy from his son—Hugh Peter who had so vehemently preached against him, Daniel Axtell who had commanded the guards in Westminster Hall, Matthew Tomlinson who had been responsible for him as a prisoner from the time he arrived at Windsor until he went to the scaffold, Francis Hacker, Robert Phayre and Hercules Hunks, the three to whom the death warrant had been directed.

Tomlinson had been careful not to sign the death warrant, and now produced the evidence of the Royalist Henry

216

Seymour that the King had spoken well of his civil behaviour. Charles II and his advisers, anxious to avoid unnecessary bloodshed, were willing to accept the excuses of any of their one-time enemies who would co-operate with the new government. Tomlinson secured a full pardon and sealed it by giving evidence against his old comrades in arms, Axtell and Hacker, both of whom were executed. Hercules Hunks bought his dishonoured life in the same way. "That poor wretch Lieutenant Colonel Hunks," said Axtell on his way to death, had been the uncivilest of all to the King, but now gave evidence to hang his fellow soldiers.[2]

Colonel Phayre, whose name on the death warrant might otherwise have cost him his life, had married the daughter of Thomas Herbert. Herbert, who had after all served the King with civility and even, in his last few days, with sympathy, now posed as his devoted attendant during the whole of his captivity. It suited Charles II to accept that claim, although it was well-known to him that Herbert had continued to co-operate with the Army and to receive benefits from Cromwell in Ireland throughout the Interregnum. Herbert was elevated to the rank of baronet, and the crime of Colonel Phayre, his son-in-law, was overlooked on his account.[3]

The new King was free with honours to men of influence who came over to him; he was prepared to accept Richard Ingoldsby's statement that Cromwell had held his hand to make him sign the death warrant. For his services at the Restoration Ingoldsby became a Knight of the Bath.[4] No other Regicide was so fortunate or so astute in changing his allegiance and blotting out his past.

Of the forty-one survivors, fifteen fled the country. Three of these, John Dixwell, Edmund Whalley, and William Goffe, crossed the Atlantic and found safety in New England. Much of the time they were in hiding, but they enjoyed the respect of their Puritan hosts, and no demands by the home government ever caused them to be betrayed. There is a persistent legend in the town of Hadley, Massachusetts, whither William Goffe had fled, that many years later, during an attack from the Indians, the Cromwellian soldier emerged, grave, venerable and authoritative, from a cave in the hills, and rallied his countrymen to victory.[5]

William Cawley, Edmund Ludlow, John Lisle, and the two clerks of the Court, John Phelps and Andrew Broughton, fled to Switzerland. All were received with honour by the Swiss, but Lisle was stabbed and killed by an Irish Royalist one Sunday morning in Lausanne on his way to Church.[6] The other four lived out their lives at Vevey. Ludlow, who lived the longest, hoped that he might return from exile after the Revolution of 1688, but he had no sooner landed in England than a warrant was out for his arrest and he returned, to die at Vevey and be buried with his friends in the parish Church of the quiet little town under the dazzling mountains.[7]

Five others, Michael Livesey, William Say, Daniel Blagrave, Thomas Chaloner and John Hewson took refuge in Germany and the Low Countries, but Thomas Scot, who fled to Brussels, thought better of it, gave himself up to the English ambassador there, and came home to face his trial and death with a resolute mind. "I bless His name that He hath engaged me in a cause not to be repented of," he said as he prepared to die, and repeated: "I say, in a cause not to be repented of."[8]

John Okey, John Barkstead and Miles Corbet, on the other hand, reached Holland only to be tracked down and cold-bloodedly betrayed by an old colleague, Cromwell's scoutmaster George Downing who was working his passage into the King's favour. All three were executed at Tyburn. "They all looked very cheerful," wrote Pepys, "but I hear they all die defending what they did to the King to be just, which is very strange."[9]

Many of the surviving Regicides surrendered. The King had offered mercy, with few exceptions, to those of his opponents who came in within forty days of his return. The Regicides who gave themselves up mostly hoped for mercy— and in some measure received it.

They made a poor showing at their trial. Some, of whom John Downes was the most insistent, pleaded that they had done all they could to prevent the King's death. Others— Robert Tichborne, Vincent Potter, Simon Mayne, Henry Smith and more—submitted that they had been ignorant, weak and misled. Augustine Garland was confronted with the additional charge of spitting in the King's face; he denied this strenuously, and was believed. The one witness against him he described as "an indigent person", which was the polite phrase used for a hired false witness.[10]

The trials of the Regicides were not grossly unfair. The overwhelming reaction in favour of the monarchy made these men scape-goats for the crimes of the nation. In the emotional atmosphere in which the Court proceeded it is surprising that standards of justice and decency were, on the whole, upheld. Vindictive Royalists, personal enemies and dubious suborned witnesses were indeed called to give evidence, but they were not always believed. In the end the only evidence that mattered was that of the prisoners' own handwriting at the foot of the King's death warrant.

Found guilty, the death sentence on these lesser men was remitted to life imprisonment, varied in some cases with an annual humiliating appearance, on the anniversary of the King's death, when they were drawn through the streets on hurdles to Tyburn and back.

A few would neither escape nor surrender; resolved to die for their cause, they waited quietly for arrest. Such were the two Fifth Monarchy men Thomas Harrison and John Carew. There were others who gave themselves up in the faint hope of mercy, but in the end faced trial without cringing. A last minute return of courage came to poor Gregory Clement, who had long been in disgrace with the Puritans. His name had been scratched out of the death warrant when

his conduct had been found unworthy: he had been caught
in bed with his maid-servant. At the Restoration he had
hidden himself in London, but was recognised "by his voice
which was very extraordinary." He at first tried to plead
not guilty, but his dishonoured name was still legible on the
warrant. Seeing there was no way out, he recovered himself,
stood to his convictions, and went to his death regretting
only that he had ever been so weak as to deny the cause he
was proud to die for.[11]

Colonel John Hutchinson, who was respected by all
parties, was persuaded in the interests of his family to profess
repentance for his part in the King's death. He purchased
liberty with an unquiet conscience but was arrested two years
later on suspicion of complicity in plots against Charles II.
He remained in prison, untried, until his death. The government knew what they were about. This fine, proud man,
with a splendid presence, would have won sympathy from
spectators. It was wiser and it appeared more merciful to let
him waste away in obscurity.[12]

Unexpected mercy was shown to Harry Marten. He
made a typical but useless defence at his trial by pointing out
that his name was wrongly spelt in the indictment—so he
could not be the same person as the accused. There was no
doubt of his dangerous republican principles, but he had so
often in the past intervened in Parliament with some sly
good natured quip to help some persecuted Royalist—even
to save one at least from death—that it seemed needlessly
cruel to hang him. He spent the long remainder of his days
a prisoner at Chepstow Castle. Some malicious busybody
seized on his papers and published his love-letters to the
mistress with whom he had lived for many years, thinking to bring him into disrepute. But this sensible, kind
and affectionate correspondence did him more good than
harm.[13]

In the end only nine of the Regicides suffered the hideous
death designed by the law for traitors—the ghastly business

of half hanging followed by disembowelling and quartering while still alive. They were Cromwell's brother-in-law Colonel John Jones, Adrian Scroope, Thomas Harrison, John Carew, Thomas Scot and Gregory Clement, and, after their recapture two years later, Okey, Barkstead and Corbet.

Four who had not signed the death warrant were also executed: John Cook, Hugh Peter, Daniel Axtell and Francis Hacker. Cook had no hope of mercy. This strange, bitter, eccentric man—half visionary, half practical reformer—died with complete faith in God and in the political justice of his cause. Shortly before he died, he wrote to his wife:

> We are not traitors, nor murderers, nor fanatics, but true Christians and good Commonwealth men, fixed and constant to the principles of sanctity, truth, justice and mercy, which the Parliament and Army declared and engaged for; and to that noble principle of preferring the universality, before a particularity, that we sought the public good and would have enfranchised the people, and secured the welfare of the whole groaning creation, if the nation had not more delighted in servitude than in freedom.[14]

No doubt he often addressed his wife in this hortatory vein, but he had gentler words when she came weeping to him before he died. "Let us not part in a shower," he said, "God hath wiped away all tears."[15]

One of his companions in death, Colonel Jones, carried his exultation in martyrdom even higher and said to a friend who stood by, "I could wish thee in the same condition with myself, that thou mightest share with me in my joys."[16]

Of the remaining victims, Axtell and Hacker died with the resigned courage of soldiers; Axtell spoke briefly and with dignity for both of them, because Hacker had little command of words.[17] He had been boorish with the King, but after all his lack of breeding was not his fault.

Hugh Peter was perhaps the most to be pitied. It was true

he had exulted in the King's death, but he had really done nothing to procure it. Bustling about in a state of enthusiasm and preaching ferocious sermons do not amount to murder. At his trial a great deal of play was made with the popular fable that he had himself been the executioner. This he denied. He also denied that he had ordered staples to be fixed on the scaffold to tie down the King if he struggled. But he had no hope of acquittal. He had been too deeply engaged with the Regicides, and he had become to many a symbol of the hypocritical, zealous Saint. His appearance too was against him. Poor "Jack Pudding" Peter was too plump and well-fed, too coarse and red-faced to excite pity. He was also physically a coward, and knew it, and was afraid he would disgrace his cause at the end. Yet he faced his horrible end with unexpected courage and even a certain dignity.[18]

Of all the Regicides it was the fanatic Thomas Harrison who made the deepest impression at his trial and death. He had profited little by the triumph of the Army. He was one of those who abhorred the establishment of Cromwell's government when he had hoped for—and believed in— the thousand year rule of the Saints on earth. But he still believed that the destruction of the King had been according to the will of God whatever came afterwards.

"I do not come to be denying anything," he said to his judges, "but rather to be bringing it forth to the light. . . . It was not a thing done in a corner. I believe the sound of it hath been in most nations. I believe the hearts of some have felt the terrors of that presence of God that was with his servants in those days. . . . I followed not my own judgment; I did what I did, as out of conscience to the Lord. . . . Maybe I might be a little mistaken, but I did it all according to the best of my understanding, desiring to take the revealed will of God in his Holy Scriptures as a guide to me." He had spoken for some time before the judge interrupted him: "Know you where you are, Sir, you are in an assembly of

Christians; will you make God the author of your treasons and murders?"

Harrison offered a worldly authority for the King's trial as well as a Heavenly one—the Parliament of England and the Commons of England. He offered a material reason for the King's execution—his making war on his people and shedding their blood. He knew that neither would be accepted and had no hope of anything but the death sentence. At least he had spoken out; he had not denied the act or weakened in his conviction that the "presence of God was with his servants in those days."

He went to his death with equanimity, the first of the Regicides to suffer. The crowd was hostile and derisive. "Where is your Good Old Cause now?" they jeered. "Here in my bosom," said Harrison, "and I shall seal it with my blood." His courage astonished and impressed the onlookers, and a story later went round among the missionary prophets who still had their following in the poorer streets of London that he would shortly rise again, to judge his judges, and bring in the Rule of the Saints on earth.[19]

But, gradually, the fierce fanaticism went underground; the political shock was absorbed. The King's death was seen to be more startling in itself than in its consequences. In fifty years the fate of King Charles would no longer be remembered by any as a part of their living experience; with later generations the horror, excitement, exultation or anguish of those January days would become the stuff of political argument or dramatic imagination.

Other men with other creeds and other interests would adapt the story to their political arguments, their moral or religious needs, would venerate King Charles or condemn him, would admire the Regicides or execrate them. In other Revolutions, in other Civil Wars the King's name and Cromwell's would become catchwords for parties and doctrines that neither the King nor Cromwell would have understood. The most real thing in their situation—the guidance of God—was to become the least real to ensuing generations.

"This man against whom the Lord hath witnessed", Cromwell had said in justification of the act. But the King had read the will of the Almighty in a different sense and had been equally sure that he had "a just cause and a Gracious God".

THE END

BIBLIOGRAPHICAL NOTE

NOTES AND REFERENCES

INDEX

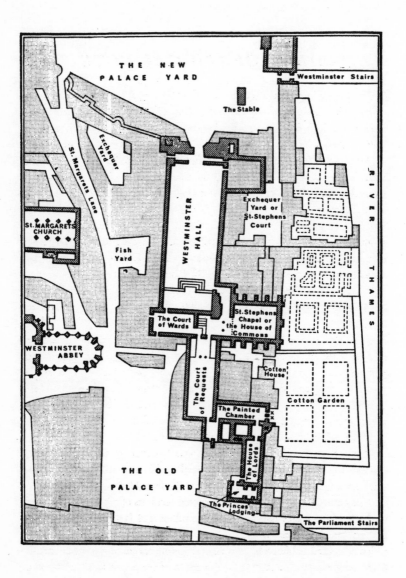

BIBLIOGRAPHICAL NOTE

Texts of the King's trial are to be found in Nalson, *A true copy of the journal of the high court of justice for the trial of King Charles I* (1684); *State Trials* volume IV; J. G. Muddiman, *Trial of King Charles the First* (1928); and the Folio Society's *Trial of Charles I*, edited by Roger Lockyer (1959).

John Nalson, a devoted Royalist and Anglican, published the minutes made by the Clerk, John Phelps, of the meetings of the High Court in the Painted Chamber and in Westminster Hall. As these are mere summaries in so far as the trial is concerned, Nalson interspersed them with fuller reports taken from contemporary printed sources and added numerous pious comments of his own. The result is a confusing and rather irritating text, but valuable because the minutes of Phelps are the only day-to-day account we have of what went on in the Painted Chamber.

Volume IV of *State Trials* reprints Nalson's text, and gives also the text of *A Perfect Narrative*, the main account authorised by Gilbert Mabbott in 1649.

J. G. Muddiman, who edited the trial for the *Famous British Trials* series in 1928, had considerable and detailed knowledge of the newspapers and pamphlet literature of the period; he used as a basic text a document in the Public Record Office (see below) which he called "Bradshaw's Journal" and filled out the picture with interpolations from other sources. His work, which contains much of interest, is marred by the violent Royalist prejudice which frequently obscures his judgement.

The attractive volume edited by Roger Lockyer for the Folio Society contains the trial as printed by Rushworth, who used *A Perfect Narrative*; this is accompanied by the relevant part of Thomas Herbert's *Memoirs*.

The nature of the contemporary printed accounts of the trial is described in this book on pages 123-7. By far the fullest is *A Perfect Narrative* which is often referred to as "Mabbott's account", because he appears not only to have licensed it but to have been responsible for editing it. The initials C.W. which appear on it are probably those of the principal taker of notes, but this shadowy figure does not seem to be otherwise identifiable. In some places *A Perfect Narrative* can be supplemented by comparison with other contemporary sources.

Besides the printed sources, two MS sources exist—the official text of the minutes of John Phelps now in the House of Lords (see page 233) and a MS in book form among the State Papers for 1649 at the Public Record Office. This appears to be the record of the trial as prepared for presentation to Parliament. The Public Record Office document contains both the minutes made by Phelps of the meetings in the Painted Chamber and the full record of the trial. The text has been carelessly copied in places, so that some paragraphs are duplicated; some amendments have also been made to Bradshaw's side of the business; one of his most inept replies to the King (see page 140) has, for example, been quietly omitted. For this reason I regard this MS text as evidently later and slightly less reliable than the printed *Perfect Narrative* of Mabbott.

The best-known engraving of the trial is the frontispiece to Nalson's book (1684). It is very clear and handsome but was of course engraved many years after the King's death. I have preferred to reproduce a smaller and less elaborate but to my mind more interesting engraving. The effect of crowding and the makeshift appearance of the spectators' galleries with other details suggest to me that this was probably done from sketches made in the Hall while the trial was actually in progress.

It should perhaps be added that the English calendar was still unreformed. The month date in England was ten days behind the Continent, and the year was reckoned from March 25th. Thus King Charles, by European dating, died on February 9th, 1649, but by English dating on January 30th, 1648. I have followed the usual historian's custom of accepting the English month date but regarding the year as beginning on January 1st. (To make confusion worse, the English *did* celebrate New Year's Day on January 1st, though most of them dated their letters by the old year for another three months.) It will be noticed on page 204, that 1648—not 1649— was the date put on the King's coffin.   C.V.W.

NOTES AND REFERENCES

Note: Where a contemporary pamphlet or tract is followed by a reference in parentheses—e.g. (E.537.54)—this identifies the relevant volume of the Thomason Tracts in the British Museum.

CHAPTER ONE

1. *A Plea for the King and Kingdom.* London, November 1648. This pamphlet was written by the editor of the clandestine Royalist newspaper *Mercurius Pragmaticus*, probably at this time Marchamont Nedham, a fluent and at times a brilliant polemical writer who in the course of the Civil War had served many masters.

2. Nalson, *A true copy of the journal of the high court of justice for the trial of King Charles I.* London, 1684, p. 118.

3. John Cook, *King Charles, his Case or an Appeal to all Rational Men concerning his Tryall,* London, February, 1649.

4. Abbott, *Writings and Speeches of Oliver Cromwell.* Cambridge, Mass., 1937, I. p. 719.

5. William Allen, *A Faithful Memorial, in Somers Tracts.* VI, p. 501.

6. John Canne, *The Golden Rule or Justice Advanced,* London. 1649.

CHAPTER TWO

1. *The Whole Works of James Ussher,* ed. Elrington, Dublin, 1864, XIII, pp. 357, 361; *A Message from the Isle of Wight,* London, 1648, (E.473.32).

2. *The Sermons of John Donne,* ed. Simpson and Potter, VI, Sermon XII; Fuller, *Church History,* ed. J. S. Brewer, Oxford, 1845, VI, p. 26.

3. Warwick, *Memoires of the Reign of King Charles I,* 3rd edition, London, 1703, p. 329.

4. J. A. Gotch, *Architectural Review,* June, 1912; *Herbert's Narrative* in Stevenson, *Charles I in Captivity,* London, 1927, pp. 90-1.

5. Clarendon, *History of the Great Rebellion,* IX, 194; *Kingdom's Weekly Intelligence,* Dec. 26-Jan. 2.

6. Peck, *Desiderata Curiosa,* London, 1779, II, p. 392.

7. *Clarendon State Papers,* II, pp. 425ff.

8. Wagstaffe, *A Vindication of King Charles the Martyr,* London, 1711, Appendix pp. 152ff.

9. *Clarendon State Papers,* II, p. 442; Carte, *Life of James Duke of Ormonde,* Oxford, V, p. 25.

10. Warwick, p. 326.

11. *Clarendon State Papers,* II, pp. 430-1.

12. Petition of Ireton's regiment to the Lord General, 1648 (E.468.18).

13. E. Walker, *Historical Discourses,* London, 1705, pp. 14, 24; *The Moderate,* Oct. 31-Nov. 7 and Nov. 14-21; *The True Informer,* Oct. 7-Nov. 8; *Mercurius Militaris,* Nov. 1-8.

14. Abbott, *Writings and Speeches of Oliver Cromwell,* Harvard, 1939, seq., IV, p. 473.

15. Ibid, I, pp. 676-8.

16. Two versions of the Northern Army's declaration occur in the Thomason collection (E.472.6 and 20). Cromwell's presence is implied in the second of these.

17. *The Clarke Papers,* ed. C. H. Firth, London, 1894, II, p. 260 (Appendix B, Lilburne, *Legal Fundamental Liberties*).

18. Several of the Army petitions emphasise their unwilling oppression of the people: e.g. the petition of Fleetwood's regiment (E.470.32).

19. *The Representations of the General Council of the Army*, (E.473.3,5); Gardiner, IV, pp. 236-7, 242.

20. The letter also signed by Harrison, Desborough and Grosvenor, is quoted *in extenso* in Ramsey, *Henry Ireton*, London, 1949, p. 124.

21. *His Majesty's Declaration of November 17th from the Isle of Wight*, (E.473.5); Wagstaffe, p. 163; *Calendar of State Papers, Domestic Series, 1648-9*, pp. 323-4; *Old Parliamentary History*, XVIII, pp. 152, 240. The King suggested that the Army should lay their demands before Parliament, and that he would offer a general pardon and oblivion. This was in effect a rejection, barbed with irony, as Parliament would be hostile to the Army's demands and an act of oblivion indicated that he thought they stood in need of his pardon.

22. The full text of the Remonstrance, with the covering letter, is given in *Old Parliamentary History*, XVIII, pp. 160-238.

23. Ibid, p. 239; *Mercurius Pragmaticus*, Nov. 21-28.

24. For several of these petitions see the regiments see Thomason Tracts E.473. Between November 21st and 24th the heads of the Remonstrance were printed in *The Moderate* (Nov. 21st); *The Perfect Weekly Account* (Nov. 22nd); *Packets of Letters* (Nov. 22nd); *The Moderate Intelligencer* (Nov. 23rd); *Perfect Occurrences* (Nov. 24th) and a day or two later in *The Kingdom's Weekly Intelligencer* and *A Perfect Diurnall*. *The Moderate* also advertised a separate issue of the text of the Remonstrance. For the character of the London Press see Chapter II.

25. *Clarendon State Papers*, II, pp. 449, 453.

26. *Old Parliamentary History*, XVIII, p. 240.

27. *Abbott*, I, pp. 696-9

28. *Clarke Papers*, II, p. 53.

29. Royston, *Works of Charles I*, p. 137.

30. Ibid, p. 136; *A Royalist's Notebook* (Sir John Oglander) ed. F. Bamford, London, 1936, p. 126.

31. N. Ferne, *A Sermon preached before his Majesty*, (E.473.38).

32. Cooke's and Firebrace's narratives in Stevenson, *Charles I in Captivity*, pp. 145ff.

33. Cooke's and Firebrace's narratives, in Stevenson, pp. 143, 158; *Perfect Occurrences*, Dec. 1-8; *The Moderate*, Nov. 28-Dec. 5.

34. F. Peck, *Desiderata Curiosa*, London, 1779, II, p. 411.

35. Herbert's narrative in Stevenson, p. 165.

36. *Clarke Papers*, II, p. 64.

37. *Commons Journals*, Dec. 16.

38. Abbott, I, pp. 630-1.

39. *Clarke Papers*, II, p. 58; *Declaration of the Lord General*, (E.474.13).

40. *Commons Journals*, Dec. 1; Bodleian Library, *Clarendon MSS*, vol. XXXIV, No. 2964, Lawrans to Nicholas, Dec. 4.

41. *Commons Journals*, Dec. 1.

42. Ibid, Dec. 4; *The Moderate*, Nov. 28-Dec. 5.

43. *Clarendon MSS*, Bodleian Library, vol. XXXIV, No. 2964, Lawrans to Nicholas Dec. 4.

44. *Commons Journals*, Dec. 5; *Old Parliamentary History*, XVIII, pp. 302-447; Ludlow, p. 208; *Mercurius Pragmaticus*, Dec. 5-12.

45. C. Walker, *History of Independency*, London, 1649, pp. 29-31; Ludlow, I, pp. 209-10; *Mercurius Pragmaticus*, Dec. 5-12.

46. *The Moderate*, Dec. 5-12; *The Staffe set at the Parliament's owne Door*, (E.475.29).

47. *Clarke Papers*, II, p. 137; Collins, *Historical Collections*, London, 1752, p. 200; *Commons Journals*, Dec. 6; *The Moderate*, Dec. 5-12; *Mercurius Elencticus*, Dec. 5-12; *The Humble Proposals of the Lord Fairfax*, (E. 475.25); *Parliament*

under the Power of the Sword, (E.476.I).

48. Ludlow, *Memoirs,* ed. C. H. Firth, Oxford, 1894, I, pp. 211-12.

49. *Mercurius Pragmaticus,* Dec. 5-12.

50. *Military Intelligencer,* Dec. 7-14; *A declaration Concerning a supply of Bedding* (E.475.40).

51. *Commons Journals,* Dec. 13; *Clarke Papers* II, pp. 132-3, 272.

CHAPTER THREE

1. *Clarendon State Papers,* II, p. 249.

2. *Rump Songs,* London, 1874, I, pp. 291-2.

3. *Aubrey's Brief Lives,* ed. Oliver Lawson Dick, London, 1949, p. 63.

4. Thorold Rogers, *History of Agriculture and Prices,* Oxford, 1887, V. pp. 826-7; Ernle, *English Farming, Past and Present,* ed. A. D. Hall, London, 1936, p. 448; *A Royalist's Notebook* (Sir John Oglander) pp. 121-2.

5. Frank, *Beginnings of the English Newspaper,* Cambridge, Mass., 1962, p. 146.

6. Ibid, p. 25.

7. Ibid, p. 150.

8. Ibid, pp. 152-8; see also Clyde, *The Struggle for the Freedom of the Press,* Oxford, 1934, pp. 145-6.

9. Frank, pp. 160-4; Clyde, pp. 158-9.

10. *The Moderate,* Jan. 2-9.

11. Bodleian Library, *Clarendon MSS,* Vol. XXXIV, No. 2973 (*Clarendon State Papers,* II, p. xix) Lawrans to Nicholas, Dec. 26; the printed version of this letter describes the injury inflicted on Brereton as "cudgelladoes," and this word has been written by a later hand above the original word in the MS which is quite clearly "cuchilladoes"—a Spanish word from "cuchillo" a knife—and meaning cuts or thrusts, not, as the amendment suggests, blows with a stick.

12. For Prynne and Walker's pamphlets see Thomason Tracts E.537.

See also C. Walker, *Anarchia Anglicana* or *The History of Independency,* the second part, 1649, p. 32 for the earliest use of the term "Rump."

13. *The Moderate,* Jan. 9-16 cites Calamy, Burgess, and "Jenkings" as very active opponents; see also Baxter, *Reliquiae,* London, 1696, Part I, p. 67.

14. Bodleian Library, Clarendon MSS, Vol. XXXIV, No. 2964, Lawrans to Hyde, 4 Dec, 1648.

15. *Perfect Weekly Account,* Dec. 27-Jan. 3; *Perfect Diurnall,* Dec. 25-Jan. 1. The sermon entitled "God's Anatomy upon Man's Heart" was printed by Watson (E.536.7) but with the offensive matter removed.

16. *A Declaration Collected,* etc. Dec. 13-20.

17. Goodwin, *Right and Might Well Met* (E.536.28).

18. William Sedgwick, *A Letter to Fairfax,* 1648 (E.536.16); see also the same author's *Justice upon the Armie* (E.475.34).

19. Lilburne, *Legal Fundamental Liberties,* as printed in Appendix to the *Clarke Papers,* II, pp. 255, 256-8.

20. Ibid, pp. 259-62.

CHAPTER FOUR

1. *Perfect Occurrences,* Dec. 8-15; *Heads of a Diary,* Dec. 20-7.

2. *His Majesty's Declaration concerning the Treaty,* (E.476.13): some versions give the phrase as "sincere and absolute," but in this earliest version the word is "serene."

3. Herbert's *Narrative* in Stevenson, p. 170.

4. *The Moderate,* Dec. 19-26; Whitelocke, *Memorials,* London, 1682, p. 359.

5. *Clarke Papers,* p. 417.

6. *Perfect Occurrences,* Dec. 23-30; Herbert in Stevenson, pp. 173-5. I have on the whole preferred the account of what was said by Harrison in *Perfect Occurrences* to

that given by the rather unreliable Herbert. Admittedly Henry Walker, the editor of *Perfect Occurrences*, may have invented his version or altered the report he had of it. But the words he attributes to Harrison sound to me more like his laconic style than Herbert's version.

7. *Perfect Occurrences*, Dec. 23-30.
8. *The Visible Vengeance*, (E.476.40).
9. *Perfect Occurrences*, Dec. 23-30; the story is also given with slightly different details in other sources, including Clarendon, and by Newburgh himself at Harrison's trial, *State Trials*, v, p. 1020.
10. *Terrible and Bloody News from Windsor*, (E.536.1).
11. *Mercurius Melancolicus*, Dec. 25-Jan. 1; *Mercurius Pragmaticus*, Dec. 12-19; *Moderate Intelligencer*, Dec. 19-26; Burnet, *Memoirs of the Lives of the Dukes of Hamilton*, London, 1679, p. 379.
12. Burnet, *loc. cit.*
13. *Perfect Occurrences*, Dec. 23-30.
14. The King had made this statement about Strafford as early as 1645. See Wedgwood, *The King's War*, p. 402.
15. Bodleian Library, *Clarendon MSS*, Vol. xxxiv, No. 2977, Lawrans to Nicholas, Dec. 18; No. 2968 Lawrans to Nicholas, Dec. 21.
16. *Mercurius Pragmaticus*, Dec. 19-25.
17. *Kingdom's Weekly Intelligencer*, Dec. 26-Jan. 2; *Heads of a Diary*, Dec. 26-Jan. 2.
18. *Perfect Weekly Account*, Dec. 27-Jan. 3; *Perfect Occurrences*, Dec. 23-30, and Dec. 29-Jan. 5.
19. *Clarke Papers*, ii, pp. 140-6.
20. Whitelocke, p. 359; Rushworth, iv, ii, p. 1376; Herbert's *Narrative* in Stevenson, p. 185. Herbert confuses dates and details but is probably trustworthy in his account of the King's behaviour.
21. *Clarke Papers*, ii, pp. 141, 267-8; *Commons Journals*, Dec. 15.
22. *Perfect Occurrences*, Dec. 29-Jan. 5.

Apart from these letters from the Queen it would appear from the King's last letter in Wagstaffe, dated Dec. 30, that an occasional message did still reach him from loyal friends. For Herbert's character and conduct see the interesting articles by Norman Mackenzie in *The Bulletin for the Institute of Historical Research*, xxix, to which I am much indebted.

23. *Kingdom's Weekly Intelligencer*, Dec. 26-Jan. 2.
24. *Mercurius Pragmaticus*, Dec. 19-26.
25. Lilburne, *Foundations of Freedom*, (E.476.26).
26. *Clarke Papers*, pp. 73 ff; *Diary and Correspondence of John Evelyn*, ed. Bray, London, 1859, iii, p. 34.
27. *Clarke Papers*, ii, pp. 262-6; Woodhouse, *Puritanism and Liberty*, London, 1952, pp. 129ff, 472ff; *A Plea for Common Right*, (E.536.22).
28. Lilburne, *A Preparative to a Hue and Cry after Sir Arthur Haslerig* (E.573.16); *Commons Journals*, Dec. 18.
29. Clement Walker, *History of Independency*, London, 1660, p. 48; *Commons Journals*, Dec. 20.
30. Bodleian Library, *Clarendon MSS*, Vol. xxxiv, No. 2968, Lawrans to Nicholas, Dec. 21; *Mercurius Pragmaticus*, Dec. 26-Jan. 9; *Mercurius Melancolicus*, Dec. 25-Jan. 1; Gardiner, x, pp. 281-2, 285-6, quoting P.R.O. Transcripts of Grignan's despatches. Gardiner accepts the story of an offer to Charles by way of Denbigh, and links it to Cromwell's supposed opposition to the King's death, but I cannot see that the evidence cited adds up to more than rumour. It is surely incredible that if Denbigh had a message he failed to convey it to the King, which is Grignan's suggestion. Rumours that Cromwell would save the King were frequent and were nearly all Royalist wishful-thinking. Cromwell's hesitations seem

to be more coherently explicable as arising from his desire to strengthen the case against the King.

31. Burnet, *Lives of the Dukes of Hamilton*, p. 379.

32. Whitelocke, *Memorials*, pp. 357-8 under dates Dec. 18, 19, 21, 22, 23.

33. Ibid, p. 359; *Commons Journals*, Dec. 23 and 26.

34. Abbott, I, p. 719.

35. *Clarke Papers*, II, pp. 150-1; Elizabeth Pool, *A Vision*, Jan., 1649 (E.537.24).

36. Blencowe, *Sidney Papers*, London, 1825, p. 45.

37. Firth and Rait, *Acts and Ordinances*, London, 1911, I, pp. 1252-3.

38. *Commons Journals*, Jan. 1.

39. *Kingdom's Weekly Intelligencer*, Jan. 2-9; the account is quoted in full in Leslie Hotson, *The Commonwealth Stage*, London, 1928.

40. *Lords' Journals*, Jan. 2; Blencowe, p. 47; *Old Parliamentary History*, XVIII, pp. 481-2; C. Walker, p. 55.

41. *Mercurius Pragmaticus*, Dec. 26-Jan. 9.

42. *Commons Journals*, Jan. 3.

43. C. Walker, *First Part of the History of Independency*, p. 171; Brunton and Pennington, *Members of the Long Parliament*, p. 49; Aylmer, *The King's Servants*, p. 368-9 points out that there is evidence that Holland had been out of sympathy with the King's policy as early as 1639.

44. Lucy Hutchinson, *Memoirs of Colonel Hutchinson*, ed. Firth, London, 1906, p. 272.

45. Ludlow, I, p. 203.

46. For the deaths of Carew, Scot, and Harrison see chapter X.

47. Goodwin, *Right and Might Well Met*, Jan., 1649, p. 31.

48. W. Haller, *Liberty and Reformation*, London, 1955, pp. 346-7.

49. *Rectifying Principles* (E.537.5).

50. *Commons Journals*, Jan. 4; Manley, *History of the Rebellion*, London, 1691, p. 190 emphasises the

necessity of this move in order to dissolve the traditional allegiance to the King.

51. *Mercurius Melancolicus*, Jan. 1-8.

52. *Clarke Papers*, II, pp. 163-9.

53. *The Petition of the Jewes*, Jan., 1649 (E.537.17).

54. Sedgwick, *An Appeal*, 1648; Stephens, *A Letter of Advice*, 1648; (E.536.16,38).

55. *Sidney Papers*, ed. Blencowe, p. 48.

56. Whitelocke, p. 361.

57. Guizot, *Oliver Cromwell*, trans. Scobie, London, 1854, I, pp. 371-3.

58. *Thurloe State Papers*, I, pp. 109-11.

59. *Commons Journals*, Jan. 6; Firth and Rait, I, pp. 1253-5.

60. *Lucifer's Lifeguard*, London, 1660.

61. *Perfect Occurrences*, Jan. 5-12.

CHAPTER FIVE

1. Carte, *Letters*, I, pp. 201-2.

2. *Kingdom's Weekly Intelligencer*, Jan. 1-9.

3. Dictionary of National Biography; articles on Henry Rolle and John Wilde.

4. *The Case of Oliver St. John*, London, 1660. In view of my contention that Cromwell had wished to avoid the forcible purging of Parliament, it is interesting that his two most active friends and colleagues, St. John and Vane, both withdrew on account of the Purge.

5. *Commons Journals*, Jan. 9; Whitelocke, p. 362; *Mercurius Pragmaticus*, Dec. 26-Jan. 9.

6. The printed list of the High Court of Justice in the Thomason Collection (669.f.13. No. 68) is dated January 11th in Thomason's handwriting.

7. The background of all the men named to serve on the Court of Justice would repay investigation. My necessarily brief comments are chiefly drawn from biographical material in Brunton and Pennington, *Members of the Long*

Parliament, Keeler, *The Long Parliament*, the relevant articles in the *D.N.B.* and some county histories of the Civil War.

8. Haslerig in 1660 made much of his absence from the trial, but he had, in the intervening years, expressed an unqualified approval. See *Brunton's Parliamentary Diary*, ed. Rutt, London, 1828, III, pp. 96, 99.

9. J. Nalson, *A True Copy of the Journal of the High Court of Justice for the Trial of King Charles I*, London, 1684. The appendix gives a useful table showing the attendance record of the members of the Court.

10. Ludlow, I, p. 208; see also Vane's evidence at his trial in *State Trials*, VI, p. 164.

11. See Nalson, *Appendix;* also Brunton and Pennington for Bond and Lowry.

12. Blencowe, p. 237.

13. See M. F. Keeler, pp. 101-2 for Baynton; Aubrey, ed. Dick, p. 61 for Chaloner. The articles in the D.N.B. on the others give the relevant references.

14. See their evidence in *State Trials*, V, pp. 1213, 1218-19; Downes, *A Humble Representation*, London, 1660; Simon Mayne, *Considerations, Somers Tracts*, Third Collection, II, London, 1751, pp. 196-7.

15. *Memoirs of Colonel Hutchinson*, p. 271.

16. *State Trials*, p. 1213.

17. Nalson, p. 5. Nalson's *Trial of Charles I* contains—somewhat confusingly set out—the whole of the minutes of John Phelps. The MS of these minutes as finally put on record and preserved is in the possession of the House of Lords. I have checked it against Nalson's version which contains a few minor verbal variations. See *Manuscripts of the House of Lords*, New Series, ed. M. F. Bond, XI, London, 1962, p. 476.

18. H. M. Colvin, *The History of the King's Works*, London, 1962, I, pp. 497-501. See also *Vetusta Monumenta*, VI, London 1842; and the articles by I. M. Cooper in the *Journal of the British Archaeological Association*, 1938-9. For the tapestries, *Harleian MSS* 4898.

19. Evelyn, *Diary*, ed. E. S. de Beer, II, p. 547. Evelyn gives the date as January 17th when the morning was given up to planning the arrangement of Westminster Hall. The presence of Peter is not recorded in the minutes but is perfectly possible.

20. *D.N.B.* John Burley.

21. *D.N.B.* Isaac Dorislaus.

22. *D.N.B.* John Cook.

23. J. Cook, *Unum Necessarium*, London, 1648.

24. *Perfect Occurrences*, Jan. 2-12; A *Proclamation for the Trial of the King*, (E.537.34); Nalson, pp. 6-8.

25. *Clarendon State Papers*, II, p. li. It is impossible not to agree with Dean Swift's brief comment on the indecisions of Fairfax set down in Burnet, *History of His Own Time*— "Fairfax had hardly common sense." (Burnet, I, p. 80 n).

26. *Clarendon State Papers*, II, p. li.

27. Nalson, p. 11.

28. Ibid, p. 9.

29. J. Cook, *The Case Against King Charles*, London, 1649, pp. 1, 2, 38.

30. Nalson, pp. 9, 13, 16.

31. Ibid, pp. 14-15.

32. Cook mentions threats to his life in *The Case Against King Charles*, p. 41, and Bradshaw's famous hat can be seen to this day in the Ashmolean Museum at Oxford.

33. *A serious and faithfull Representation . . . of Ministers of the Gospel*, London, January 1st, 1648, (E.538.25).

34. John Geree, *Katadynastes: Might Overcoming Right*, London, 1649, (E.538.24).

35. See chapter II, p. 59.

36. *Commons Journals*, Jan. 15; *The*

Moderate, Jan. 9-16; *A Petition of the Common Council of London*, London, 1649.

37. *Clarke Papers*, II, pp. 178, 181-2; *Old Parliamentary History*, XVIII, pp. 519 ff.

38. Nalson, pp. 18-19, 22; *Clarke Papers*, II, pp. 186-7.

39. Nalson, pp. 16, 20, 23, 25.

40. *A Declaration and Protestation of William Prynne and Clement Walker against the present proceedings of the Army*, Jan. 19th 1649. *Thomason Tracts* 669.f.13(74).

41. The petition is in *Thomason Tracts*, 669.f.13(75); *Commons Journals*, Jan. 18.

42. *Old Parliamentary History*, XVII, pp. 503ff. The declaration is also in the *Thomason Tracts*, B.538.23.

43. Herbert's *Narrative* from Stevenson, *op. cit.*, pp. 176-80. Though Herbert is inaccurate in many details and deceitful in others, I see no reason to doubt the truth of his trivial recollections about the lost seal, the accidental fire, or the King's attendance at the chapel. Peter complained later that the King had refused to hear him preach, and it seems most probable that Peter's suggestion and the King's refusal would have occurred at Windsor.

44. Herbert, p. 180.

45. Ibid, p. 180-1; *State Trials*, v, p. 1125.

46. Ibid, p. 1126.

CHAPTER SIX

1. Nalson, p. 24.

2. *Commons Journals*, Jan. 20; see also *Perfect Diurnall*, Jan. 19-22.

3. See William Haller, *Liberty and Reformation in the Puritan Revolution*, New York, 1955, p. 334.

4. Blencowe, p. 52.

5. *Diaries and Letters of Philip Henry, 1631-1696*, ed. Matthew Henry Lee, London, 1882, p. 12.

6. *Perfect Weekly Account*, Jan. 17-24.

7. Herbert's *Narrative* in Stevenson, p. 188; evidence at the trial of Hacker, *State Trials*, v. p. 1179. Herbert says the soldiers were *not* in the same room, but several contemporary news-sheets (e.g. *Perfect Occurrences*, Jan. 18-25) assert that they were; so also Clarendon. The bad behaviour of the soldiers was emphasised by the Royalists and denied by the Army. Hunks, who gave evidence against his old comrades, Hacker and Axtell, in 1660 asserted that they had let the troops behave badly. Axtell and Hacker both implied on the scaffold that Hunks had borne false witness, and Axtell is reported as saying that Hunks was more uncivil to the King than anyone. *State Trials*, v, pp. 1289-90. None of this evidence is worth much, but I am inclined to think that the rude behaviour of the soldiers has been somewhat exaggerated. The maintenance of a reasonable civility towards the prisoner was the evident intention of Cromwell and the other leaders.

8. *State Trials*, v, p. 1201.

9. Nalson, p. 25.

10. Ibid, appendix.

11. The watchers sitting on the window-sills are depicted in the engraving reproduced to face p. 180 which I believe to have been done from sketches made on the spot. For Axtell's occasional exclusion of some spectators or inclusion of others see *State Trials*, v, p. 1152.

12. Frank, p. 175; for Jennings's career as messenger and scout master see *Perfect Occurrences*, Apr. 16-23, 1647.

13. *The King's Tryal*, (B.538.26).

14. Clement Walker, *History of Independency*, 1661 edition, p. 98.

15. *State Trials*, v, pp. 1018-19 and elsewhere.

16. I shall deal with the three principal interruptions—two by Lady Fair-

fax and one by John Downes—as they arise. I am not attempting to whitewash the licensers who were perfectly capable of suppressing evidence, but there is no *contemporary* reference even in private letters or by Royalists to this intervention of Lady Fairfax, and I think it is therefore a justifiable assumption that it was not very noticeable.

17. See plate to face p. 180.

18. *Clarendon* XI, 235 gives the shorter version; the longer and less convincing version is interpolated into Rushworth, p. 1395. A woman's voice would not carry very far in Westminster Hall, and Phelps was—it can safely be assumed—reading fast partly to get the roll-call over before the King came but still more to cover up the fact that less than half the Commissioners were present. At the trial of Axtell in 1660 there was considerable confusion as to the time, nature, and even the *day* on which the famous interruptions of Lady Fairfax were made. See *State Trials*, V, pp. 1152-3.

19. *The King's Tryal*, (E.538.26).

20. *State Trials*, V, p. 1153, where his name is given as "Jeonar." For his previous career see Fuller, *Church History*, VI, p. 349.

21. All quotations and incidents at the trial are from Mabbott's *Perfect Narrative* unless otherwise stated. The earlier versions are best for Jan. 20, 22, 23, but the later edition is best for Jan. 27. See bibliographical note.

22. *The King's Tryal.*

23. *The Moderate*, Jan. 16-23.

24. Nalson, pp. 29-32.

25. *Perfect Weekly Account*, Jan. 17-24.

26. Bodleian Library, *Clarendon MSS*, No. 3003, Lawrans to Nicholas, Jan. 26.

27. *The King's Tryal*, (E.538.26). The editor of this account apologises for inadequate reporting at this point because of the disturbance caused by the crowding in of new spectators. H. G. Muddiman in his edition of the Trial suggests that this disturbance to his text in reality masks the famous interruption of Lady Fairfax and the branding of Anna de Lyle. After careful comparison of the evidence I have come to the conclusion that the more famous of the two interruptions of Lady Fairfax did not occur until January 27th. As for the extraordinary story of the branding of Lady de Lyle I find it wholly unconvincing. The evidence is contained in letters to Sancroft (Harleian MSS 3784, Nos. 270, 271, 273, 287). Anna de Lyle asserted in 1666—when she was in prison for debt after failing to pay damages to a woman in whose face she had smashed a glass of wine—that she had raised her voice on the King's behalf and had been branded in open Court by Colonel Hewson. No explanation was offered for the remarkable handiness of a red-hot iron in Court. Sancroft, to whom the story was told, sent the poor woman some money but clearly did not believe her. Had the story been true it could not have failed to come out at the trials of the Regicides.

28. In the *Perfect Narrative* the King is described as looking at the *sword*. Nalson, p. 37, gives his words, from the House of Lords MS, as "I do not fear that bill," meaning the charge.

29. *Perfect Narrative.*

30. The King's reasons for not answering the Court (printed illicitly before Feb. 5 and re-printed both in Nalson, Rushworth, and *State Trials*) were clearly written *before* January 22nd when he, unavailingly, tried to utter them. On Sunday he was at prayers most of the day. The obvious time for

him to prepare this paper was the evening of the 20th when he would have all his impressions fresh in his mind. The illicit version is in the Thomason Collection in the British Museum, numbered 669.f.13/81. Charles may have smuggled it out by way of Bishop Juxon. The nameless printer was probably Royston.

31. *Perfect Occurrences*, Jan. 18-25; Herbert's *Narrative* in Stevenson, p. 188.

32. *State Trials*, v, pp. 1090, 1127.

33. *The Moderate*, Jan. 16-23.

34. Stephen, *History of English Common Law*, I, 279.

35. Nalson, pp. 38-9; Ludlow, I, p. 216. Ludlow makes the meeting take place *after* the session on the 20th. He is perhaps confusing it with some private consultation between those principally concerned.

36. The quotations from the proceedings are from *Perfect Narrative* as before.

37. *State Trials*, v, pp. 1085-6.

38. Herbert, p. 189. It is however possible that he invented the incident basing it on the King's conduct as recorded in the Press on the last day of his trial.

39. Lilburne had made his sufferings very well known by constantly alluding to them in his pamphlets. Atrocity stories about the ill-treatment of prisoners, with or without the King's knowledge, were frequently published during the war; see also the evidence given on p. 149.

40. Herbert, pp. 189-190. I do not mention Mildmay among those whose faces the King knew as he did not attend the Court except on January 23rd.

41. Nalson, pp. 50-1; it is clear that they had not yet thought of postponing the sentence because at the end of the Tuesday session the Court was adjourned until Wednesday at 10 o'clock in Westminster Hall, indicating that the last session was definitely planned for Wednesday; the change of arrangements must have occurred late on Tuesday evening. See Gardiner, IV, pp. 305-7.

42. H. Walker, *Collections of Notes*, (E.539.4).

43. The confused reporting of this part of the trial was evidently due to interruptions and the mingling of the King's words with Bradshaw's. Clement Walker in his *History of Independency* (p. 98) suggests that something the King said was here suppressed; but in view of the highly damaging nature of the King's statements which were authorised for publication this does not seem likely.

44. The King's last rejoinder "I see I am before a power" is omitted in Mabbot's account (*The Moderate* and *A Perfect Narrative*) and in the newspapers which stem from it. Mabbott presumably realised its critical implications. Dillingham (*Moderate Intelligencer*) evidently realised something had been suppressed and invented a new rejoinder of his own. From this I deduce that Dillingham was in the Hall although he depended like all the journalists on the official text for the bulk of his account. Henry Walker (*Perfect Occurrences*), though very hostile to the King, printed this last rejoinder, as did Mabbott's co-censor Theodore Jennings (*Perfect Summary*); neither of them apparently thought it as damaging as Mabbott appears to have done.

45. *Moderate Intelligencer*, Jan. 18-25.

46. Muddiman, p. 100. Muddiman's intensely Royalist glosses on the accounts of the trial are to be accepted with the greatest caution, but this does indeed seem to be the likeliest explanation of the Crier's unprecedented formula.

CHAPTER SEVEN

1. Nalson, p. 59.
2. The phrase is quoted from Thomas Jordan's ballad *The Anarchy* in *Rump Songs*, p. 292.
3. Nalson, p. 60.
4. *Clarendon State Papers*, II, appendix, p. li. "The general was baited with fresh dogs all Tuesday night to bring him into the Hall on the morrow."
5. Francis White, *The Copies of Severall Letters . . . to Fairfax and Cromwell* (E.548.6).
6. For the numerous publications of these January days see *Catalogue of the Thomason Tracts*, London, 1908, I, pp. 717-18.
7. *Perfect Occurrences*, Jan. 18-25.
8. *Perfect Summary*, Jan. 20-7.
9. Nalson, pp. 61, 63-81.
10. *Perfect Diurnall, Perfect Summary* and *Perfect Occurrences*, all printed the evidence or parts of it.
11. Nalson, p. 63.
12. *Perfect Occurrences*, Jan. 26-Feb. 2; *Commons Journals*, Jan. 26; see also Fry's own account *The Accuser Sham'd* printed in February 1649 (E.544.7). Fry later satisfied the House that he had not denied the divinity of Christ, although it is pretty clear that he was an anti-Trinitarian.
13. Mary Pope, *Behold, here is a word*, (E.539.8); *Perfect Occurrences*, Jan. 26-Feb. 2.
14. *Perfect Summary*, Jan. 22-9.
15. *Mercurius Melancolicus*, Dec. 25-Jan. 1.
16. Rushworth, p. 1428.
17. Carte, *Letters*, I, pp. 195-7.
18. *Perfect Summary*, Jan. 22-9; Madame de Motteville, *Mémoires*, Paris, 1855, II, pp. 250 ff. See also an English pamphlet on the state of Paris, *A Letter from Paris*, (E.538.9).
19. Cary, *Memorials of the great civil war*, London, 1842, II, pp. 105, 108; *Perfect Occurrences*, Jan. 26-Feb. 2.

20. Nalson, pp. 81-2.
21. *Historical MSS Commission*, Report XV, appendix II, p. III.
22. Nalson, pp. 52-5.
23. *Perfect Narrative*, which I have followed except where otherwise stated.
24. *State Trials*, V, pp. 1150, 1152-3. Clarendon and Rushworth, both published long after the Restoration, do not indicate that the identity of Lady Fairfax was ever in question, but the evidence given at Axtell's trial makes it clear that she cannot have been known to many.
25. Downes gave two accounts, one at his trial (*State Trials*, V, pp. 1211-13) and one in a pamphlet (*A True and Humble Representation*, London, 1660); the evidence of Harvey is in *State Trials*, V, p. 1197, and that of Waite in the same volume, p. 1218. For Nicholas Love's alleged conduct in the Painted Chamber see his petition of 1660 in *Historical MSS Commission*, VIII, p. 119.
26. Ludlow, *Memoirs*, I, p. 217.
27. The King's exclamation is recorded in Mabbott's *Perfect Narrative*. We know from subsequent events that he wished to make an answer, and I hope it is justifiable to see this part of the speech as the highly damaging attack that he saw he ought to contradict, no doubt by denying his responsibility for the war.
28. *Perfect Occurrences*.
29. Joiner's evidence at Axtell's trial, *State Trials*, V, p. 1153.
30. *Herbert's Narrative* in Stevenson, p. 192; *Kingdom's Weekly Intelligencer*, Jan. 30-Feb. 6.
31. Nalson, p. 93. Downes gave the impression at his trial that he had withdrawn for the rest of the day after the scene at the adjournment. His name however appears on the roll-call when the Commissioners reassembled after giving sentence.

The poor man cannot be regarded as a reliable witness, but I think it probable that he really *did* withdraw for the last half of the trial and the sentence. No-one would have urged him to come back into the Hall for fear of more disturbance.

32. *Kingdom's Weekly Intelligencer,* Jan. 30-Feb. 6.

CHAPTER EIGHT

1. Isaiah, XIV, 18-20; *State Trials,* v, p. 1132; *Massachusetts Historical Society Collections,* 3rd Series, IX, *Correspondence of John Winthrop,* p. 286.

2. *Herbert's Narrative,* pp. 248-9; Rushworth, p. 1426.

3. *The Moderate,* Jan. 23-30.

4. Loc. cit.; *State Trials,* v, p. 1180; John Ashburnham subsequently claimed that he had had a plan to rescue the King which was foiled by his removal from Whitehall.

5. *Herbert's Narrative,* pp. 249-51. Herbert's chronology is inaccurate; I have taken what seems to me the likeliest sequence.

6. Wedgwood, *King's War,* p. 358.

7. *Herbert's Narrative,* pp. 247-8. For the behaviour of the Elector Palatine during the Civil War see Wedgwood, *King's War,* p. 380. It is, admittedly, a conjecture that the King refused, on the Elector's account, to receive a group of people whom he might otherwise have admitted, but it seems probable as he was extremely attached to Richmond and had had to part from him hurriedly and unhappily in the Isle of Wight.

8. *Herbert's Narrative,* pp. 250-1; W. Sanderson, *Life and Raigne of King Charles,* London, 1658, p. 1135.

9. *Old Parliamentary History,* XXII, p. 402; *Historical MSS Commission,* VII, p. 123. Tomlinson in his evidence against Hacker (*State Trials,* v, p. 1179) asserts that he admitted Seymour at Whitehall on the morning of the King's execution, but the time sequence given by Herbert seems for once more probable.

10. Clement Walker, *History of Independency,* p. 110; at least two newspapers, *The Moderate* and *The Kingdom's Faithful Scout* carried a story that Fairfax was said to have propounded a plan for saving the King's life to the Army Council. If he did so it is strange that he never subsequently spoke of it.

11. Bodleian Library, *Clarendon MSS,* Vol. XXXIV, No. 3001; *History,* XI, 229. The earliest reference to the Prince's offer is in W. Harris, *Life and Reign of Charles II,* 1766, I, p. 40. The British Museum possesses a blank paper sealed and signed by Prince Charles (*Harleian MSS* 6988). It is endorsed in an eighteenth century handwriting as his "carte blanche to save his Father's Head." But it is more probably a blank issued in connection with his current enterprises in Ireland.

12. The Dutch despatch is printed in Guizot, *History of the English Revolution,* trans. Coutier, Oxford, 1838, appendix to Vol. II. An interesting German printed version also exists: *Vollständiges Englisches Memorial,* 1649. No place of printing is given for this German account of the trials of Strafford, Laud, and Charles I which also contains a full translation of Pauw's and Joachimi's despatch. Schönle (in his edition of Gryphius) identifies it as a pirated edition of a work which was first printed in Amsterdam. See also *The Moderate Intelligencer,* Jan. 25-Feb. 1.

13. Guizot, *loc. cit.; Englisches Memorial; Commons Journals,* Jan. 29;

Calendar of State Papers, Venetian Series, 1647-52, pp. 90-1.

14. *The Moderate*, Jan. 23-30.

15. *London County Council Survey*, XIII, pp. 30-1.

16. For a description of this MS now in the House of Lords see *MSS of the House of Lords*, New Series, XI, *Addenda*, 1514-1714, ed. Maurice F. Bond, London, 1962, pp. xviii-xix, 476.

17. Gardiner, IV, pp. 308-11.

18. Nalson, pp. 108-9.

19. *D.N.B.* Richard Ingoldsby.

20. *State Trials*, V, p. 1200.

21. Nicholas Love and William Heveningham successfully resisted pressure to sign (*Historical MSS Commission*, VII, pp. 119, 125); Edward Harvey stayed away, and the same trick was attempted less successfully by Thomas Waite (*State Trials*, V, 1198, 1219). Tomlinson escaped scot free in 1660. He asserted that he had never attended the Court and that his name appeared in error as present on the 27th. He certainly did not sign the warrant.

22. *State Trials*, V, 1219. I assume that, as the Painted Chamber meeting was at eight, and only 48 Commissioners came, Cromwell would have gone down to the door of the House at about eleven which—to judge by contemporary references to the difficulty of getting a quorum—was about the time that the late-comers arrived.

23. *State Trials*, V, p. 1217.

24. *Herbert's Narrative*, p. 250-1.

25. Wedgwood, *King's War*, p. 589.

26. Nalson, pp. 105-7.

27. *Herbert's Narrative*, p. 254; Nalson, *loc. cit.*

28. *State Trials*, V, p. 1179.

29. *Herbert's Narrative*, pp. 277-8. Again, Herbert's sense of time and chronology is confused. Juxon, he says, stayed some hours after darkness, which may mean anything as in January it is dark by

six o'clock. The King read and prayed alone for at least two more hours. He was awake two hours before daylight—about five, say; he slept soundly for about four hours. This suggests that he was not in bed until at least midnight.

30. Lindsey was himself a competent translator from the French.

31. See Delamaine's own book, *The Mathematical Ring*, London, 1631.

32. The account of the King's last morning is from *Herbert's Narrative*, pp. 278-81, with the additional details of the dream which he added in his letter to Dr. Samways in 1680 printed in Fuller, *Church History*, VI, pp. 937-8.

33. *Herbert's Narrative*, p. 282.

34. *King Charles his Speech*, (B.540.17); Nalson, pp. 112-13. State Trials, V, p. 1179.

35. Blencowe, p. 96.

36. *Abraham van der Doort's Catalogue of the Collection of Charles I*, ed. Oliver Millar, *Walpole Society*, 1960, pp. 2-4.

37. *Herbert's Narrative*, pp. 282-3.

38. The innumerable rumours about the execution of Charles I are summarised in Philip Sidney, *The Headsman of Whitehall*, Edinburgh, 1905, a pamphlet intelligently compiled but unhappily without references. Among the more unlikely candidates was Lord Stair, the Scottish judge. Various eccentric hermits in the later seventeenth century enjoyed a local reputation as the unknown executioner of the King, and aged exhibitionists seem to have laid claim to this sinister honour well into the eighteenth century. Fairfax and Cromwell occur in F. de Marsys, *Le Procez . . . du Roy d'Angleterre*, Paris, 1649, p. 11.

39. *State Trials*, V, pp. 1186, 1192-3. *The Confession of Richard Brandon*—a pamphlet more fully discussed in Note 48 — states however that Brandon employed his usual

assistant, Ralph Jones, a rag-man.

40. *State Trials*, v, pp. 1149-50, 1180-1. Hunks places this scene just before the execution, but the details suggest an earlier hour.

41. *Commons Journals*, Jan. 30, 1649.

42. Guizot, *History of the English Revolution*, II, appendix.

43. Brian Fairfax, *Life of George Villiers, Duke of Buckingham*, London, 1778, p. 32.

44. Guizot, *loc. cit.*

45. *Herbert's Narrative*, pp. 283-4.

46. Dispute about this window is interminable. A scaffold which could be reached from one of the Banqueting Hall windows would be abnormally high, and destroying the masonry at the base of one of them would have been a heavy and elaborate task. The window indicated in a drawing of the early eighteenth century in the adjoining brick and plaster annexe is slightly lower and could have been much more easily enlarged. See G. S. Dugdale, *Whitehall Through the Centuries*, London, 1950, p. 56, and Sheppard, *The Old Royal Palace of Whitehall*.

47. *Col. S. P. Ven*, 1647-52, p. 91. *State Trials*, v, pp. 1186, 1190. Descriptions of the two executioners differ considerably. An account written at the time describes them as in seamen's clothes; one of the witnesses in 1660 said that they wore woollen habits like butchers. There is agreement about the grey hair and beard of the executioner, but his assistant is variously described as flaxen and black-bearded.

48. *The Confession of Richard Brandon*, London, 1649, (B.561.14) describing the remorseful death of Richard Brandon some months later gives a slightly different account—namely that the King had positively refused to forgive his executioner. The pamphlet

may be a pure invention, but it is noticeable that the fullest account of the execution omits the usual interchange of apology and pardon between the headsman and the victim. I incline to the belief that owing to the strangeness of the occasion and the state of Brandon's nerves, he simply forgot to say the usual formula; and this may subsequently have troubled him. Such a statement from him, referring merely to an omission, could easily have been misunderstood and elaborated into the version given in the pamphlet. My thanks are due to Miss Mary Coate for drawing my attention to this curious detail.

49. The description of the King's death is, except where otherwise stated, from the best of the contemporary pamphlets, *King Charles his Speech made upon the scaffold* (B.540.17) published immediately after his death and reproduced in Nalson, pp. 113-18, also in Rushworth.

50. *Diaries and Letters of Philip Henry*, 1631-96, ed. Matthew Henry Lee, London, 1882, p. 12.

CHAPTER NINE

1. Philip Henry, *Diaries and Letters* p. 12.
2. Herbert's *Narrative*, pp. 310-12.
3. M. A. Gibb, *The Lord General*, p. 216.
4. Perrinchief, *The Royal Martyr*, London, 1676, p. 203. The story occurs also in Baxter's *Reliquiae* and other sources.
5. Fuller, *Church History*, Book XI, pp. 348-9.
6. C. Walker, op. cit., p. 111; Fuller, p. 348.
7. *Memoirs of the Life of Mr. Ambrose Barnes*, ed. Longstaffe, *Surtees Society*, 1867, pp. 108-9; R. Sanderson, *Life and Raigne of King Charles I*, London, 1658, p. 1139.

8. Descriptions of London given by contemporaries differ extremely. The Dutch envoys reported that all the shops were open as usual; others say that they were all closed. Presumably much depended on the example set by the leading citizens in any region or street, and manifestations of grief, indifference, or support for the Army would have varied from region to region according to the wealth, religious affiliation, and social standing of the inhabitants, but it is clear that there was no unseemly rejoicing even in the most republican and sectarian districts.

9. *Calendar of State Papers, Irish*, 1647-60, p. 261.

10. This was his defence when he was accused at his trial of having been busy preparing the scaffold for the King, and even of having been the masked executioner. But his statement that he was ill all day was corroborated by a servant who had since left his service and who had no particular reason for helping his old master by swearing to an alibi. The evidence of Peter's activity on the scaffold is not borne out by any contemporary source, and the witnesses to it in 1660 are not, in the circumstances, at all convincing. *State Trials*, v, pp. 1127-8, 1134-5; Stearns, *The Strenuous Puritan*, Urbana, 1959, p. 335.

11. *Kingdom's Weekly Intelligencer*, Jan. 30- Feb. 6.

12. G. F. Russell Barker, *Memoir of Richard Busby*, London, 1895, p. 16.

13. Pepys, *Diary*, Nov. 1, 1660, on which day Pepys was embarrassed to meet an old schoolfellow whom he feared would remember this occasion.

14. Parr, *Life of Ussher*, London, 1686, p. 72.

15. Evelyn, ed. E. S. de Beer, II, p. 547.

16. Guizot, (trans. Scoble), *History of Oliver Cromwell*, London, 1854, I, appendix IV, pp. 373-7.

17. Guizot, *English Revolution*, II, appendix. *Calendar of State Papers, Venetian*, 1647-52, pp. 90-1.

18. Chéruel, *Lettres du Cardinal Mazarin*, Paris, 1883, III, p. 1099; *Calendar of State Papers, Venetian*, 1647-52, p. 91.

19. Inna Lubimenko, *Les Relations Commerciales et Politiques de l'Angleterre avec la Russie*, Paris, 1933, p. 210.

20. Collins, *Letters and Memorials of State*, London, 1746, II, p. 676.

21. H. Ellis, *Royal Letters*, Second Series, III, p. 347.

22. Madame de Motteville, *Mémoires*, Paris, 1855, II, pp. 351-2.

23. Cyprien de Gamaches, *Mémoires de la Mission des Capucins près la Reine d'Angleterre*, Paris, 1881, pp. 147-8.

24. Hyde to Prince Rupert, Feb. 18-28, British Museum, *Additional MSS, 18982*, folio 177.

25. *Calendar of State Papers, Venetian*, p. 89.

26. Cary, *Memorials of the Civil War*, London, 1842, II, p. 110.

27. *Calendar of State Papers, Domestic*, 1649-50, pp. 6-7.

28. R. Holmes, *The Sieges of Pontefract Castle*, Pontefract, 1887, pp. 213-14.

29. Balfour, *Annals of Scotland*, Edinburgh, 1837, III, p. 387.

30. Carte, *Ormonde*, v, p. 419; Carte, *Letters*, II, p. 359.

31. *Nicholas Papers*, I, p. 114.

32. Lily, *A Peculiar Prognostication*, London, 1649.

33. Fuller, *Church History of England*, ed. Brewer, London, 1845, VI, pp. 434-5, appendix, Herbert to Dugdale, Nov. 3, 1681. Trapham *said* he refused to cut off the King's hair for souvenirs, but when the body was exhumed in 1813 the hair at the back had been partly cut off.

34. Herbert's *Narrative*, p. 302; Spence's *Anecdotes*, p. 286.

35. *Commons Journals*, Feb. 8, 1649; Dugdale, *Short View*, p. 383.

36. Zachary Grey, *Examination of Daniel Neal's Third Volume of the History of Puritanism*, London, 1737, appendix, pp. 135-6.

37. Fuller, pp. 349, 435. See also Norman Mackenzie, Op. cit, p. 77. It would appear that Herbert's expenditure, which he only got back several years later, was in addition to the £500 stipulated for the burial itself.

38. Fuller, *loc. cit.* Herbert makes no direct mention of the fact that Richmond was authorised by Parliament to bury the King. He implies throughout that he was the principal organiser of the proceedings. But see the account in *The Moderate* Feb. 6-13 which makes it clear that Richmond took charge.

39. Fuller, pp. 351-2.

40. Op. cit, p. 353.

41. Fuller, p. 436.

42. Fuller, p. 350; Norman Mackenzie (op. cit., p. 53) indicates that Whichcot was a fanatical opponent of the Anglican Church. He had refused to allow the King to have his own chaplains when he passed through Windsor in July 1647, a time at which the Army was pursuing a policy of conciliation and encouragement to the King.

43. Fuller, pp. 353-4; other accounts appeared in the Press and Clarendon also describes the burial. I prefer Fuller's account as he may have had much of it from Juxon.

44. Cary, II, p. 126; for a discussion of the authorship of *Eikon Basilike* see Falconer Madan, *Bibliography of Eikon Basilike*. Oxford, 1949. Royalists are still unwilling to hear a word against the King's authorship, but scholarly opinion accepts Gauden as, substantially, the author. For the King's knowledge of it and co-operation and the change of title see Wagstaffe, *Vindication*, pp. 35-6. Wagstaffe favours the King's authorship, but none of the evidence is incompatible with the King's having supplied Gauden with material on which to work.

45. E.541.6 in the Thomason Collection; Thomason's note as to his date of purchase is 2nd February.

46. Carte, *Ormonde*, VI, p. 606.

47. *The Devilish Conspiracy*, London, 1649 (E.550.16)

48. *The Man in the Moon*, April, 1649, (E.550.26)

49. Clarendon repeats these stories; so does Fuller in his *Church History*; Montrose in his manifesto for Charles II published at Copenhagen in the year of the King's death, also refers to them. An attempt was unsuccessfully made to pin the spitting myth on to the hapless Augustine Garland at the trials of the Regicides.

50. See for instance Abraham Cowley, *Essays, Plays and Verses*, ed. A. R. Waller, Cambridge, 1906, p. 345.

51. For Bower see Whinney and Millar, *The Oxford History of English Art*, 1625-1714, Oxford, 1957, pp. 79-80; see also E. K. Waterhouse, *Edward Bower, painter of Charles I at his Trial, Burlington Magazine*, 1949, p. 18. Mr. Waterhouse draws attention to the three slightly different poses in which the King sits in Bower's different versions, suggesting sketches made at different moments in the trial. The fact that in all he is holding a paper of notes in one hand *may* possibly mean that Bower made all his sketches on one day, January 22nd, when the King tried to make his speech about his reasons for denying the authority of the Court for which he had made notes.

52. For a list and illustrations of the medals commemorating the King's death see Pinkerton, *Medallic History of England*, London, 1790, pp. 49-51.

53. K. A. Esdaile, *The Busts and Statues of Charles I*, Burlington Magazine, 1949, pp. 9-14, gives a full account of this statue and of several others.

54. Frank, *Beginnings of the English Newspaper*, pp. 192-8.

55. *The Charge against the King Discharged*, dated by Thomason February 13th, 1649 (E.542.10).

56. *An Inquisition after Blood*, London, 1649. This tract is not in the Thomason Collection. It is in the British Museum, shelf-mark 100.e.71.

57. *Commons Journals*, Feb. 9.

58. *Calendar of State Papers, Domestic, 1649-50*, p. 555.

59. John Cook, *King Charles his Case*, London, 1649.

60. The best critical editions of *The Tenure of Kings and Magistrates* and *Eikonoclastes* is in the Yale edition of the *Complete Prose Works of John Milton*, Volume III, Newhaven, 1962.

61. Underdown, *Royalist Conspiracy in England, 1649-60*, Newhaven, 1960, gives a very clear idea of the limited and ineffective character of the Royalist resistance.

62. Clode, *London in the Civil War*, II, p. 54; *Trial and Examination of the Lord Mayor* (E.549.4); *The Vindication of Abraham Reynardson* (E.550.9); G. Smalwood, *The Wicked Man's Sad Disappointment*, London, 1661. (Reynardson's funeral sermon.)

63. *Calendar of State Papers, Domestic, 1649-50*, p. 9.

64. The British Museum contains examples of translations of the trial, printed in Paris, the Hague, Florence, various parts of Germany, and Warsaw. For the French propaganda on the subject see Ascoli, *Relations Intellectuels de la France et la Grande Bretagne*, II, pp. 74ff.

65. Gryphius, *Epigrammata*, 1663; an excellent edition of his *Carolus Stuardus* is that by Hugh Powell, University College, Leicester, 1955. See also: Hugh Powell, "The Two Versions of Andreas Gryphius's Carolus Stuardus" in *German Life and Letters*, New Series, V, No. 2.

66. St. Amant, *Oeuvres*, I, p. 440.

67. Ascoli, p. 92; see also the Catalogue of the *Mazarinades*.

68. *Nicholas Papers*, I, p. 115.

69. Ludlow, *Memoirs*, I, pp. 225-6.

70. The murder of Ascham seems unreasonable; although he had written against the King he was not an important figure and not a Regicide. I believe it possible that he may have been confused by the Royalists with the mysterious Aske who, with Cook and Dorislaus, appeared in Westminster Hall against the King. A sympathetic account of Ascham has recently been written by Irene Coltman in *Private Men and Public Causes*, London, 1962.

CHAPTER TEN

1. *Commons Journals*, December 1660; Evelyn, ed. E. S. de Beer, III, p. 269.

2. *Historical MSS Commission*, Report V; *State Trials*, V, pp. 1148, 1190, 1289.

3. Mackenzie, op. cit., pp. 83-4.

4. *D.N.B.* Richard Ingoldsby.

5. Hutchinson, *History of the Colony of Massachusetts Bay*, London, 1760, pp. 213-19.

6. *D.N.B.* John Lisle.

7. Ludlow, Cawley, Phelps and Broughton are all commemorated in the Church at Vevey.

8. *State Trials*, p. 1277.

9. Pepys, *Diary*, 19th April, 1662.

10. *State Trials*, V, p. 1215.

11. Coate, *Cornwall in the Great Civil War*, p. 318.
12. *Memoirs of Colonel Hutchinson*, pp. 324ff.
13. *State Trials*, v, pp. 1200-1; Marten, *Letters to his Miss*, London, 1660.
14. *State Trials*, v. p. 1265.
15. *The Several Speeches, Disputes and Conferences betwixt the Gentlemen of the Black Robe*, London, 1661. This pamphlet which purports to be Royalist was evidently really written by a sympathiser with the victims.
16. *Loc. cit.*
17. *State Trials*, v, pp. 1289-90.
18. *State Trials*, v, pp. 1125-30; see also Raymond Stearns, *The Strenuous Puritan*, pp. 417-8.
19. *State Trials*, v, pp. 1190ff.

INDEX

INDEX